Shelagh Cluett

A Collection of Artifacts

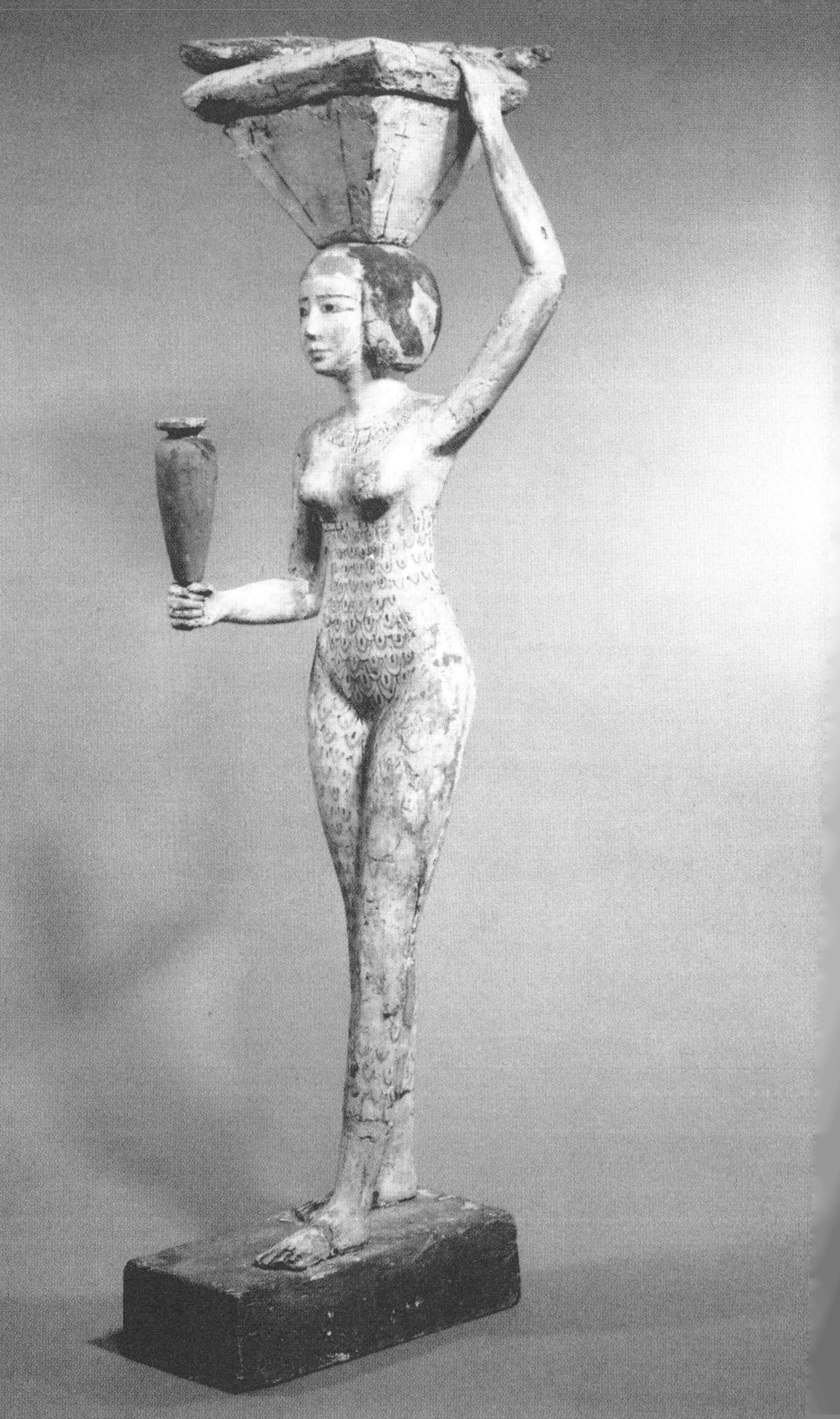

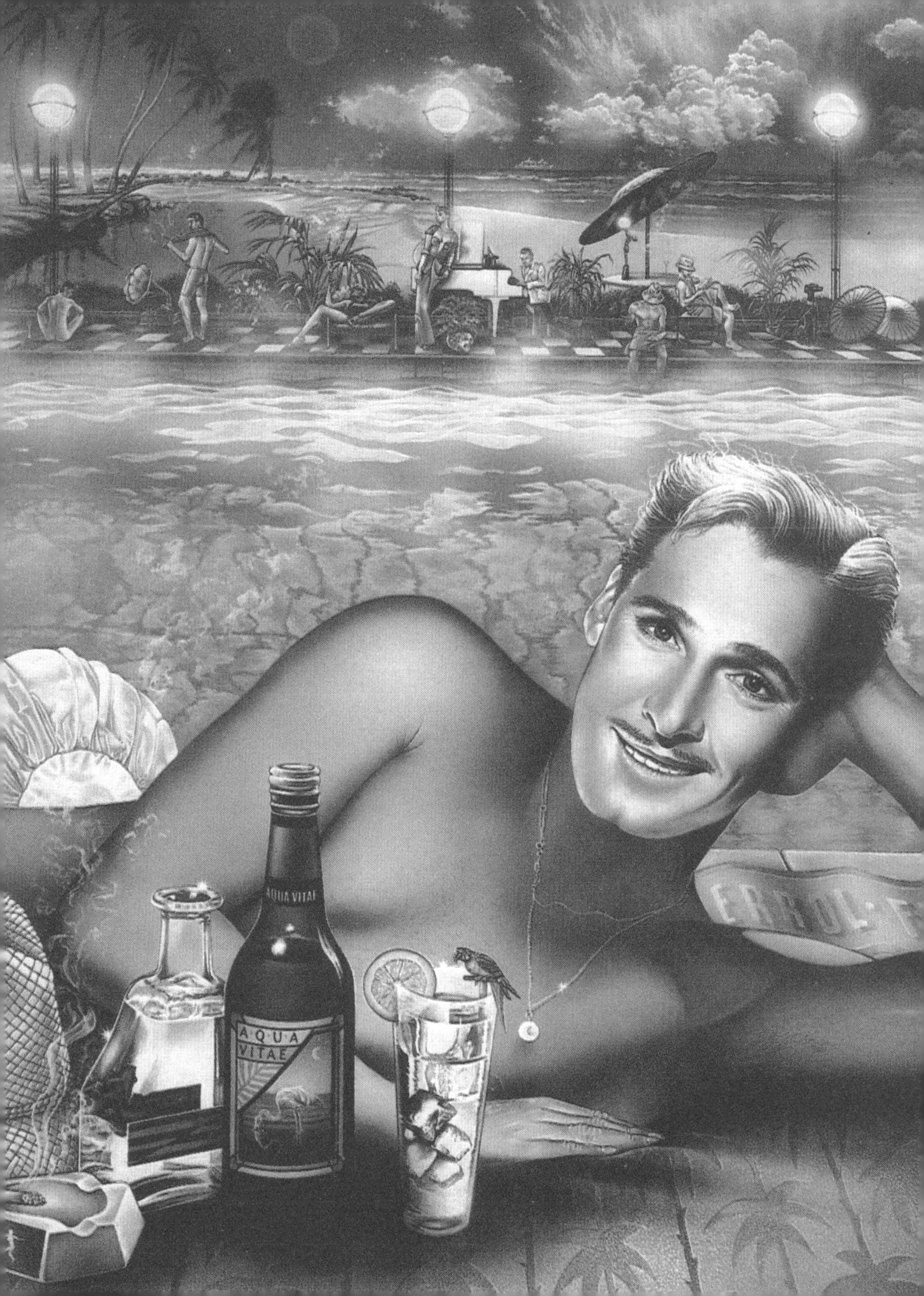
AQUA VITAE
AQUA
VITAE

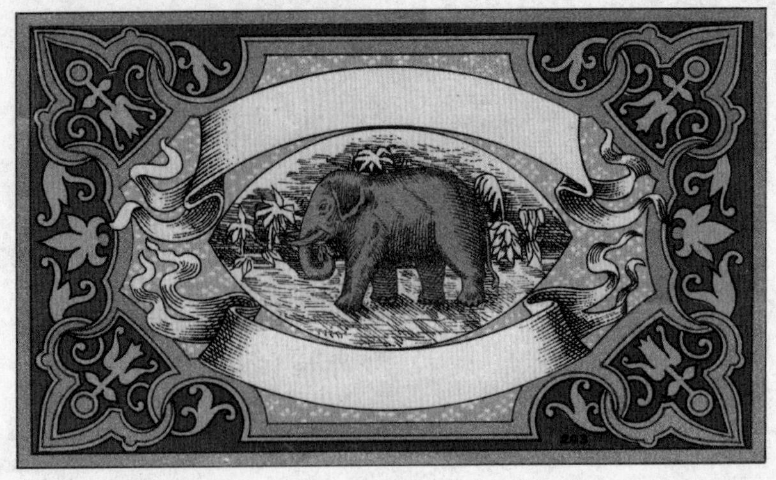

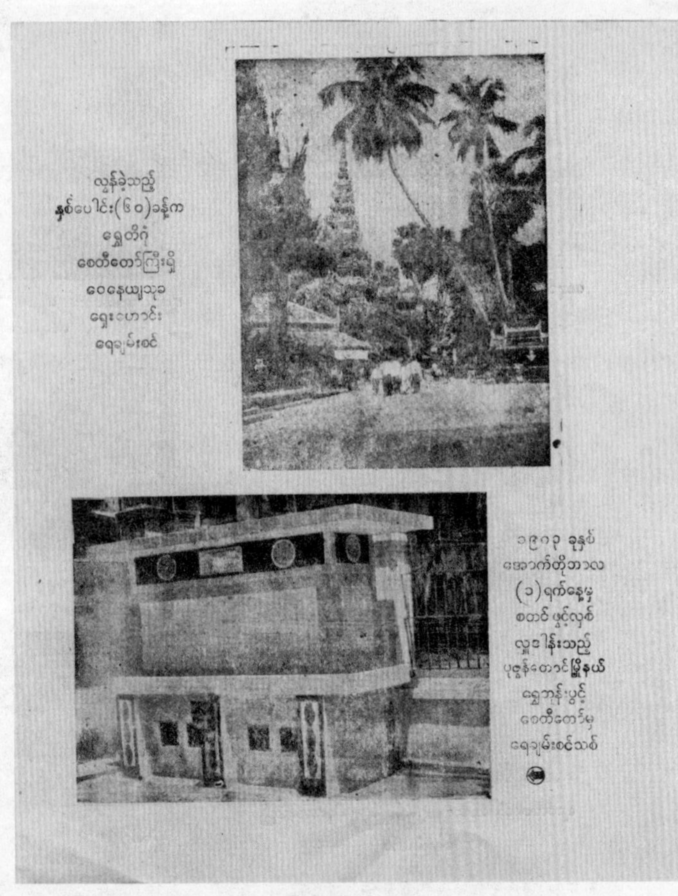

လွန်ခဲ့သည့်
နှစ်ပေါင်း(၆၀)ခန့်က
ရွှေတိဂုံ
စေတီတော်ကြီးရှိ
ဝေနေယျသုခ
ရှေးဟောင်း
ရေချမ်းစင်
၁၉၇၃ ခုနှစ်
အောက်တိုဘာလ
(၁)ရက်နေ့မှ
စတင်ဖွင့်လှစ်
လှူဒါန်းသည့်
ပုဇွန်တောင်မြို့နယ်
ရွှေဘုန်းပွင့်
စေတီတော်မှ
ရေချမ်းစင်သစ်

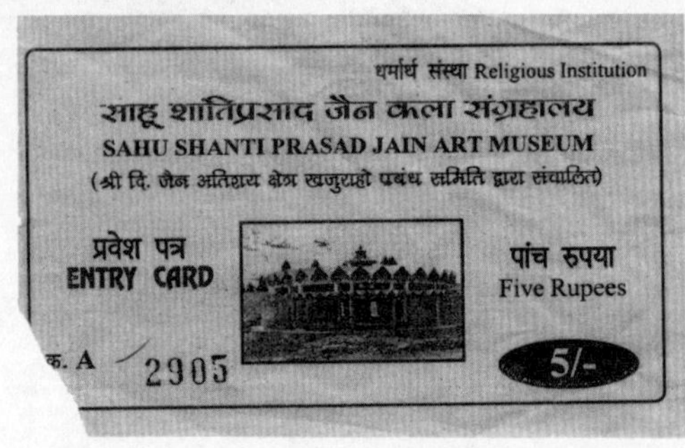

धर्मार्थ संस्था Religious Institution
साहू शांतिप्रसाद जैन कला संग्रहालय
SAHU SHANTI PRASAD JAIN ART MUSEUM
(श्री दि. जैन अतिशय क्षेत्र खजुराहो प्रबंध समिति द्वारा संचालित)
प्रवेश पत्र
ENTRY CARD
पांच रुपया
Five Rupees
क. A 2905
5/-

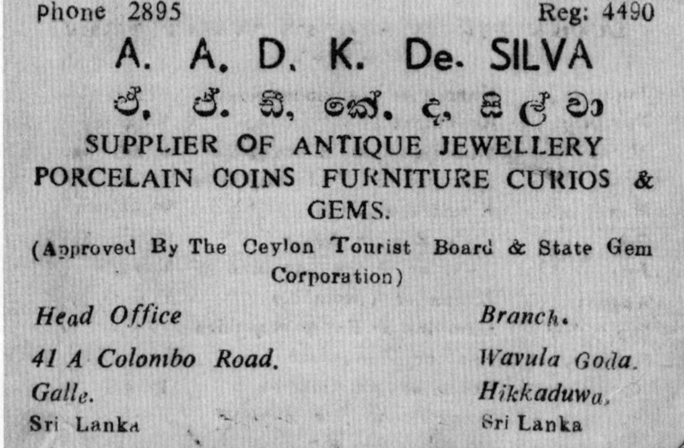

Phone 2895
Reg: 4490
A. A. D. K. De. SILVA
ඒ. ඒ. ඩී. කේ. ද, සිල්වා
SUPPLIER OF ANTIQUE JEWELLERY
PORCELAIN COINS FURNITURE CURIOS & GEMS.
(Approved By The Ceylon Tourist Board & State Gem Corporation)
Head Office
41 A Colombo Road.
Galle.
Sri Lanka
Branch.
Wavula Goda.
Hikkaduwa.
Sri Lanka

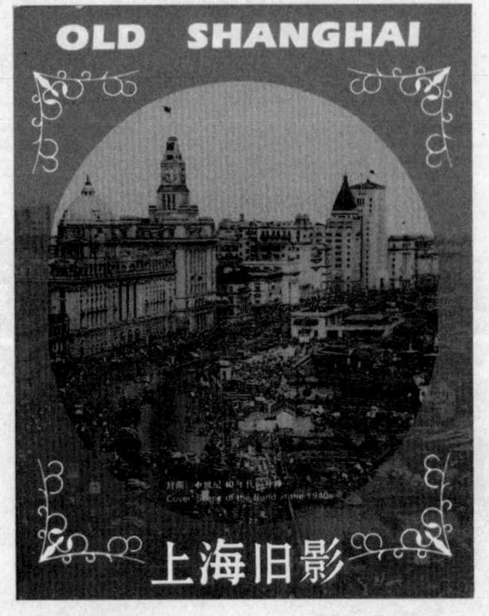

OLD SHANGHAI
上海旧影

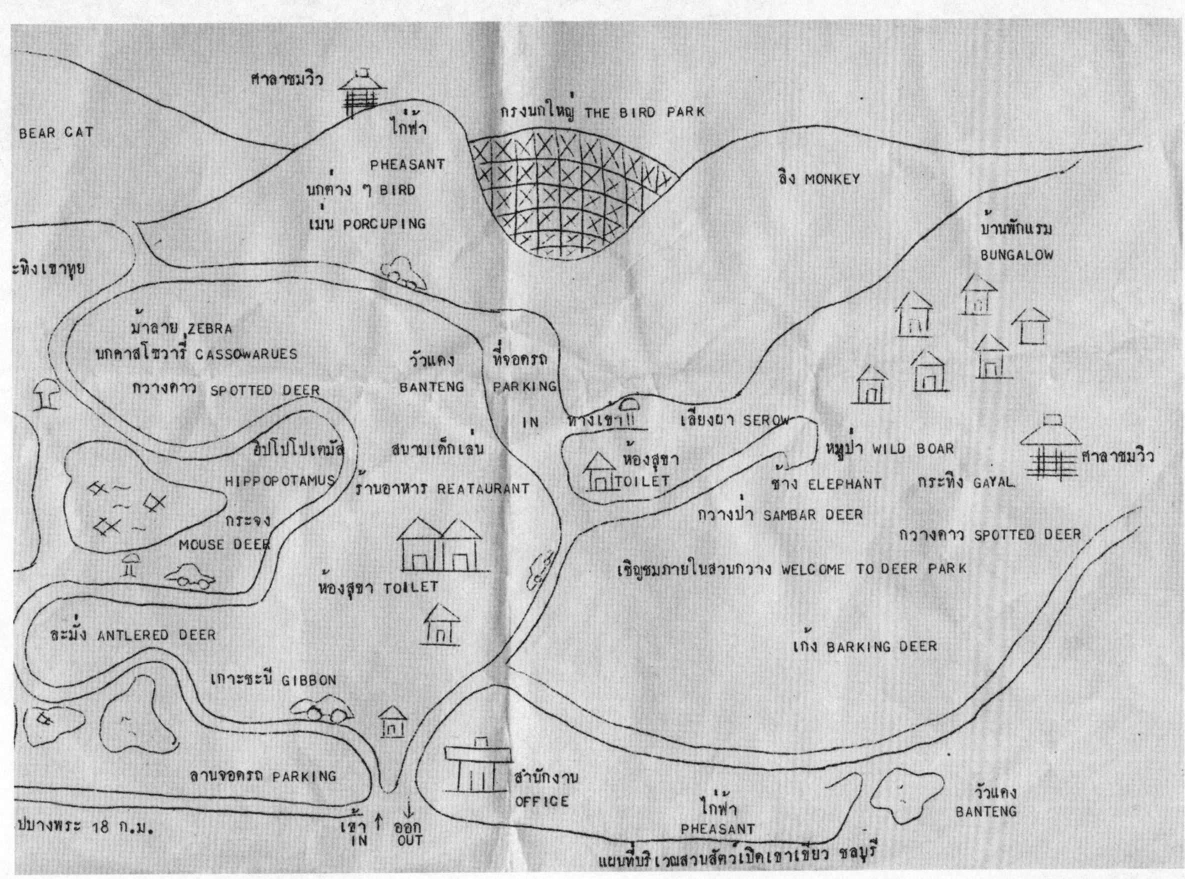

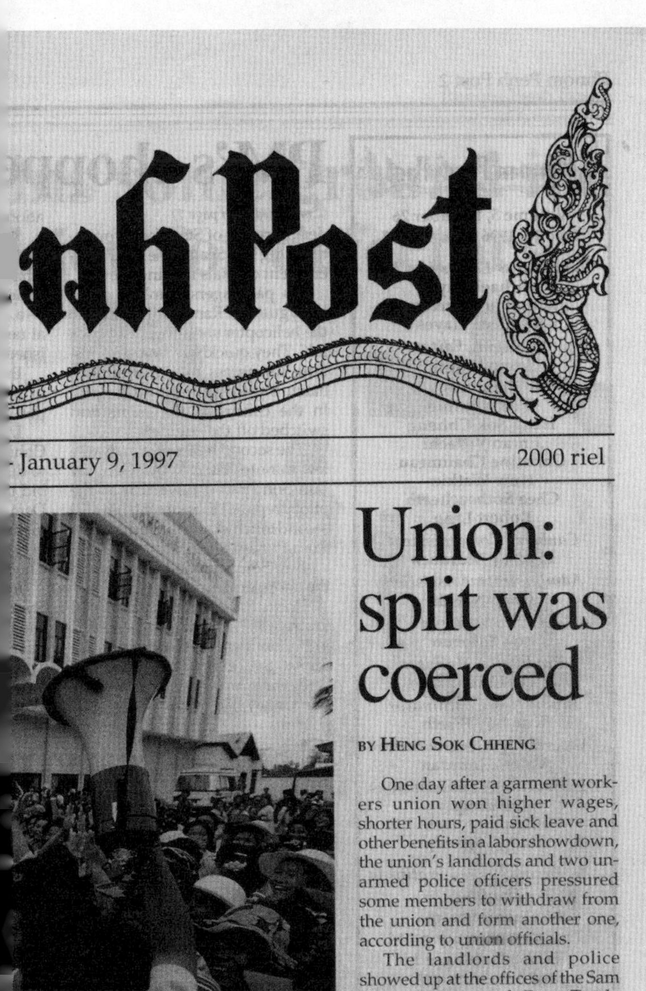

ah Post

January 9, 1997 — 2000 riel

Union: split was coerced

BY HENG SOK CHHENG

One day after a garment workers union won higher wages, shorter hours, paid sick leave and other benefits in a labor showdown, the union's landlords and two unarmed police officers pressured some members to withdraw from the union and form another one, according to union officials.

The landlords and police showed up at the offices of the Sam Rainsy-supported Free Trade Union of Khmer Workers on Dec 22, making threats and promising CPP support for the new union, said Ker Sam Oeun, the union's advisor.

"They threatened us to change the name of the union because they

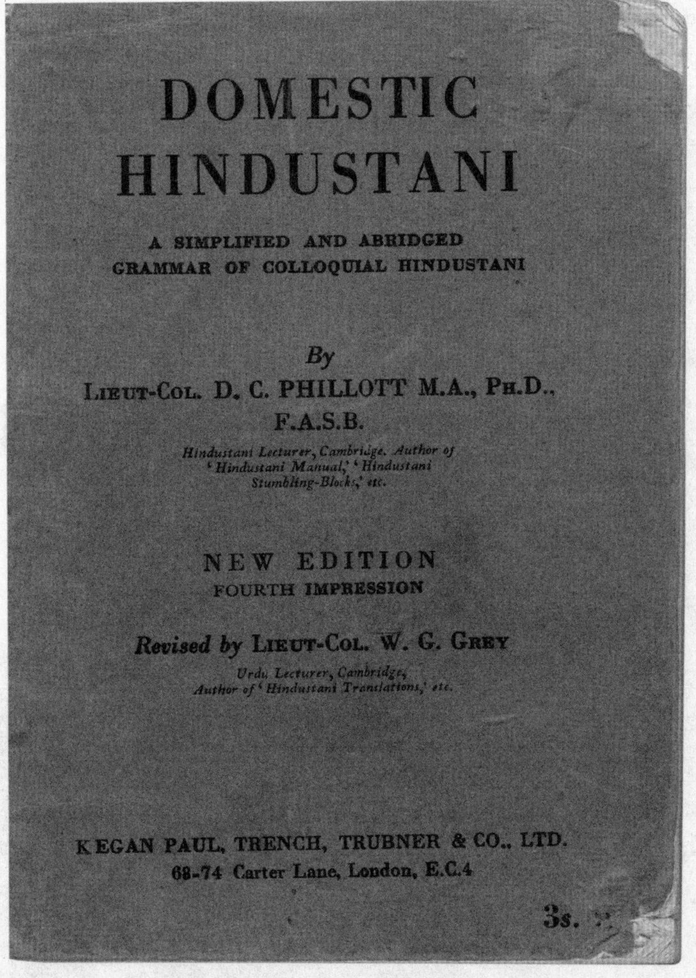

DOMESTIC HINDUSTANI

A SIMPLIFIED AND ABRIDGED GRAMMAR OF COLLOQUIAL HINDUSTANI

By

LIEUT-COL. D. C. PHILLOTT M.A., PH.D., F.A.S.B.

Hindustani Lecturer, Cambridge. Author of 'Hindustani Manual,' 'Hindustani Stumbling-Blocks,' etc.

NEW EDITION
FOURTH IMPRESSION

Revised by LIEUT-COL. W. G. GREY

Urdu Lecturer, Cambridge, Author of 'Hindustani Translations,' etc.

KEGAN PAUL, TRENCH, TRUBNER & CO., LTD.
68-74 Carter Lane, London, E.C.4

3s.

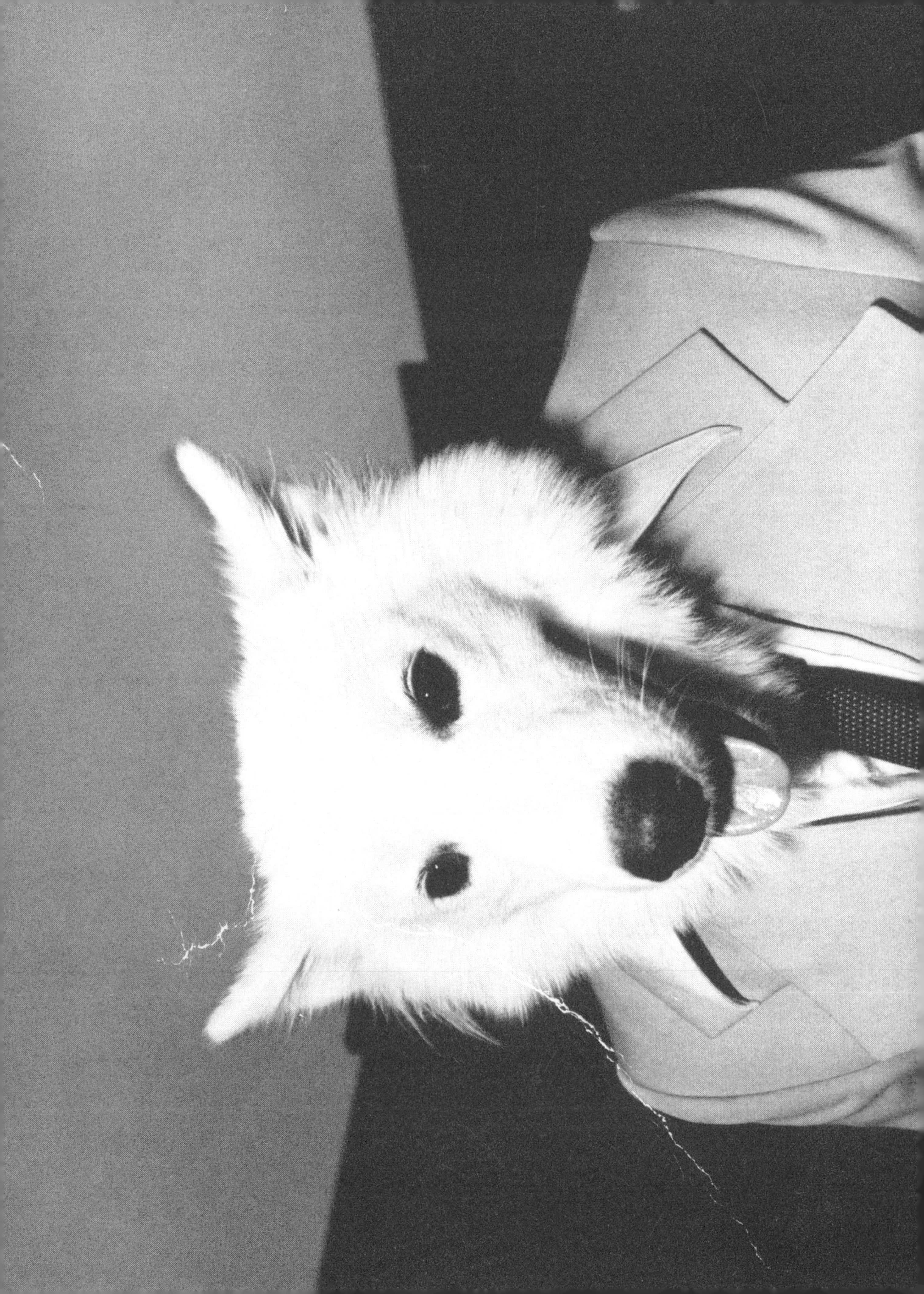

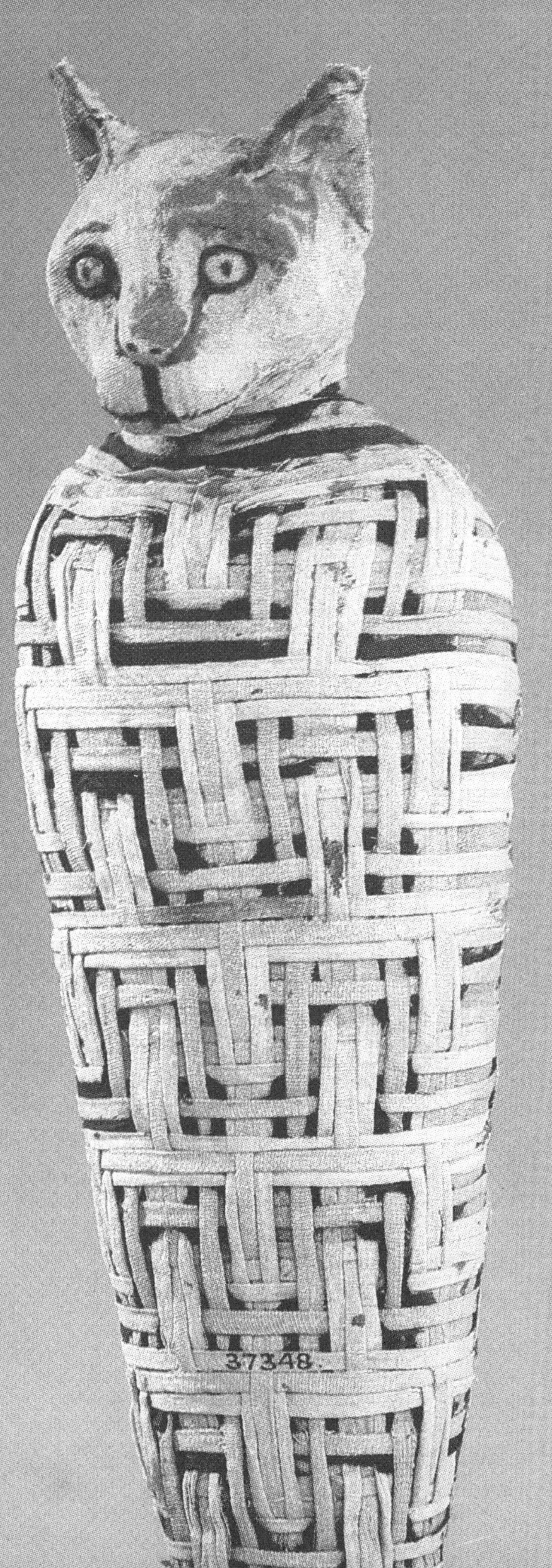
37348

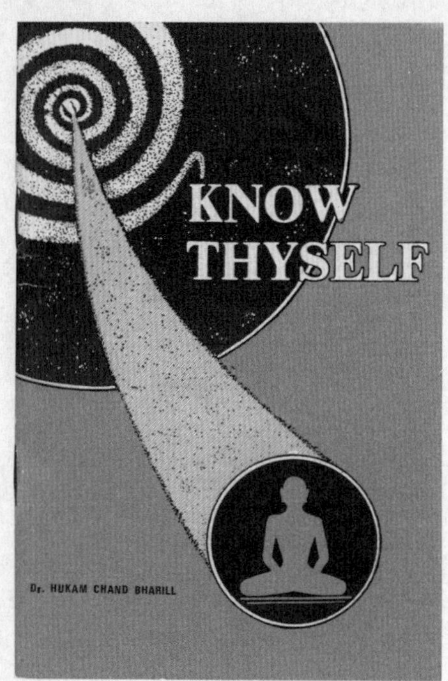
KNOW
THYSELF
Dr. HUKAM CHAND BHARILL

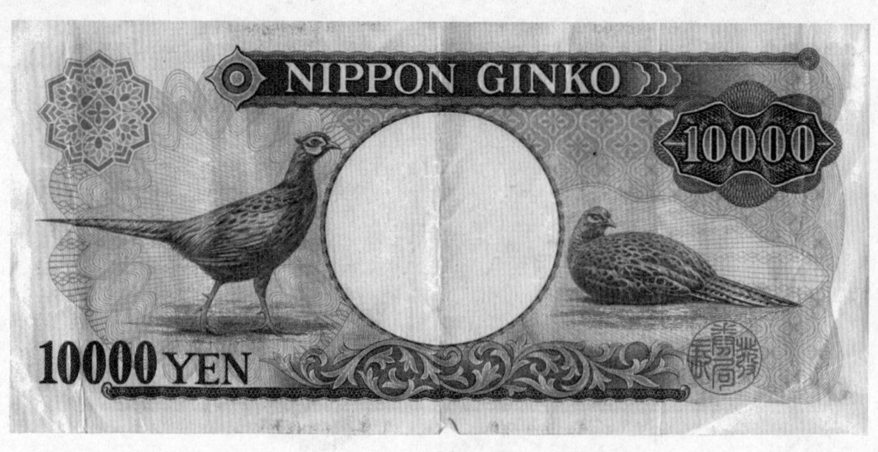
NIPPON GINKO
10000
10000 YEN

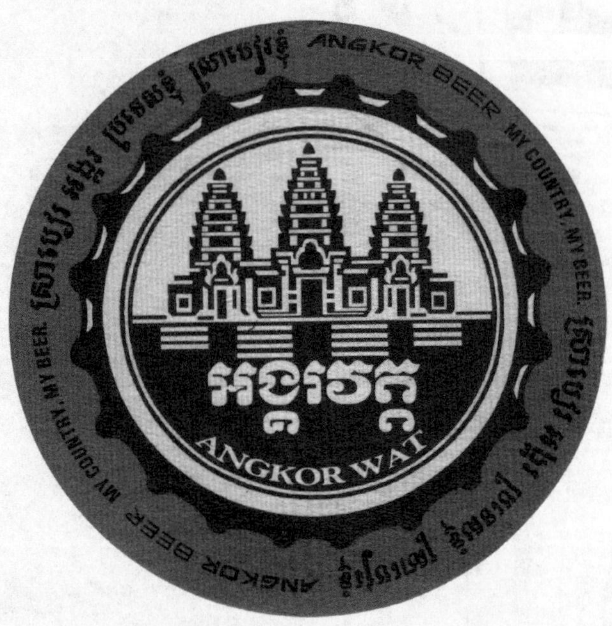
ANGKOR BEER
MY COUNTRY, MY BEER.
ANGKOR WAT
ANGKOR BEER
MY COUNTRY, MY BEER.

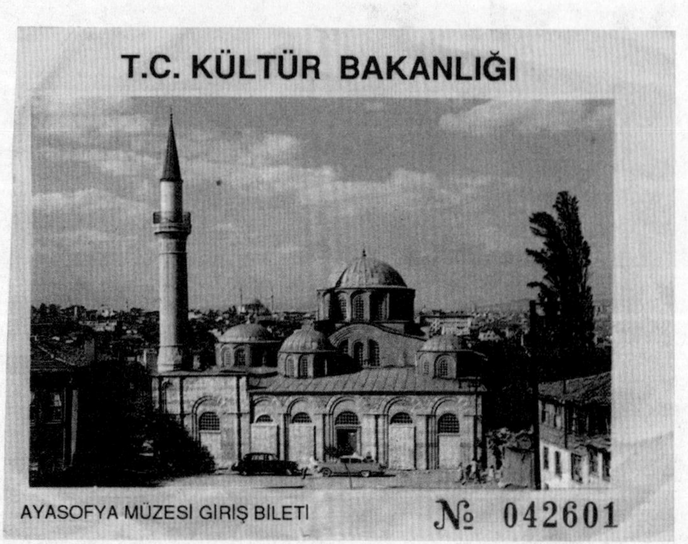
T.C. KÜLTÜR BAKANLIĞI
AYASOFYA MÜZESİ GİRİŞ BİLETİ
№ 042601

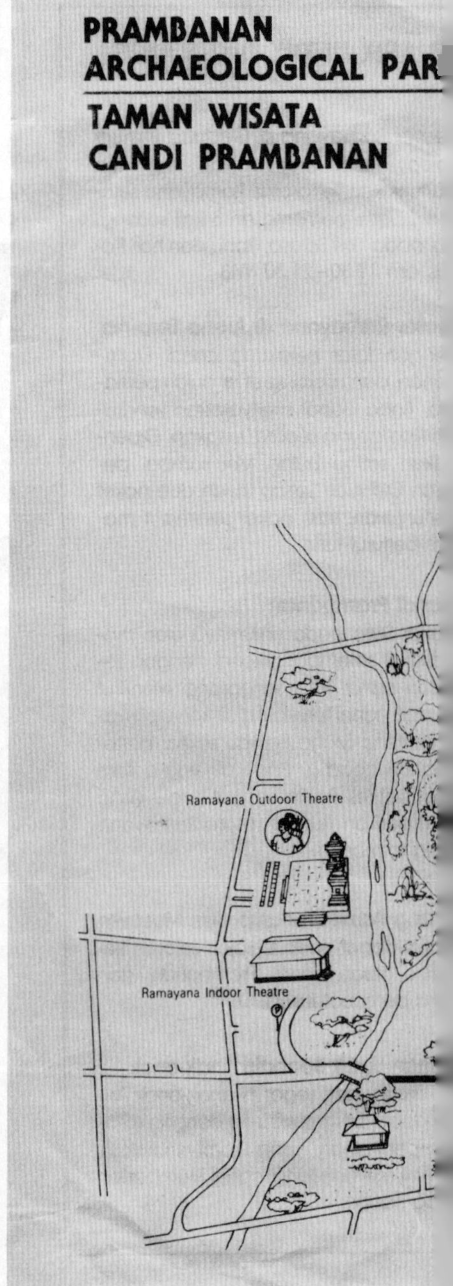
PRAMBANAN
ARCHAEOLOGICAL PAR
TAMAN WISATA
CANDI PRAMBANAN
Ramayana Outdoor Theatre
Ramayana Indoor Theatre

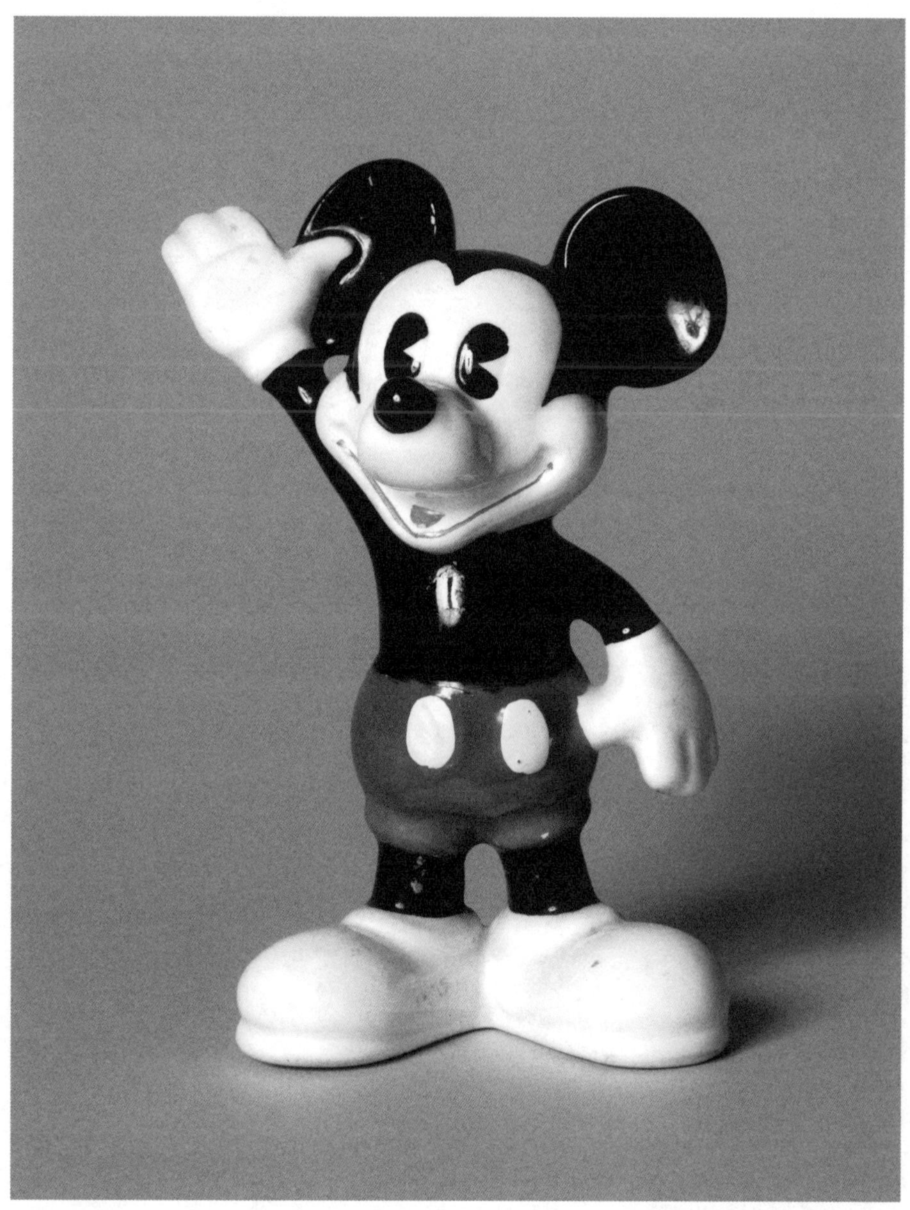

Mouse (13 cm)

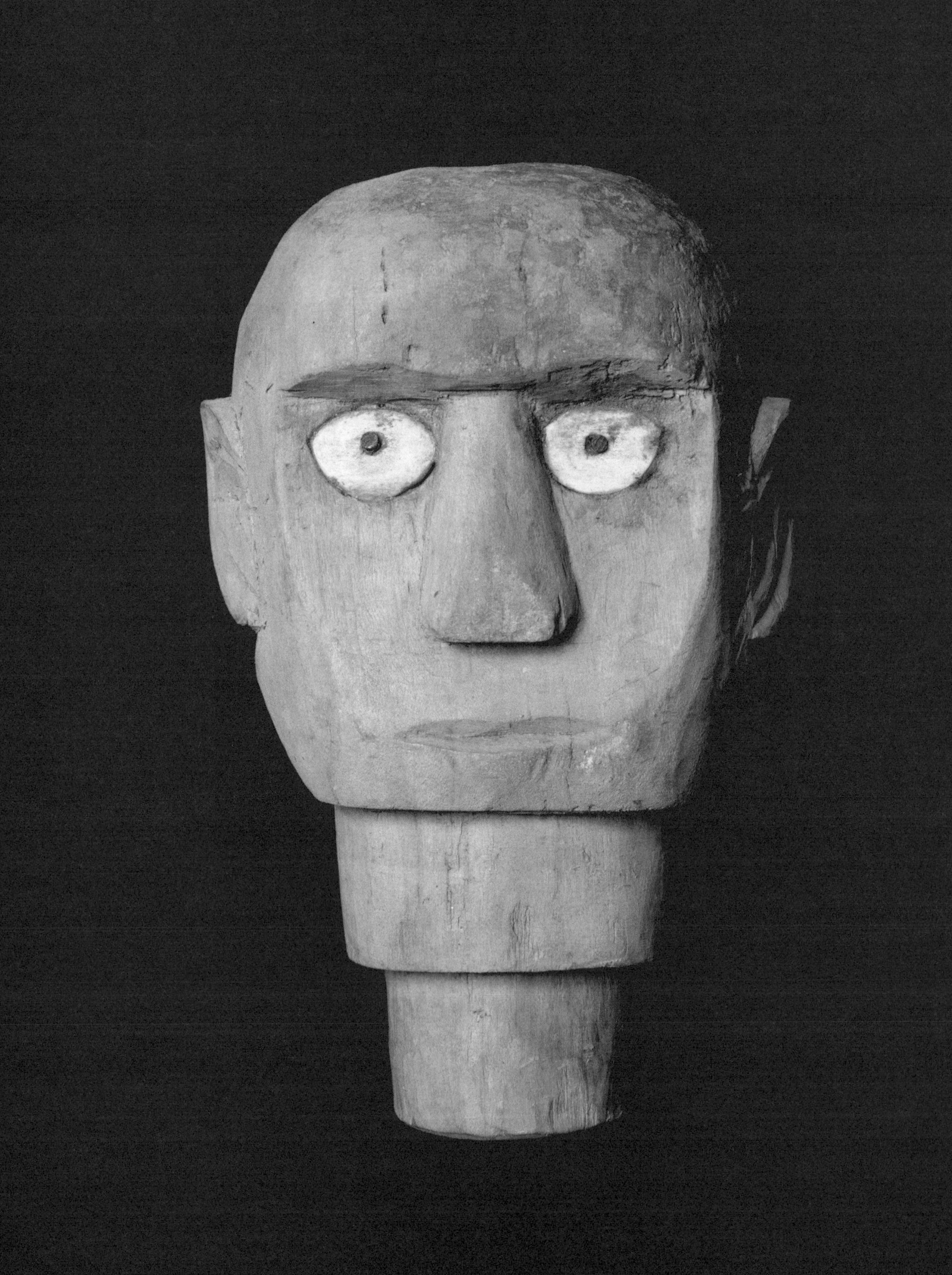

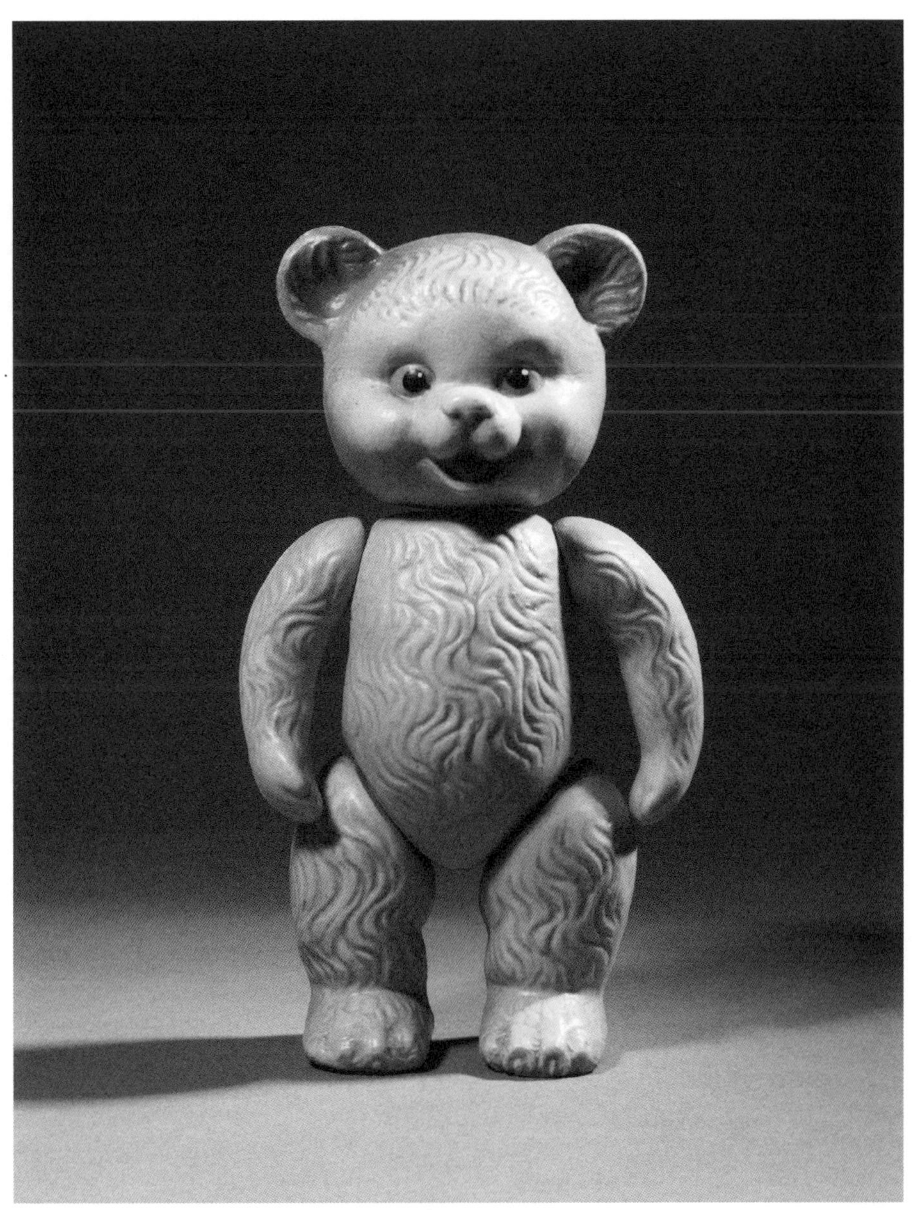

Plastic Bear (15.5 cm)

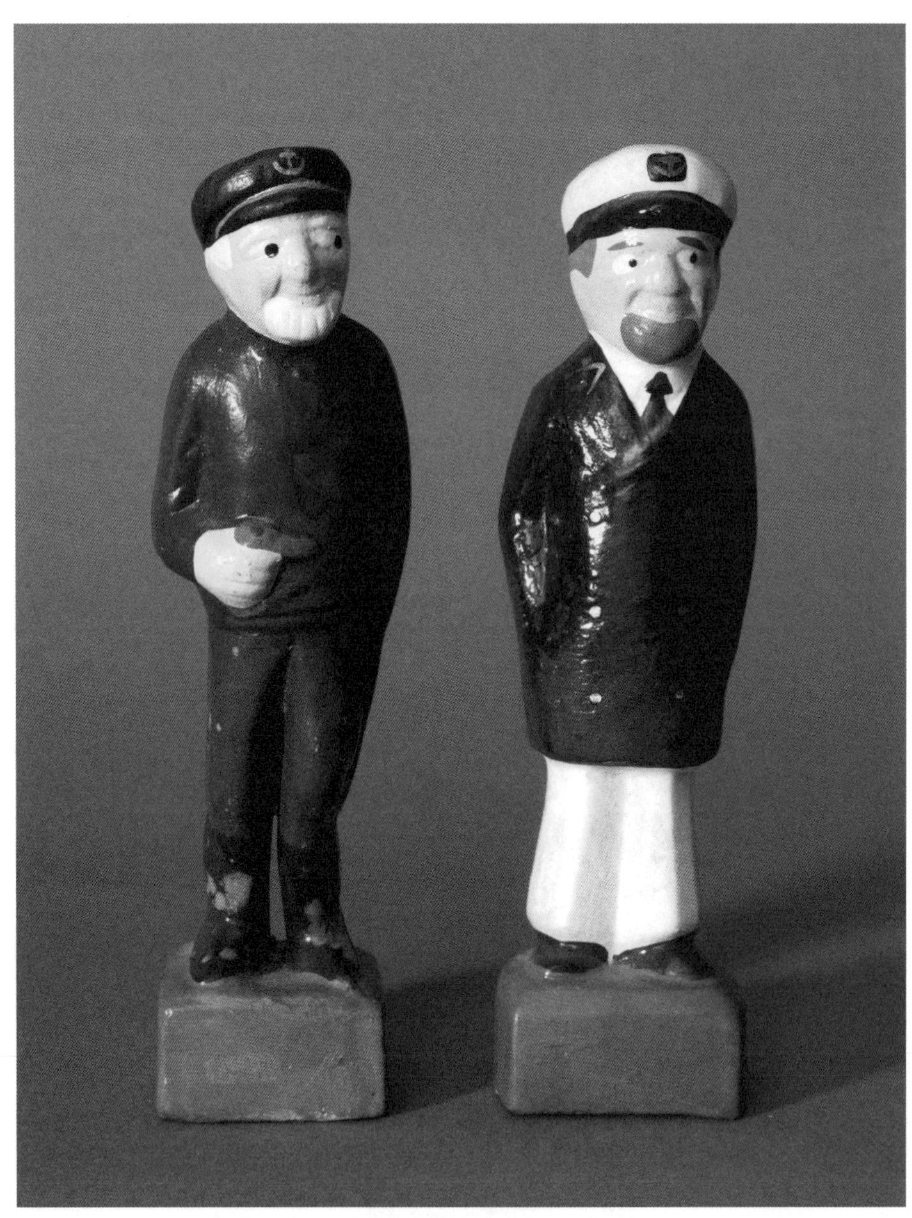

Plaster Fishermen (19.5 cm)

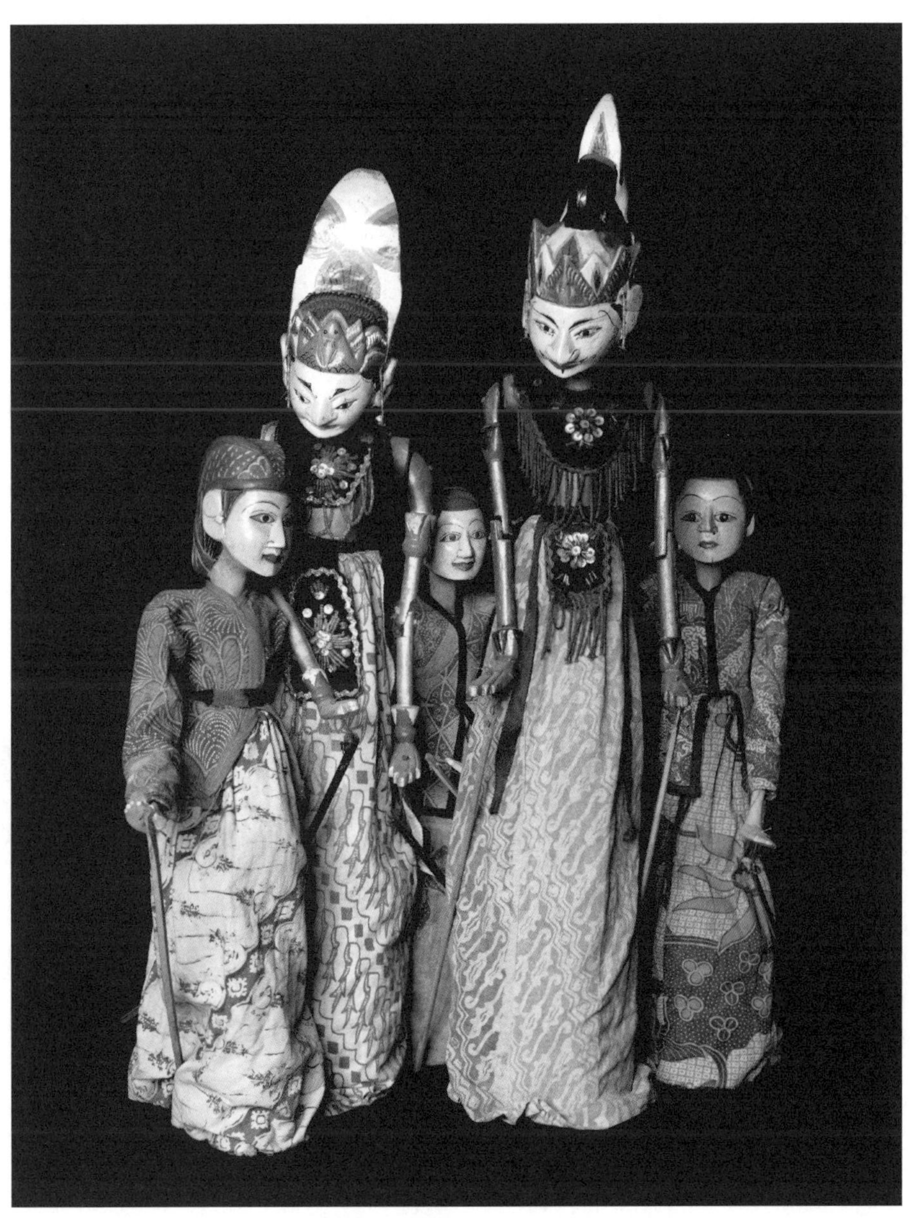

Puppets (85 cm)

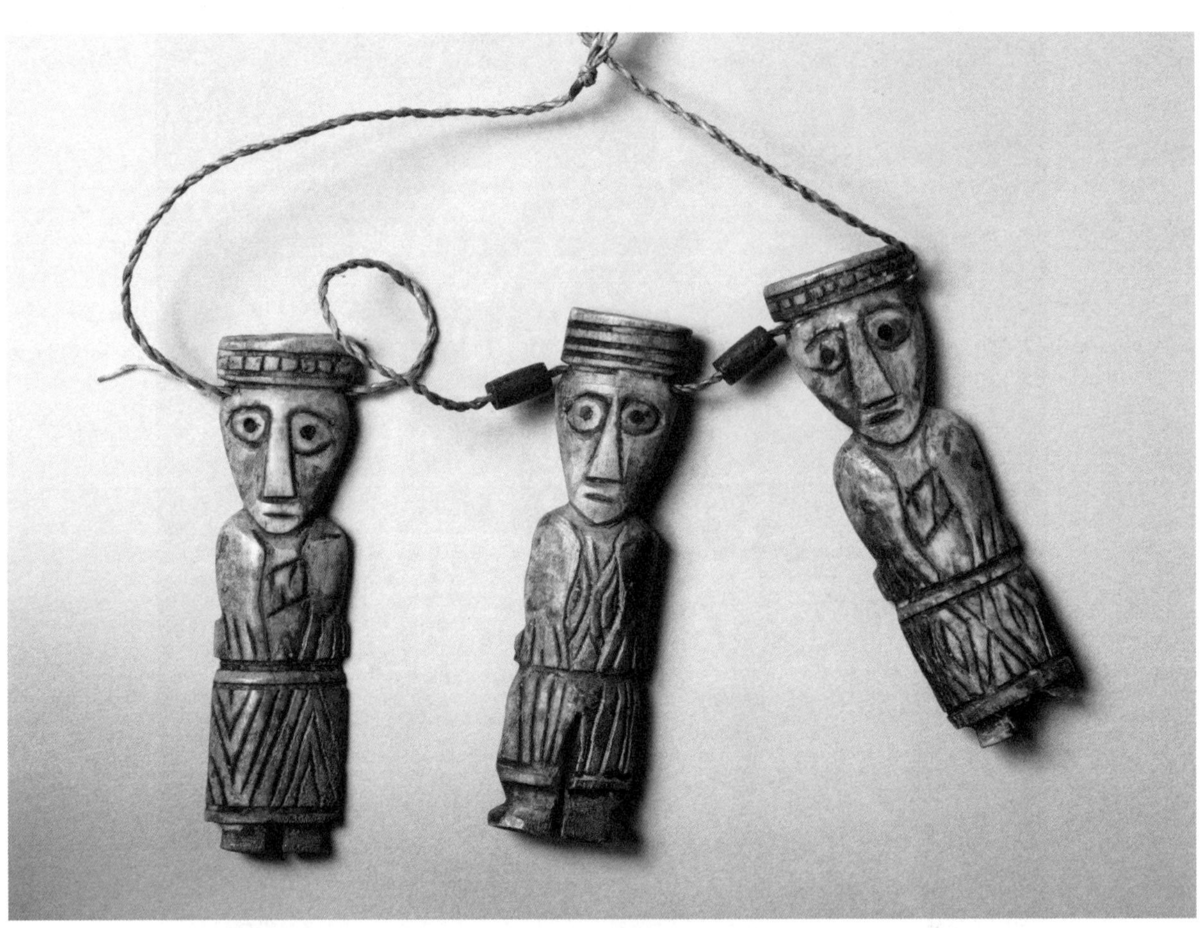

Bone Figures (8.5 cm)

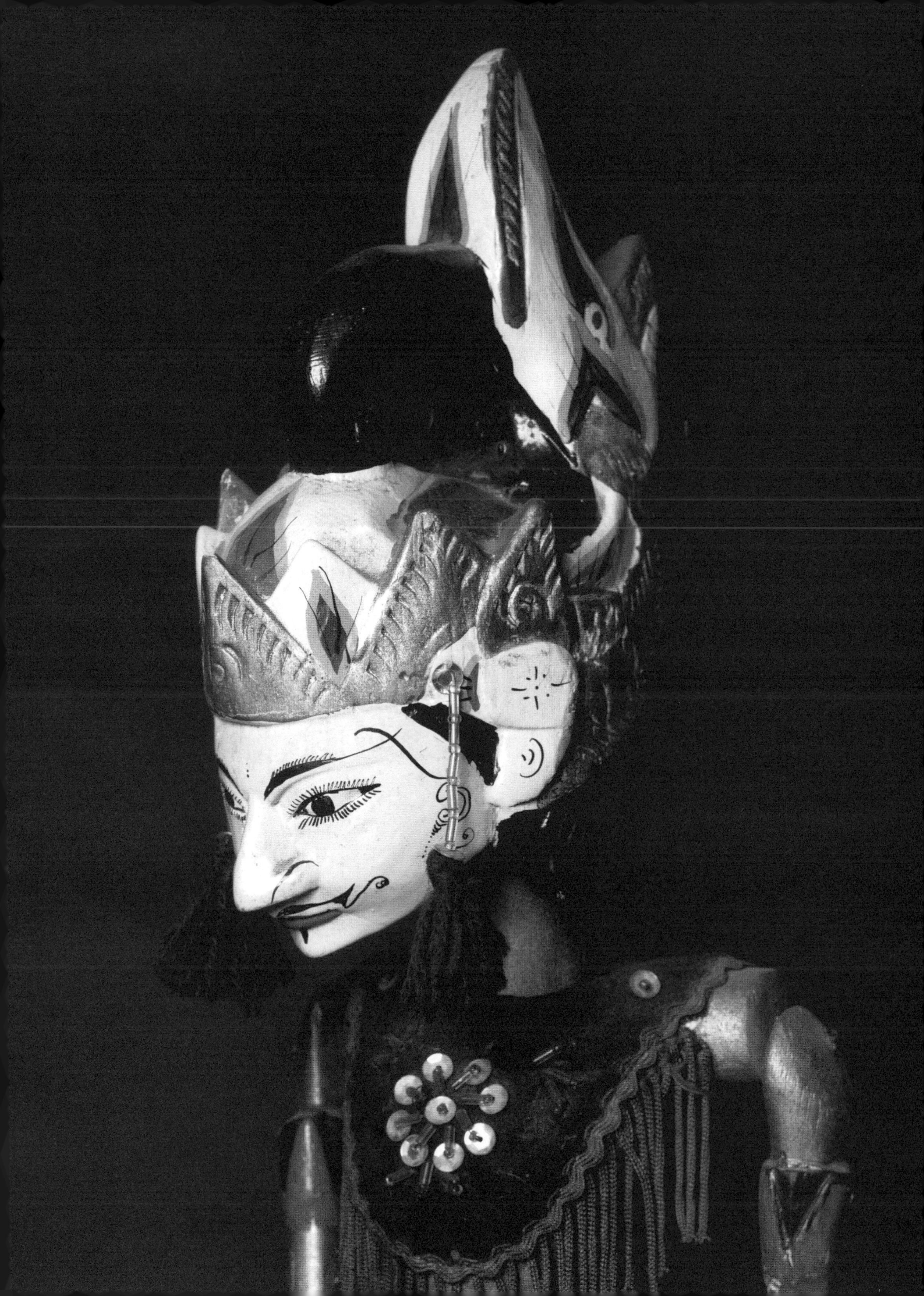

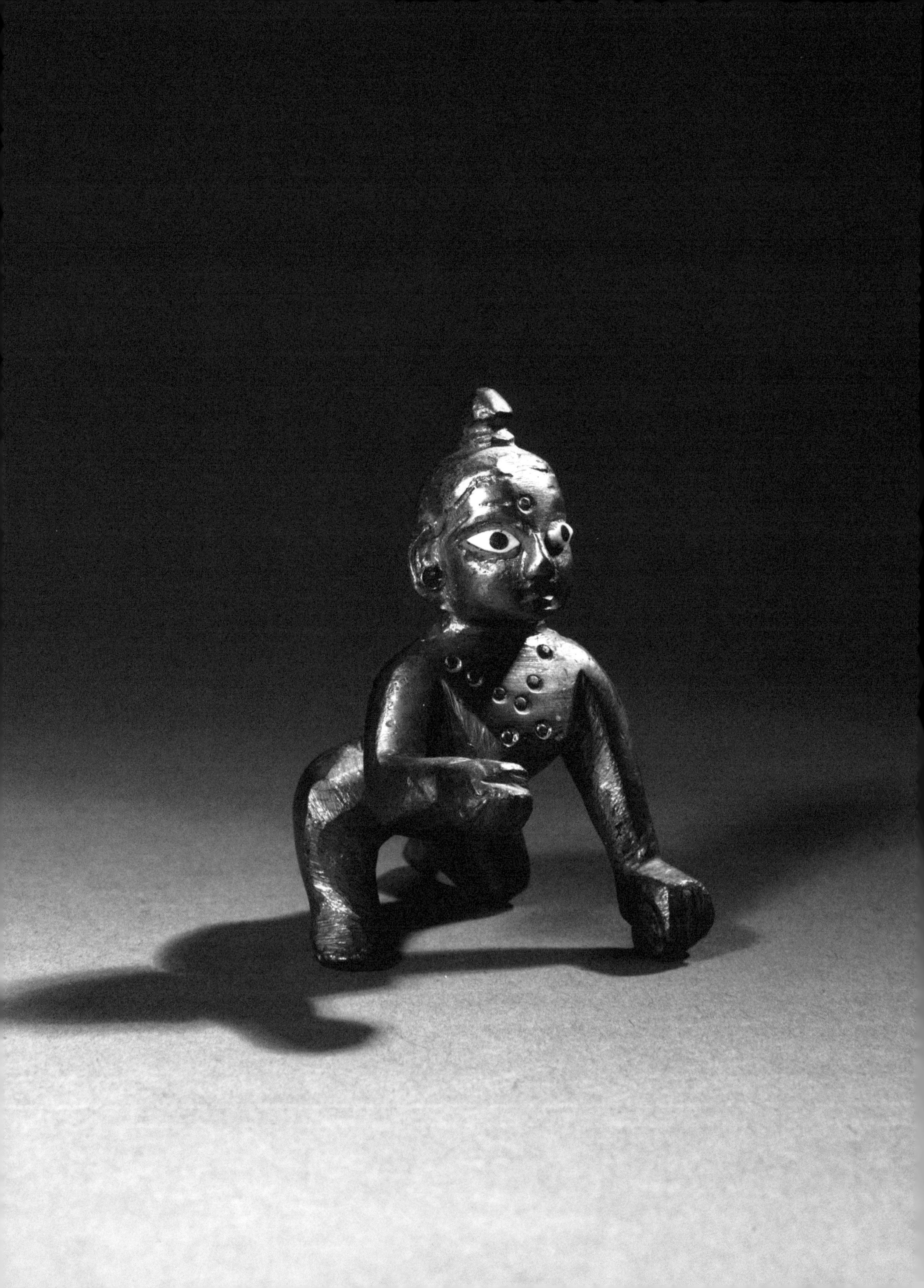

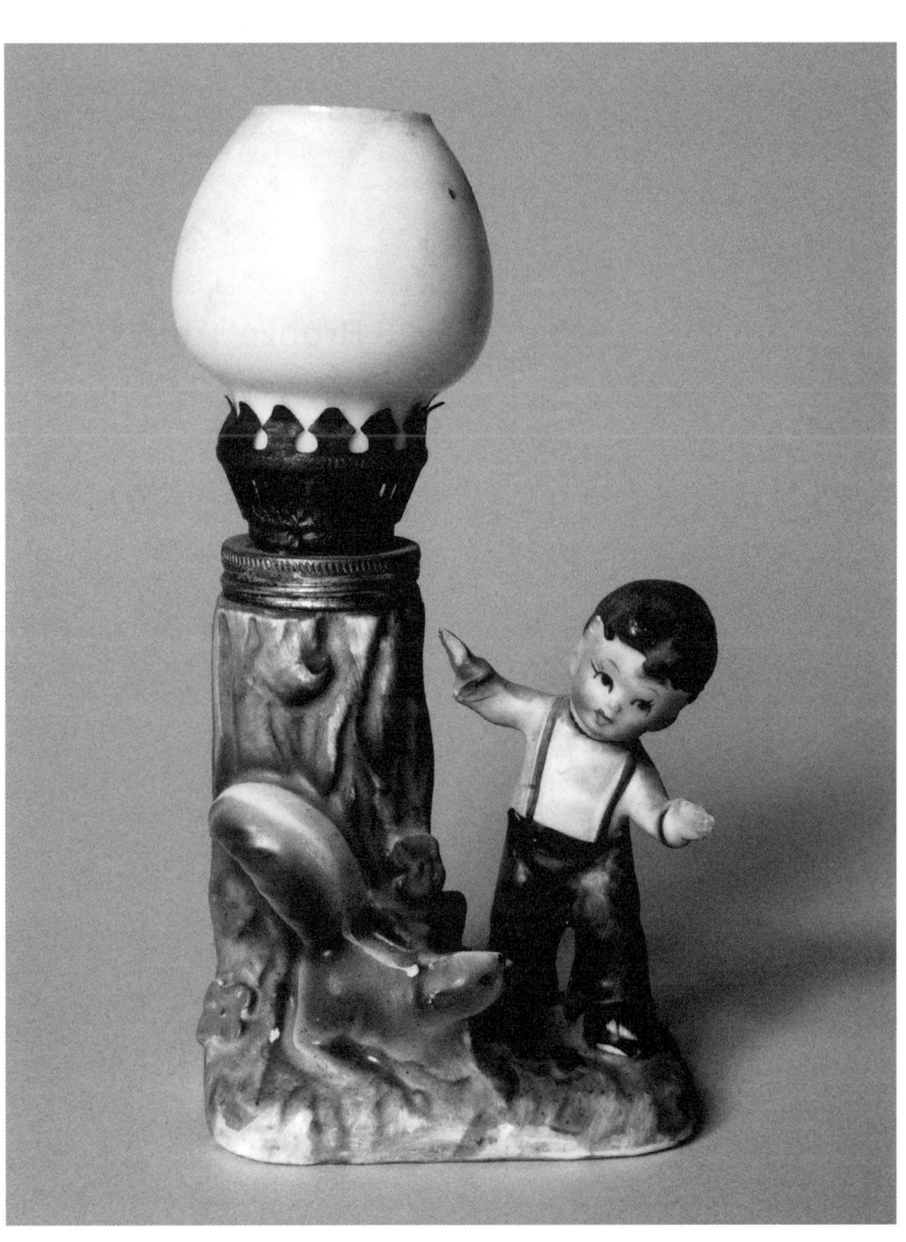

Gas Lamp (18 cm)

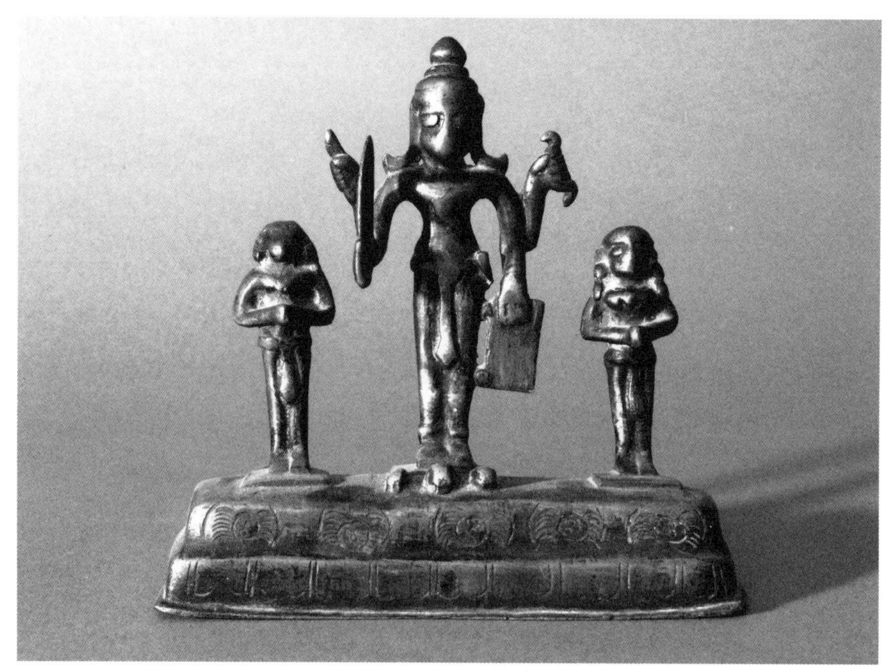
Bronze Triad (16 cm)

Brass Buddha (13.5 cm)

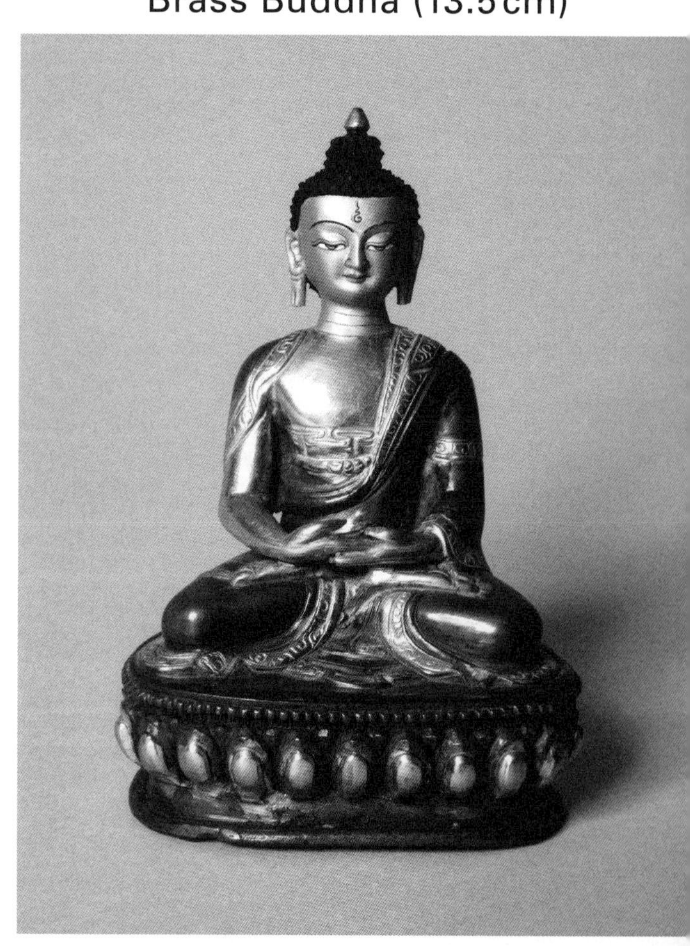

Leopard Buckle (11 cm)

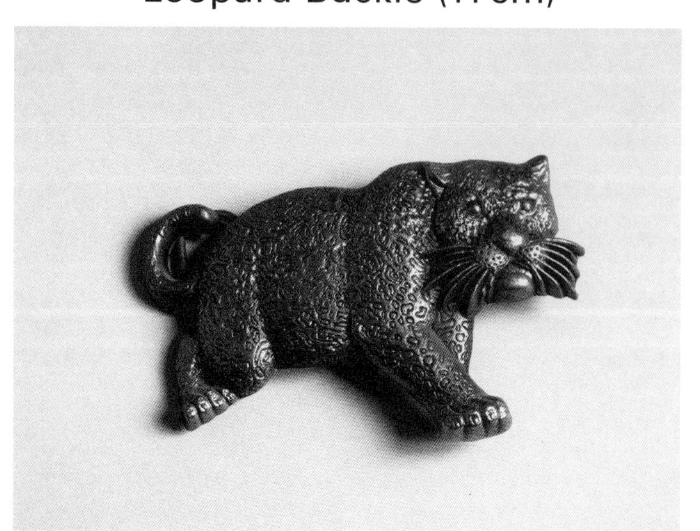

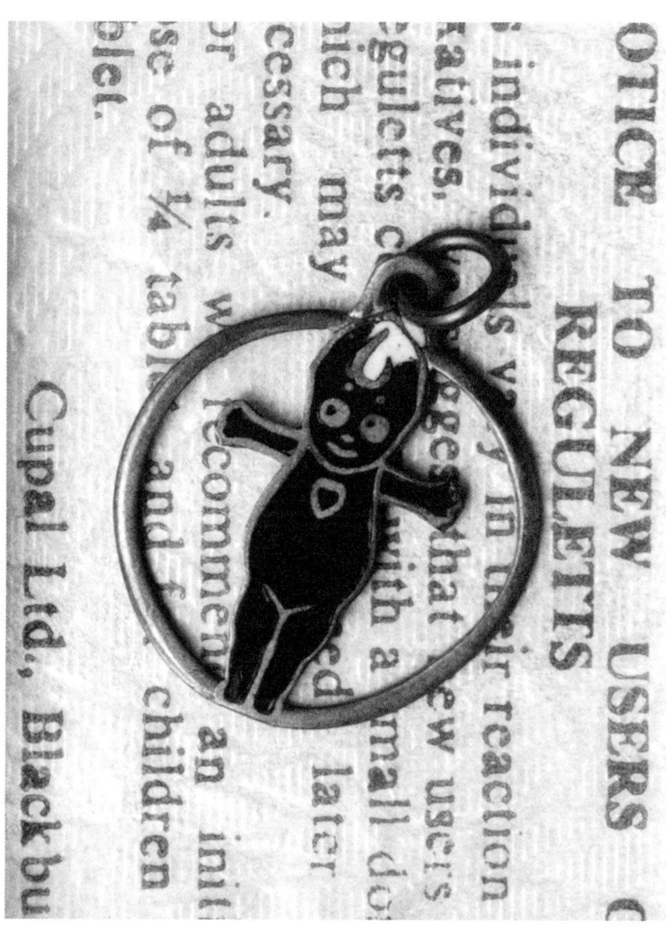

Enamel Pendant (2 cm)

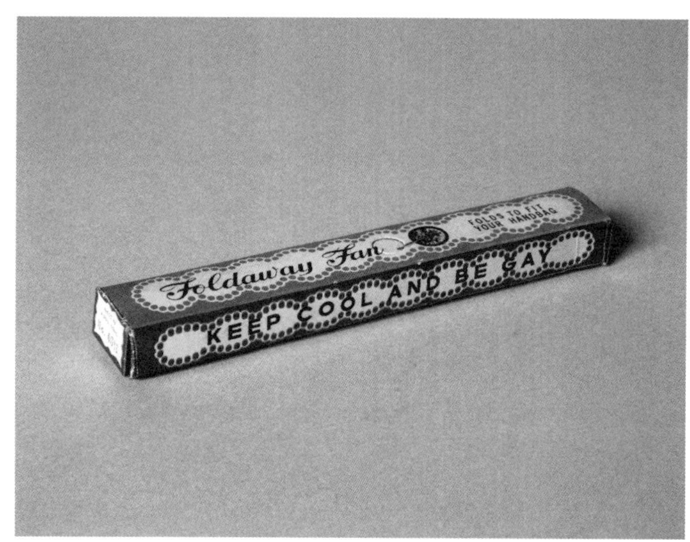

Fan Box (13.5 cm)

Bronze Figure (7 cm)

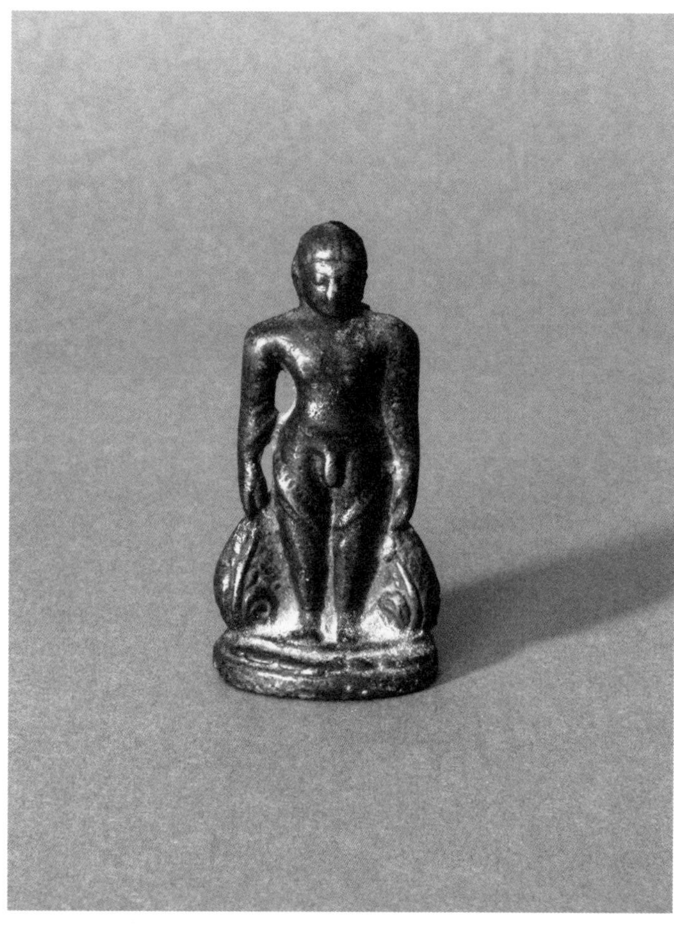

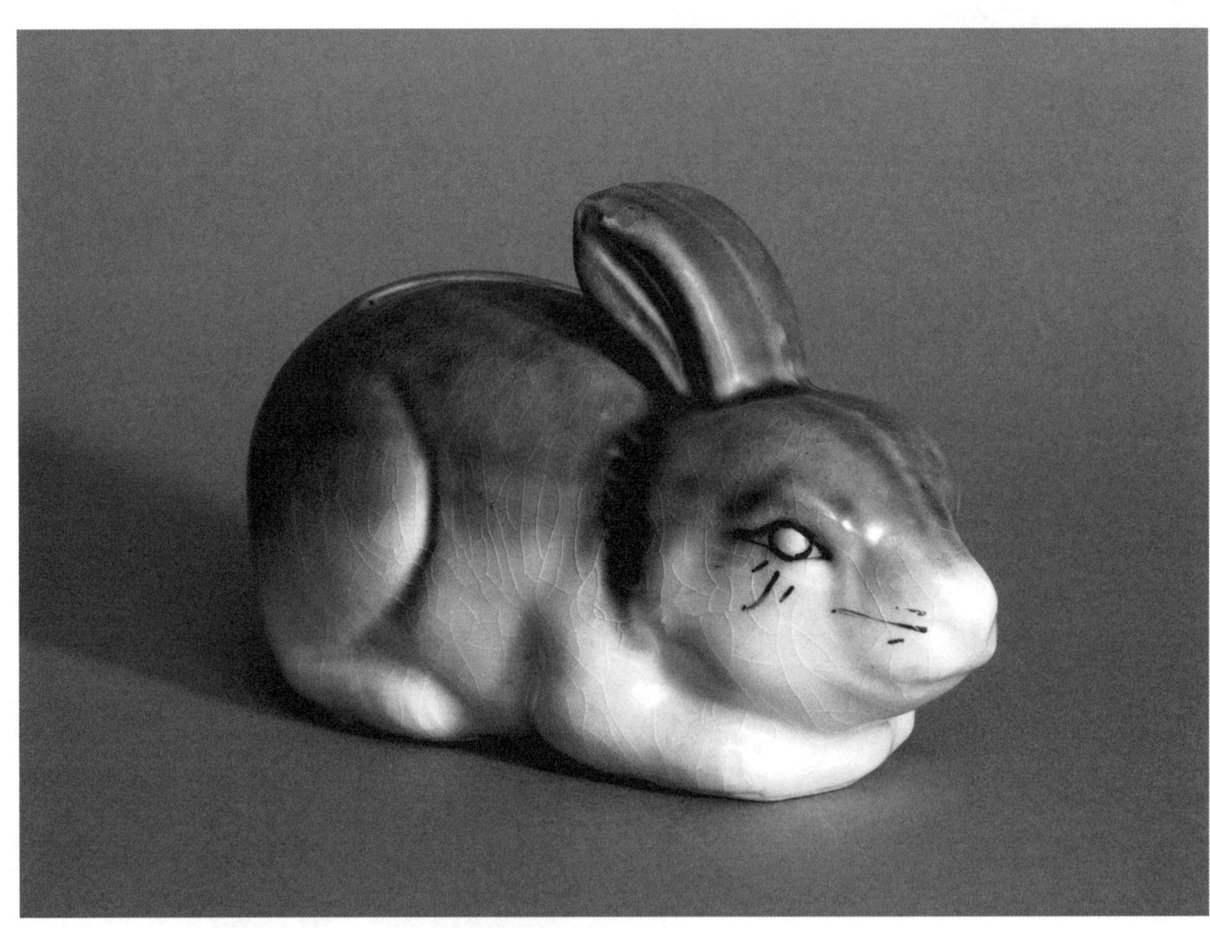

Rabbit Money Box (10 cm)

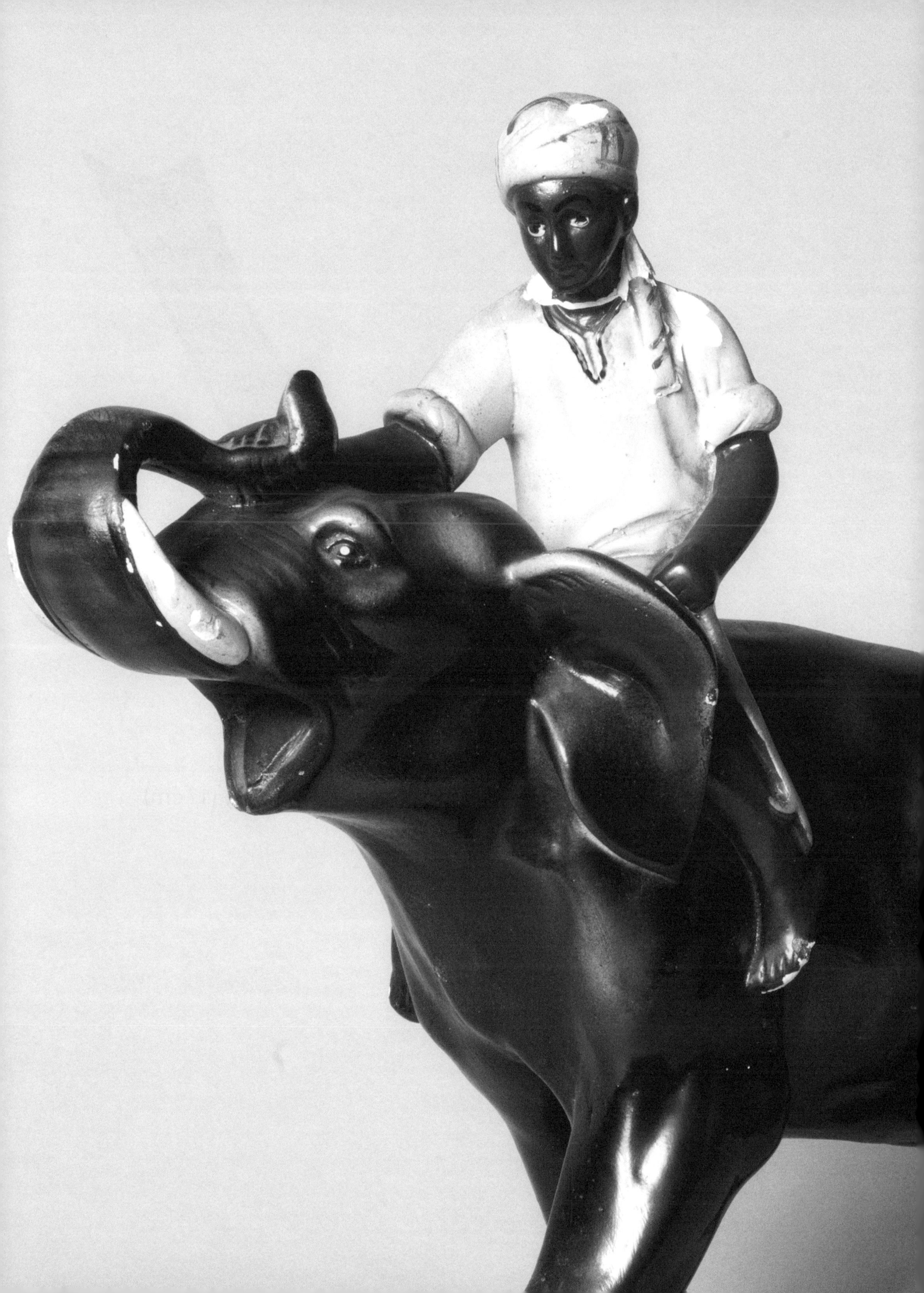

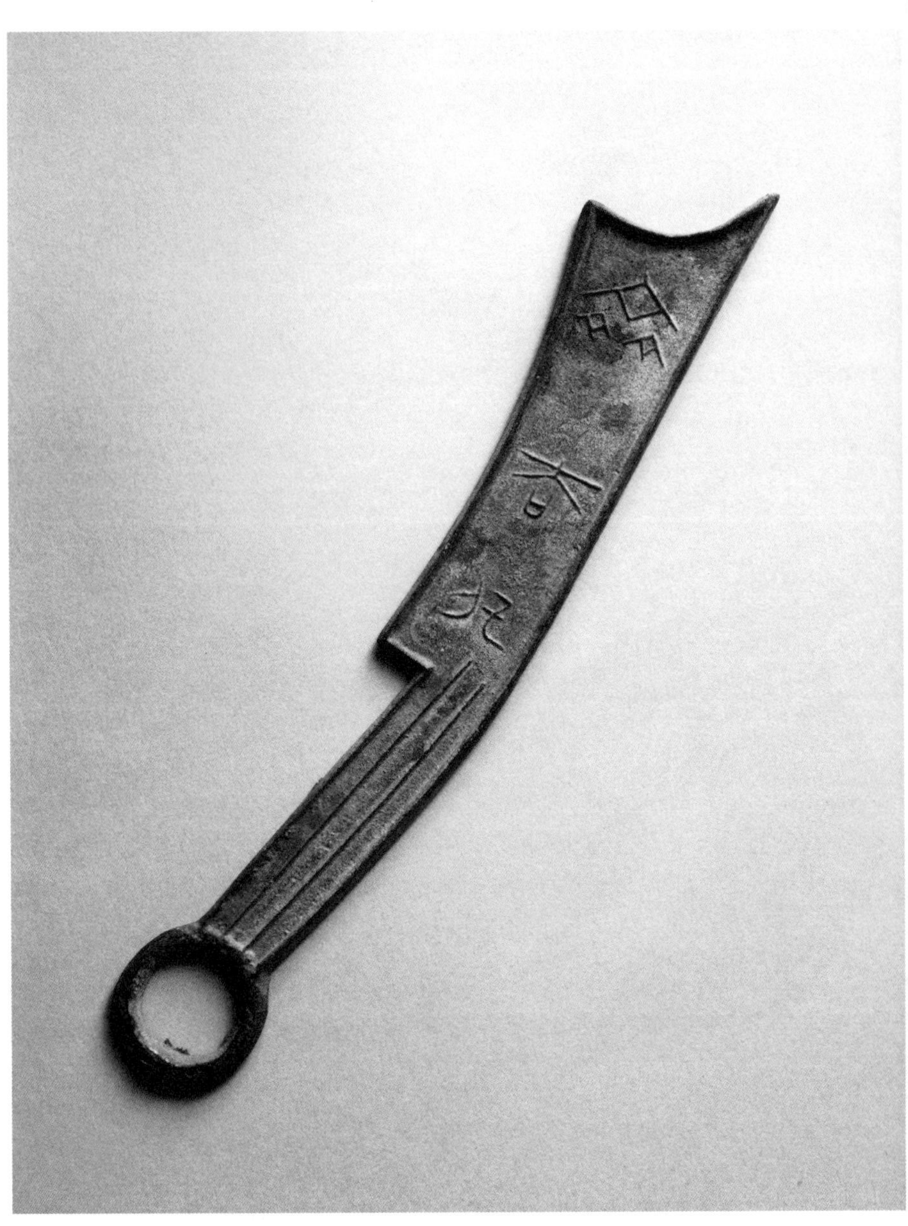

Copper Key ring (17 cm)

Bronze Cuff (10 cm)

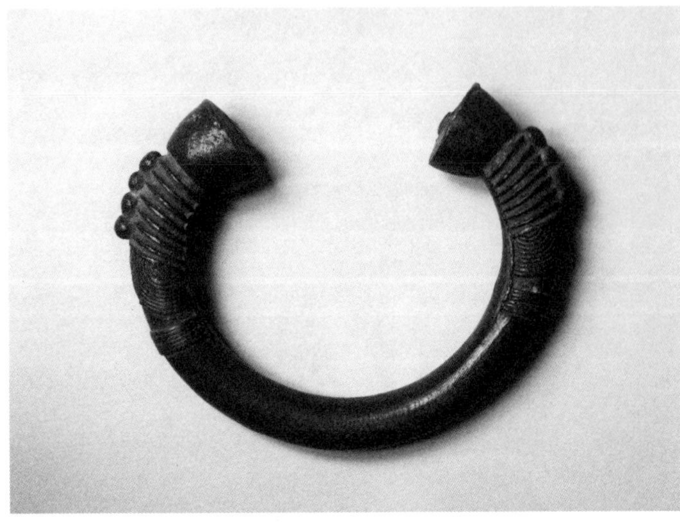

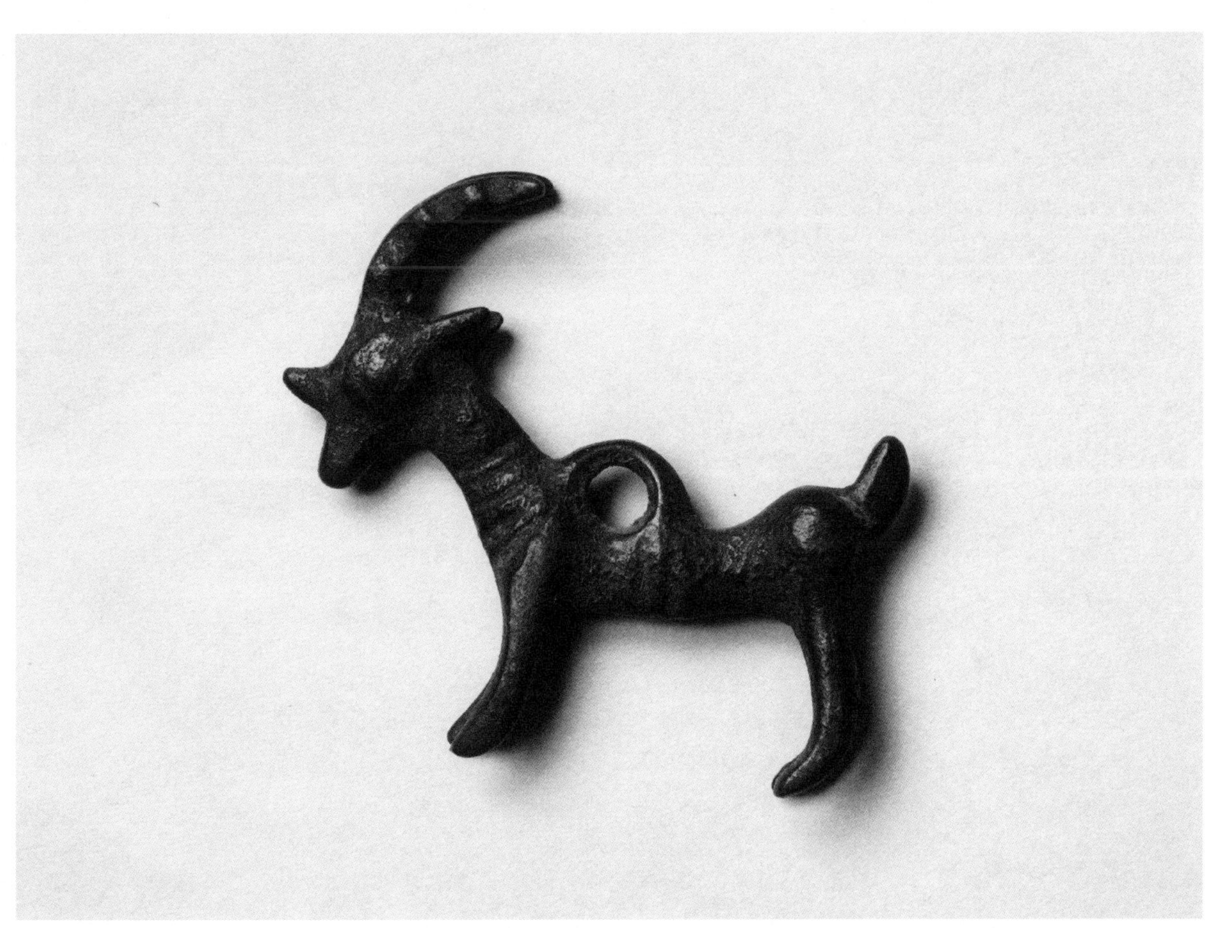

Bronze Goat (5 cm)

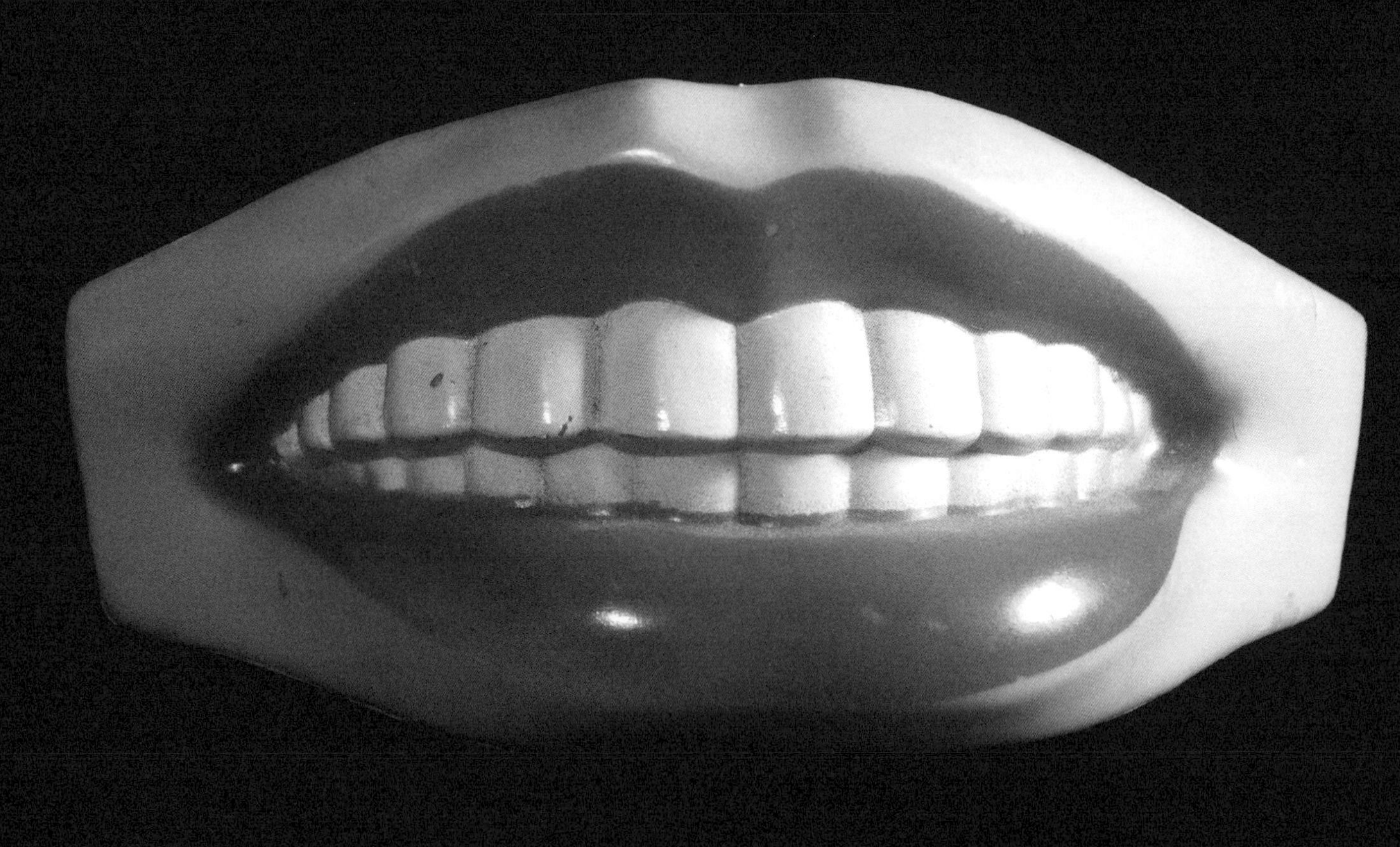

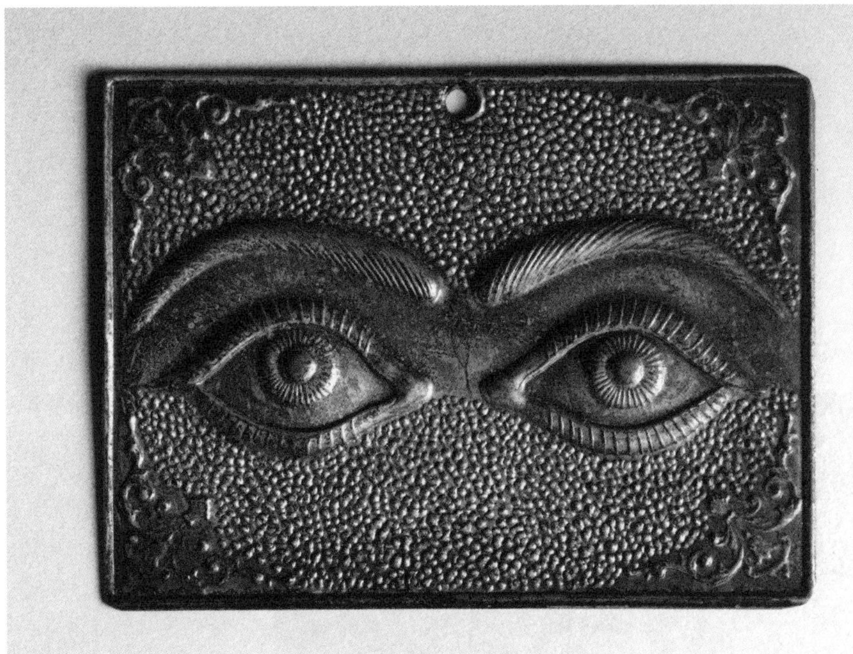

Eyes (8 cm)

Leg (12 cm)

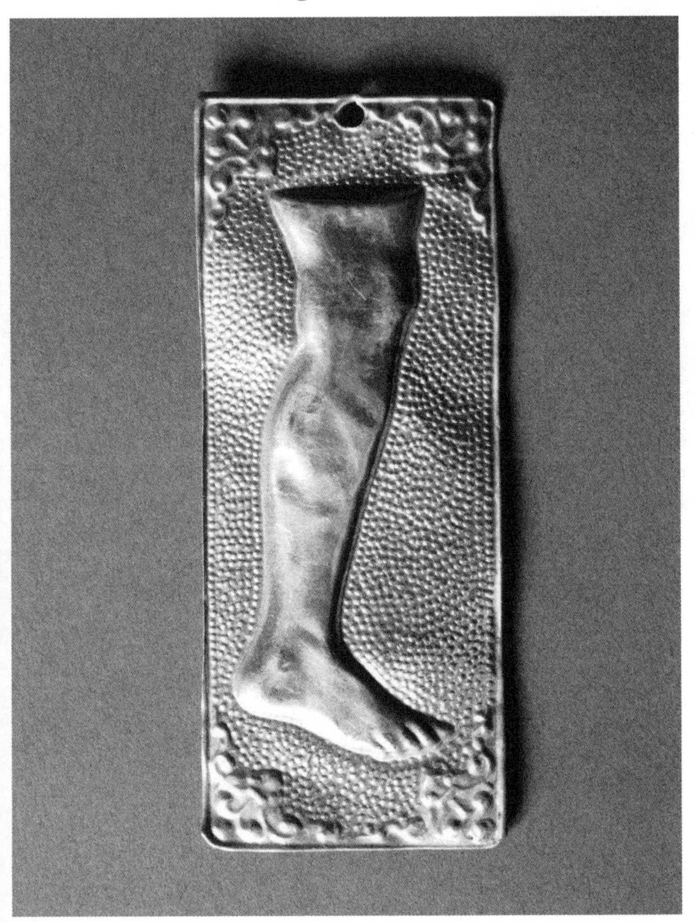

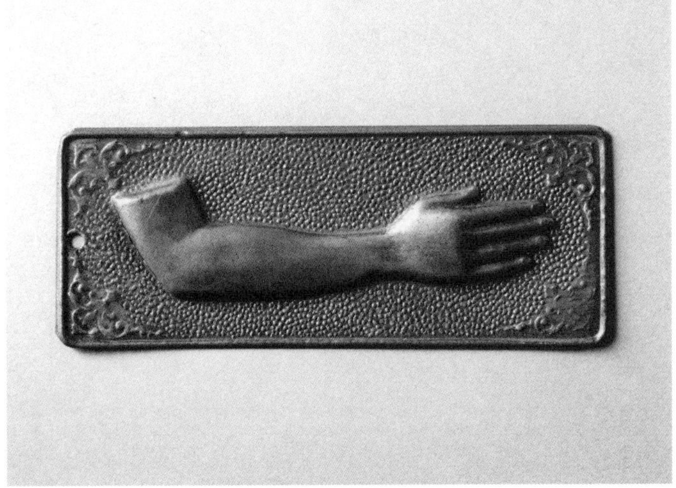

Arm (12 cm)

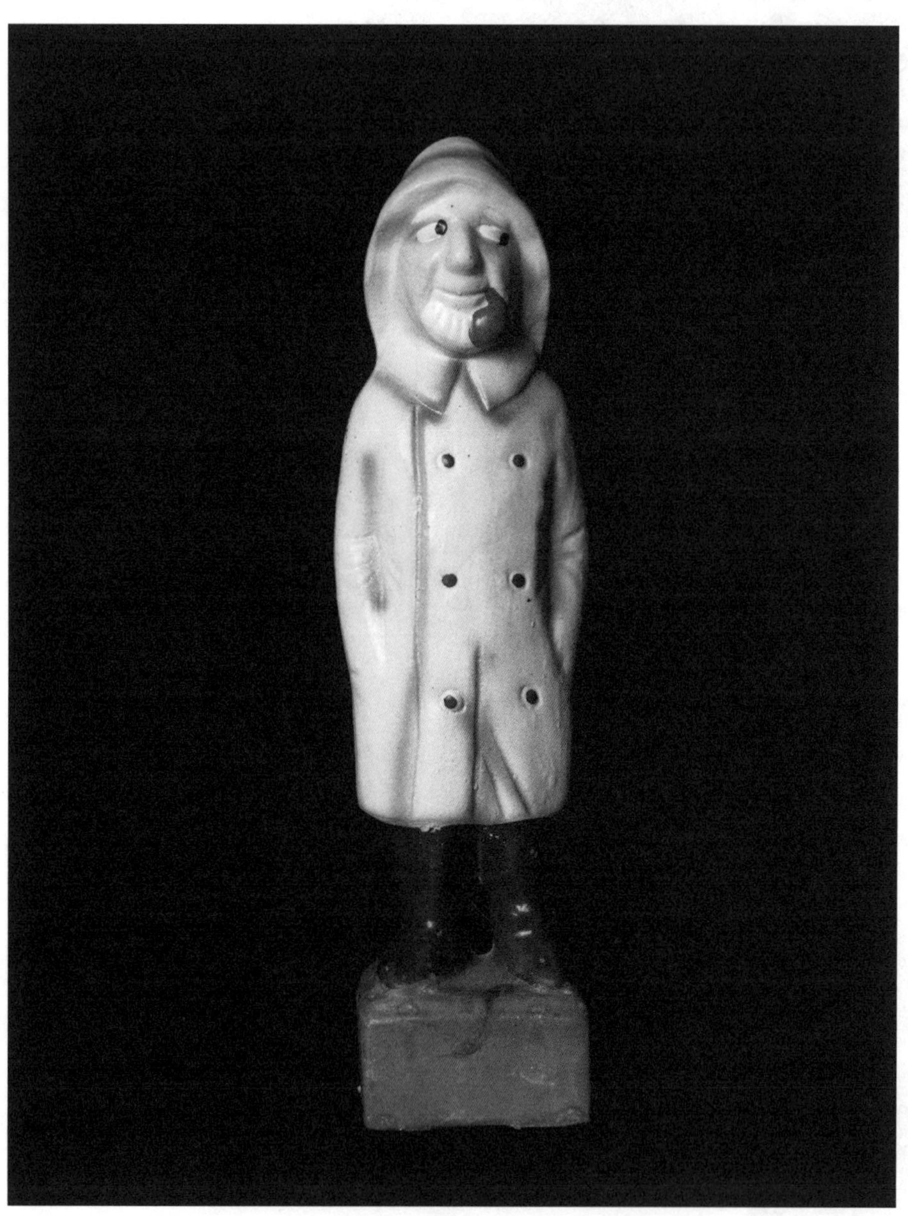

Plaster Fisherman (19.5 cm)

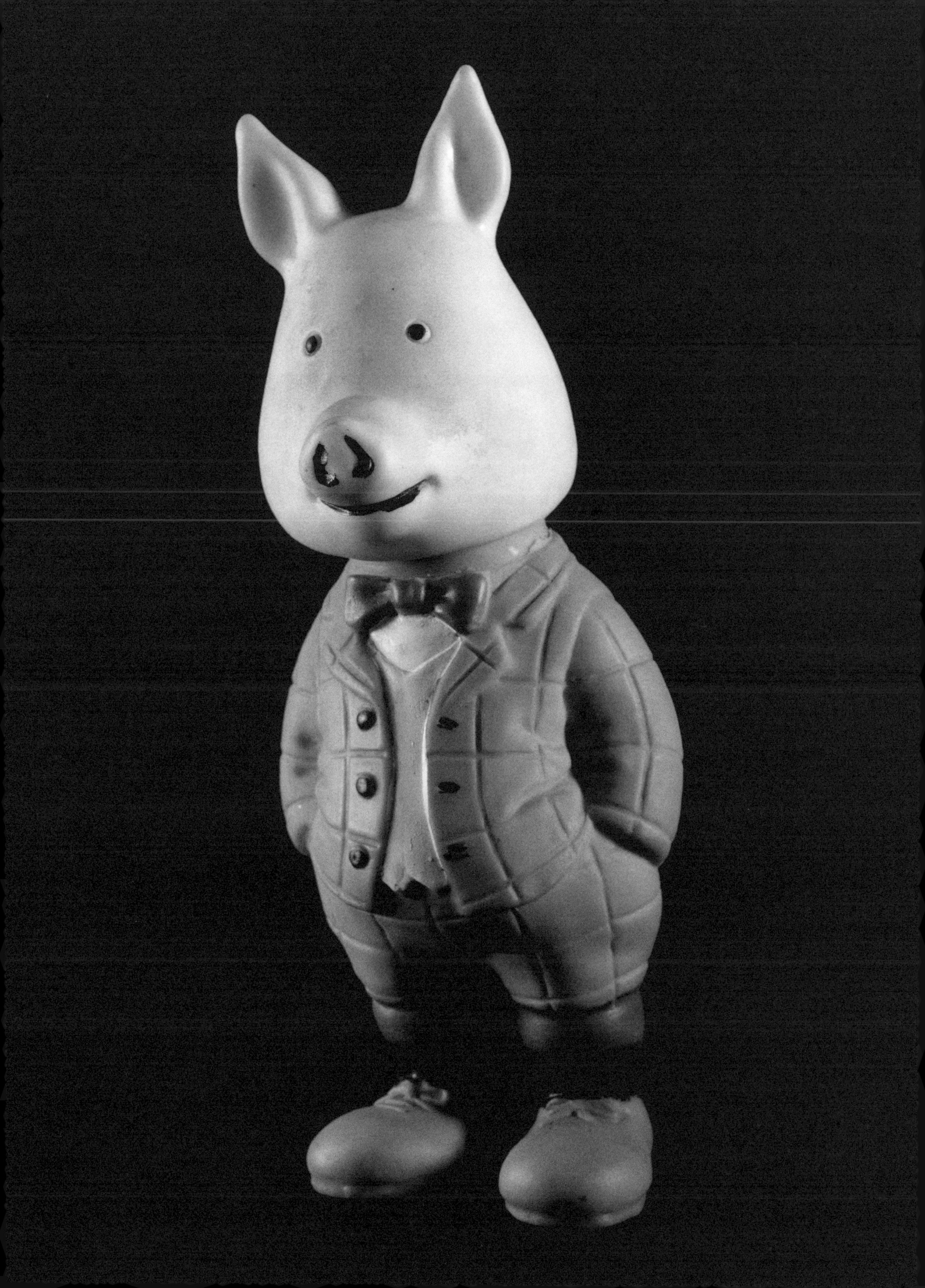

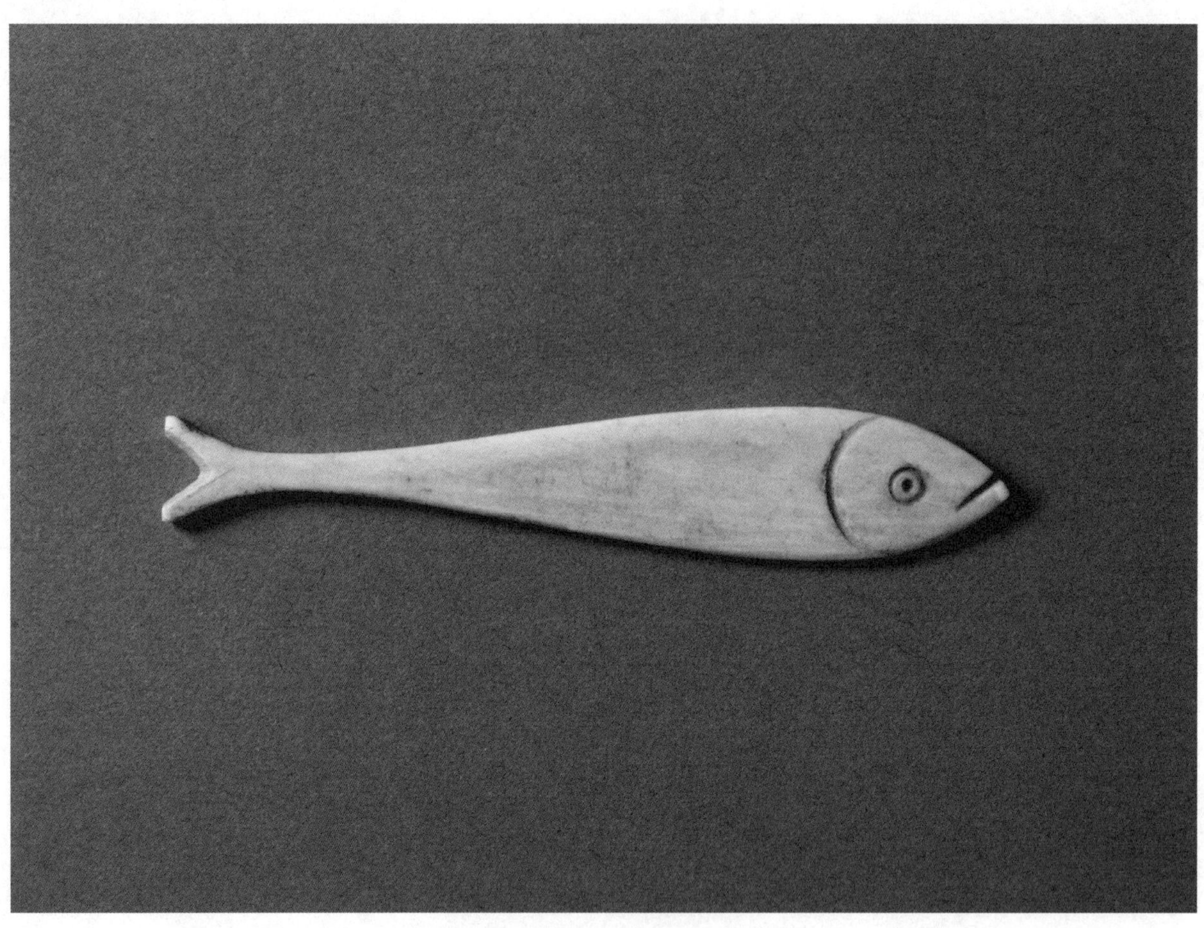

Bone Fish (7 cm)

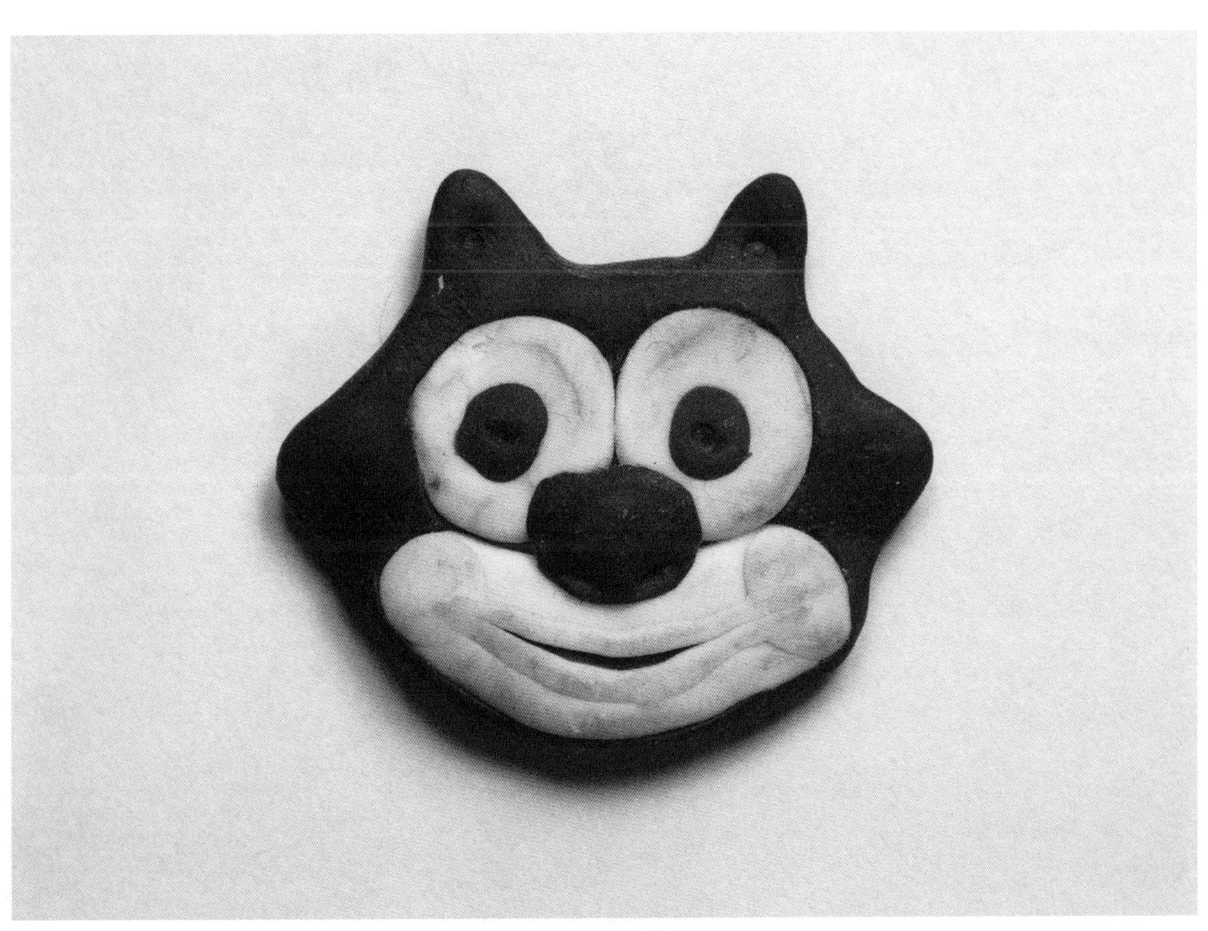

Fimo Cat (5 cm)

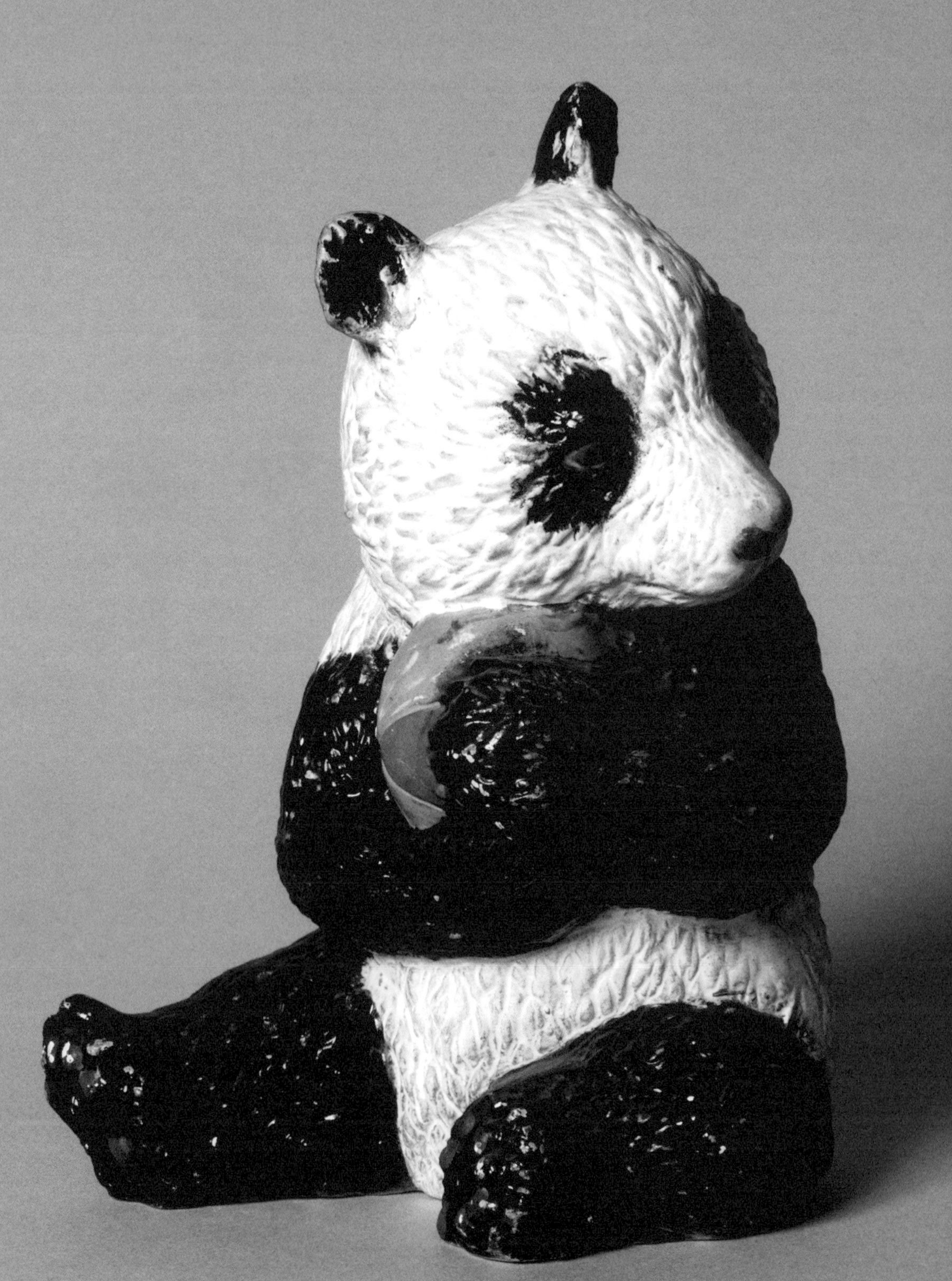

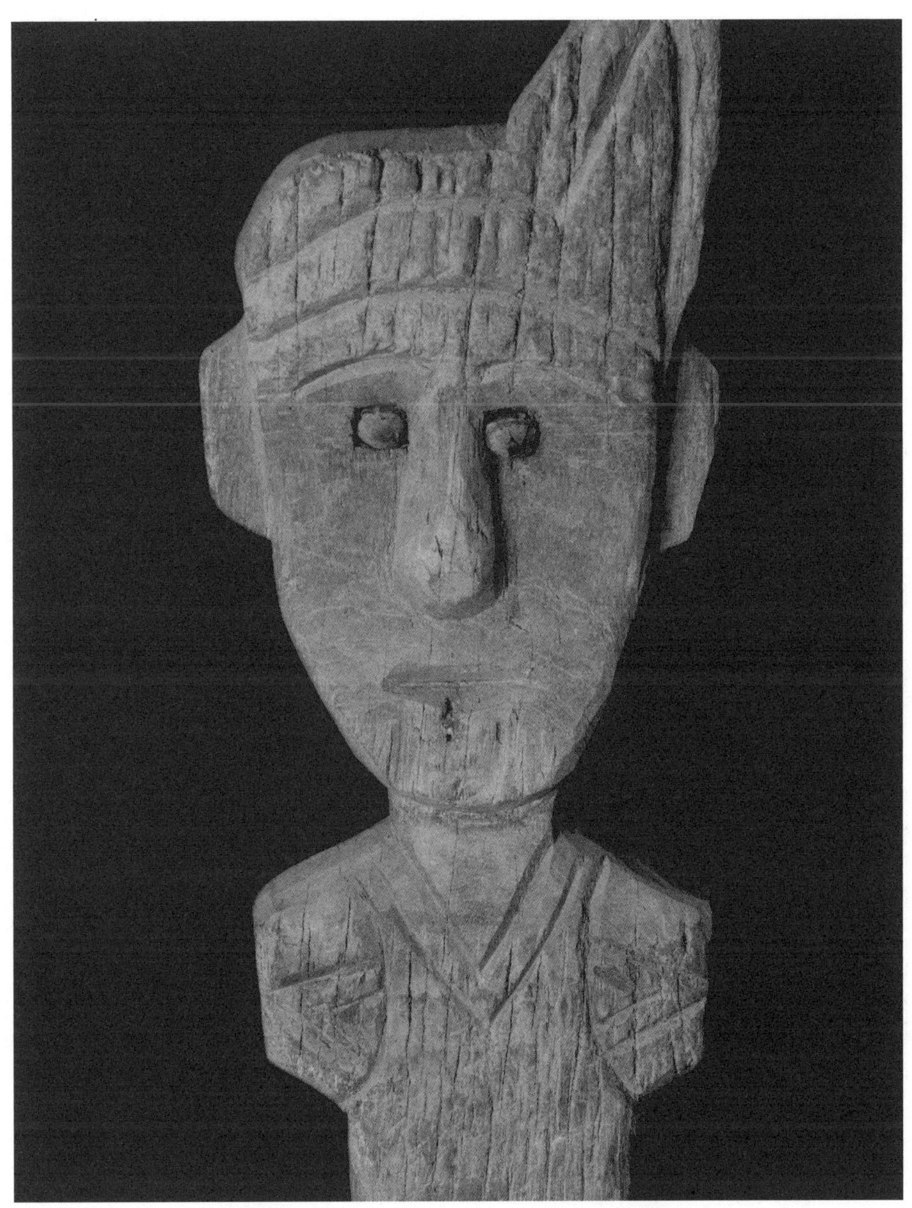

Wooden Figure (80 cm)

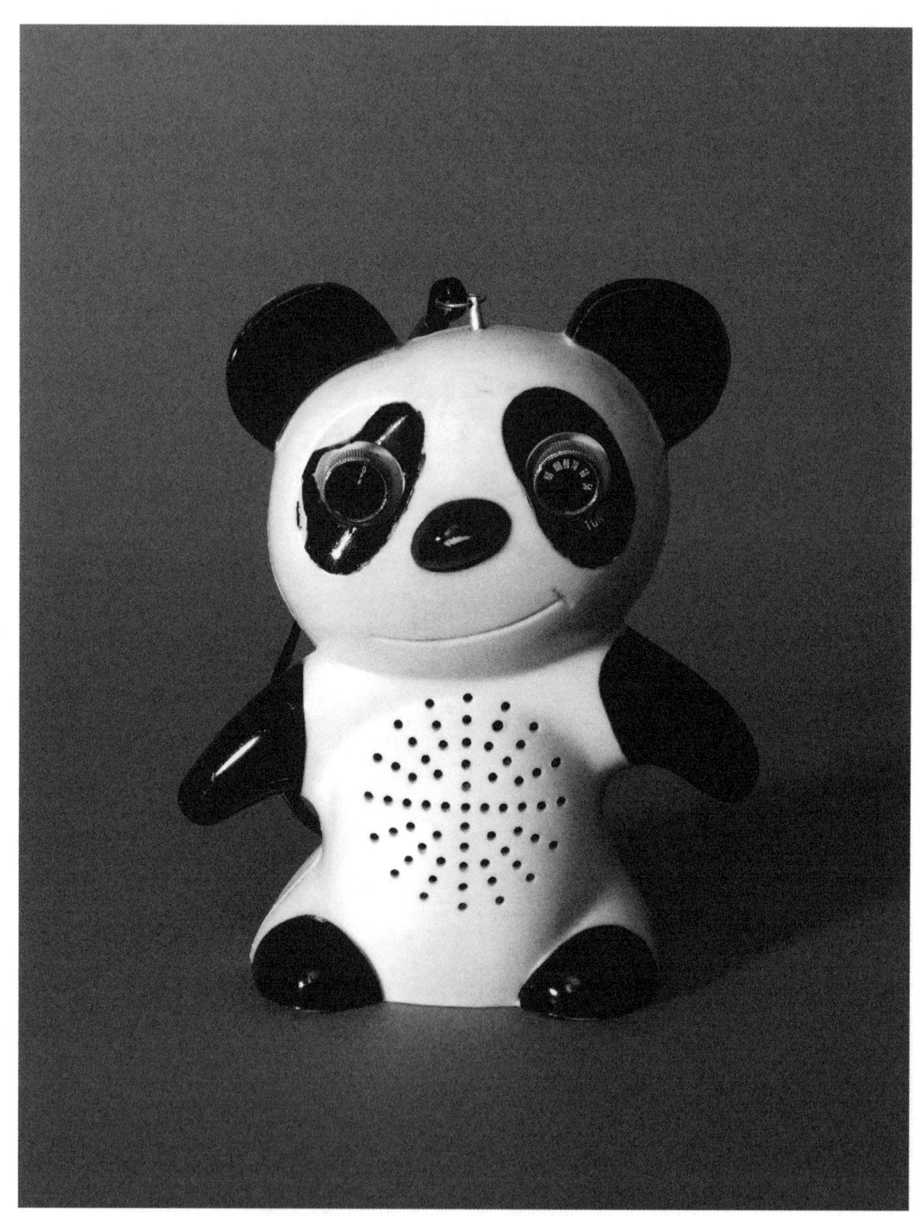

Panda Radio (15 cm)

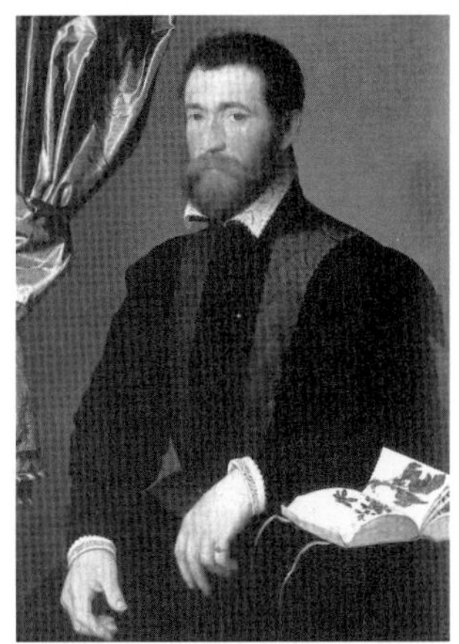

† Portrait by François Clouet of Pierre Quthe, 1562

Le CABINET De CURIOSITÉS De Mlle. CLOUETTE

'To invent you need a good imagination and a pile of junk'[1]

(Thomas A. Edison)

Many years ago in Paris, Shelagh Cluett invited me to accompany her to the Bibliothèque Nationale to check up on her ancestry, convinced that she descended from François Clouet[†], the sixteenth-century court painter. With no reliable evidence, but with much hilarity, a project was conceived for an exhibition of the collection of artifacts and objects she had found on her epic travels to be presented one day as *Le Cabinet de Curiosités de Mlle. Clouette.*

Three observations from Cluett's own texts animate this exhibition which charts her travelling, 'the backbone of her life and work',[2] through objects collected en route:

* There is a sense of journey, of mapping, of the need to locate and ground oneself yet coupled with a sense of dislocation.
* Over many visits to the Musée Guimet in Paris, I became increasingly intrigued with the energy and the vivacity of the objects and was keen to find out more about the cultural context that spawned these works.
* Sculptural objects and images are fundamental to thinking.

Artifacts and objects inspired her own practice and they perform here as agents interacting with a few reminiscences from her 'chums'. The archive of her collection and the website of her production, created

1 Citation pinned on studio door of Maderon Vriesendorp (artist and collector).
2 Charles Garrad.

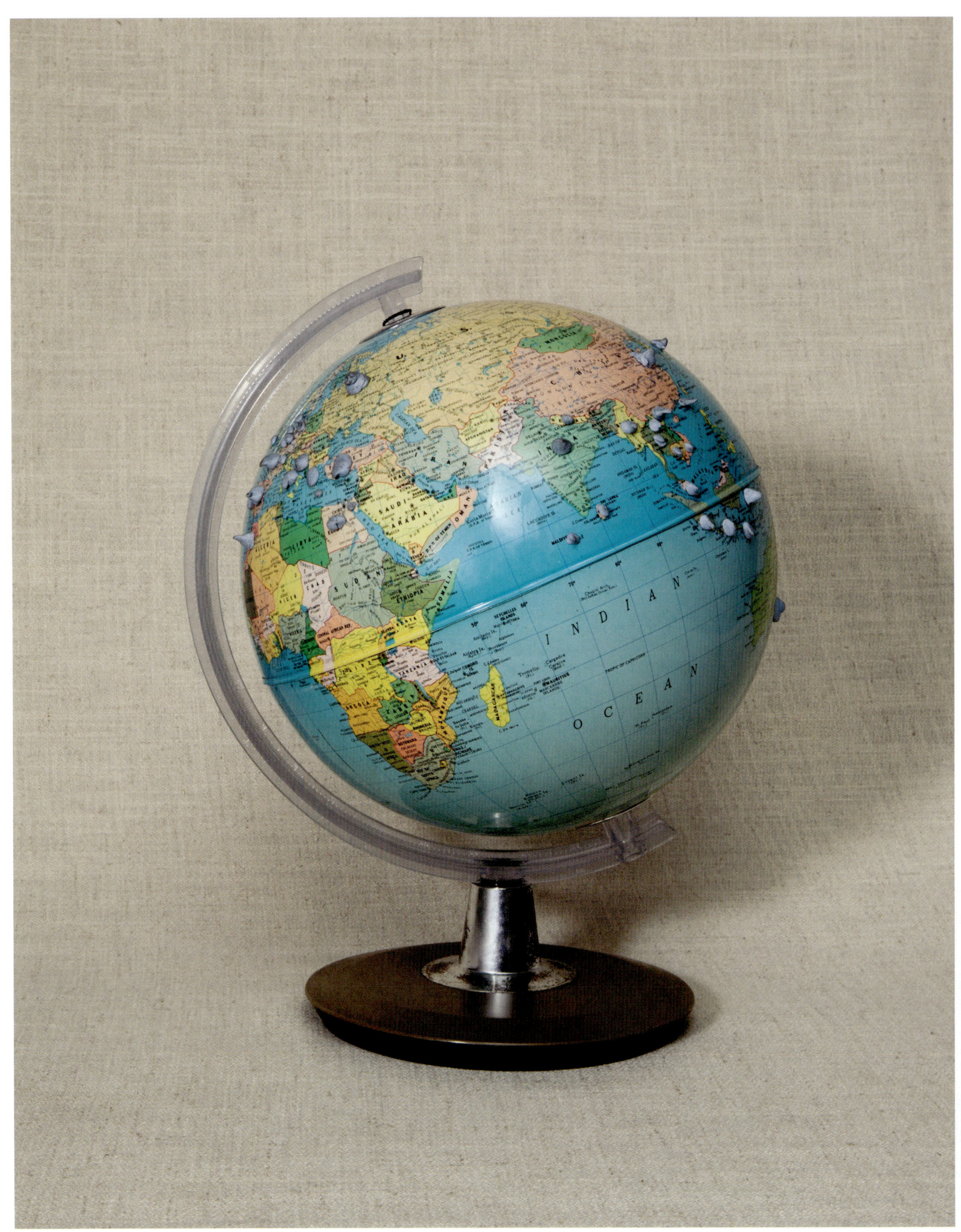

Globe (36cm)

A

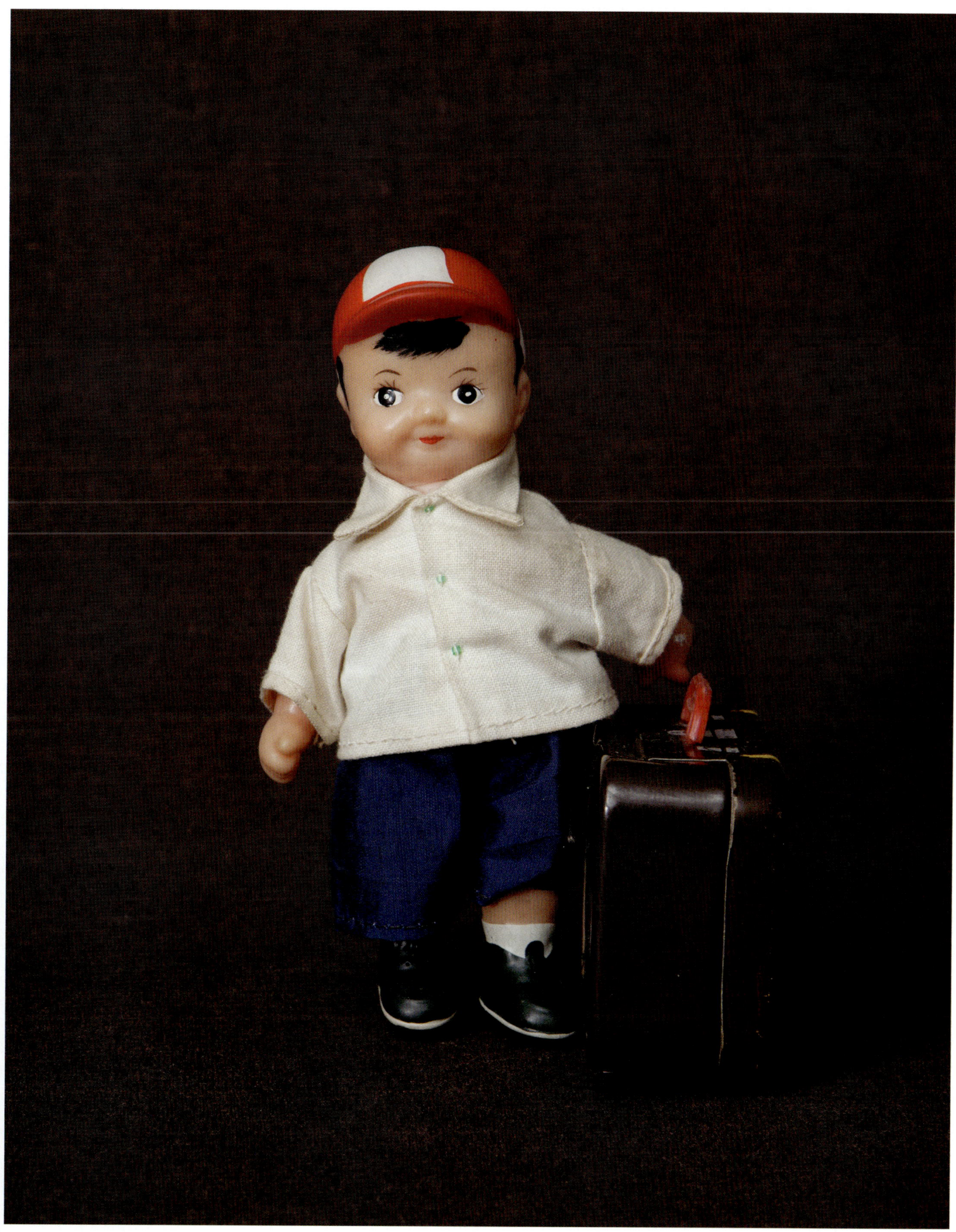

Schoolboy (12 cm)

by Jo Garrad and Jack Rugg, provides the crucial framework:

> 'As a dynamic tool the archive is far from inert. It offers the user a plethora of avenues for investigating Shelagh's diverse interests. Above all it imparts – and invites others to share in – Shelagh's passion and vitality through the medium of her work.'[3]

Dramatic juxtaposition is the strategy behind curiosity cabinets: 'the tension between entertainment and education in the idea of the marvellous [...]'[4] thus exposing the scenographer, 'it is the possessor, not the souvenir, which is ultimately the curiosity.'[5] Cluett's *mise-en-scène* reveals a fascinating persona through her heightened sense of the theatrical, as witnessed by her own performances:

> 'Picture Shelagh as one of the *Hamburgers of Calais*[†] in a Supremes Dress with a Big Mac on her head, singing from Rodin's Fast Food menu [...] then Shelagh in full fig as her favourite Rupert Bear. Plaid trousers, waistcoat and scarf, and perfectly modelled *papier-maché* head, caught on a traffic island unable to cross the King's Road because the eye alignment had been lost and she couldn't see out.'[6]

Twelve cameos of objects have been selected for their relation to sites visited and to certain pieces of her own work. At times the juxtaposition rings with relevance, at others it is obscure; chance and coincidence play their parts. 'A commodity is a thoroughly socialised thing [...] intended for exchange.'[7]

The objects Cluett collected are a motley gathering of artifacts and commodities. Both sorts have life histories, while shifts of transvaluation along their paths from production to consumption can move them into different zones of biography. Anthropologists relate objects of material culture to the capitalist mode of production, whereas artifacts

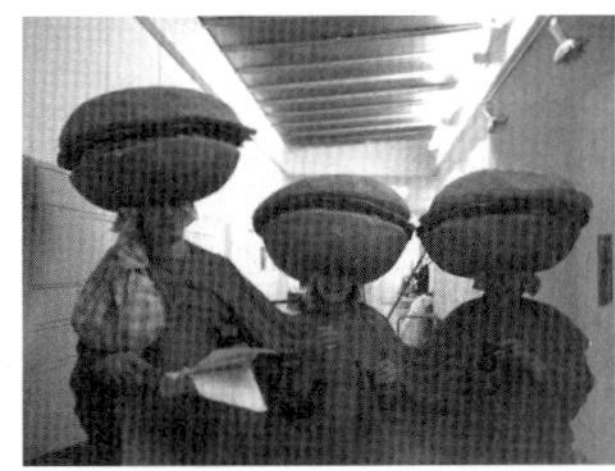

† Hamburgers of Calais

3 Jo Garrad.
4 Dion, M. *Mark Dion*, London: Phaidon Press Ltd, 1997, p.17.
5 Stewart, S. *On Longing. Narratives of the Miniature, the Gigantic, the Souvenir, the Collection*. Duke University Press, 1993.
6 Matt Rugg.
7 Appadurai, A. *The Social Life of Things*. Cambridge: Cambridge University Press. 1986, p.6.

represent aesthetic or ritual practice. However, in the contemporary art world, where context defines content, they swap places effortlessly. 'What is an art object and what is an ethnographic artifact depends on which side of the park (Central) you find yourself.'[8]

Objects as mnemonic devices, as talismans, or as the stuff of accumulation? 'In many other cultures it's not so important to keep the object but what is of value is knowing the idea or story behind it',[9] noted Boltanski. Warhol advised: 'you should try to keep track of it, but if you can't and lose it, that's fine because it's one less thing to think about, another load off your mind.'[10] As Freud's collection illustrated: 'the need to accumulate is one of the signs of approaching death'[11] – a prospect viewed with habitual sangfroid by Cluett who, when asked how she was feeling by a visiting nurse in her final days at her studio, replied:

"Well apart from dying,
I'm feeling very well thank you!"

Her two cabinets act as reliquaries for ephemera which evoke past anecdotes yet provoke contemporary reflection rather than religious veneration. It is the wittiness of her orchestration which allows for both melody and cacophony. Maybe the fact that Cluett's father had been a band-leader set the tone of her on-the-trot lifestyle, rhyming her travelling with her art practice, always ready to chant a key line from a suitable song.

Indian *citra pata*, painted scrolls, illustrate traditional legends but are accompanied by a story-teller who adapts the story to suit the social context of the spectators.[12] By the same token, these objects, dislocated from a familiar flow, are saved from melancholic preservation by new encounters in the crowded cabinets of Cluett's studio.

8 Dion, M. 1997, p.138 op. cit.
9 Boltanski, C. *Christian Boltanski*, London: Phaidon Press Ltd, 1997, p.17.
10 Warhol, A. *The Archive*. London: Whitechapel and the MIT Press, 2006. p.31.
11 Benjamin, W. *The Arcades Project, Convolute H.* Harvard University Press, 2002.
12 Current concern in western art theory with 'relational aesthetics' and the 'turn to pedagogy' would profit from a historically inter-cultural perspective.

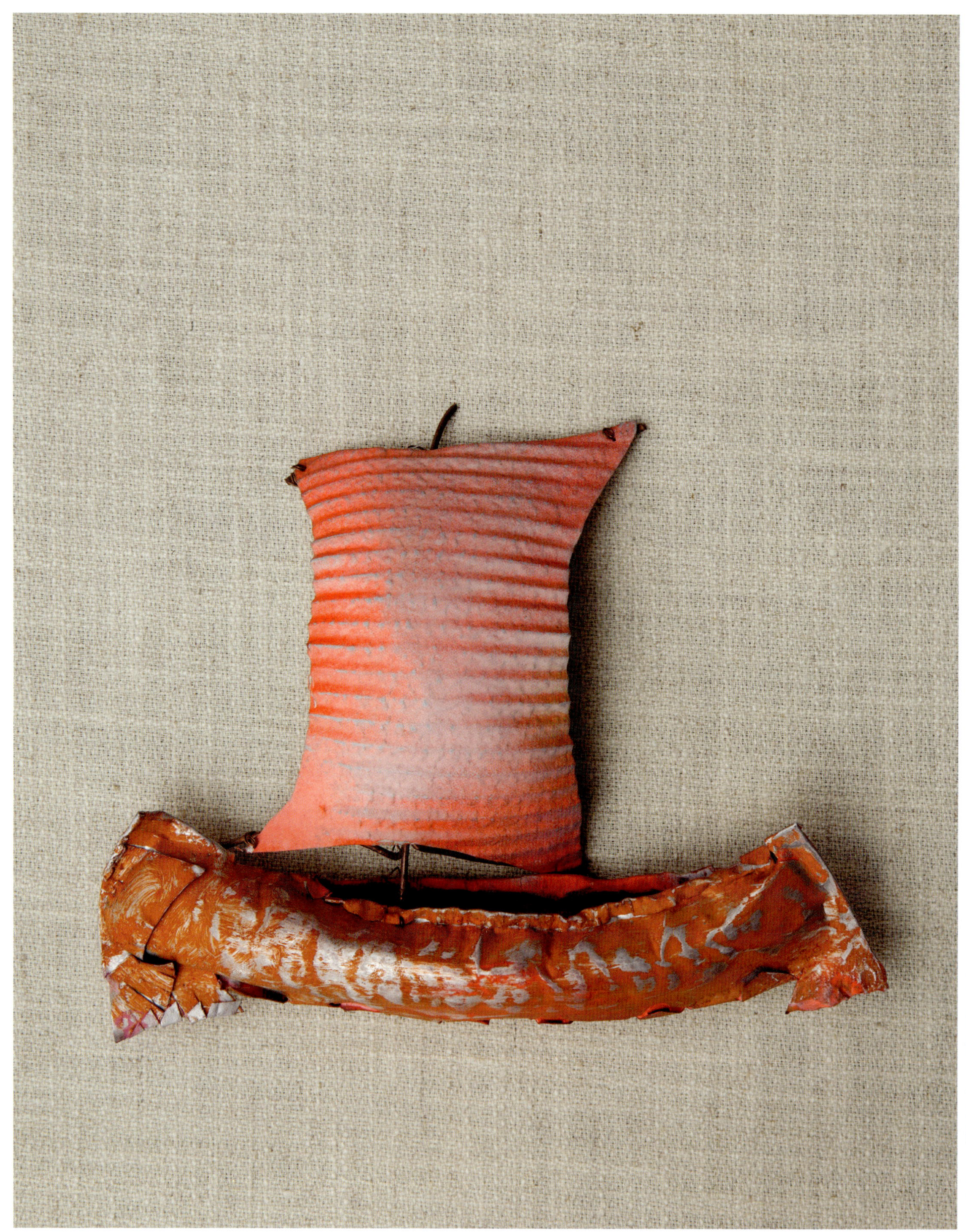

Untitled, 1984 (15×19×5 cm)

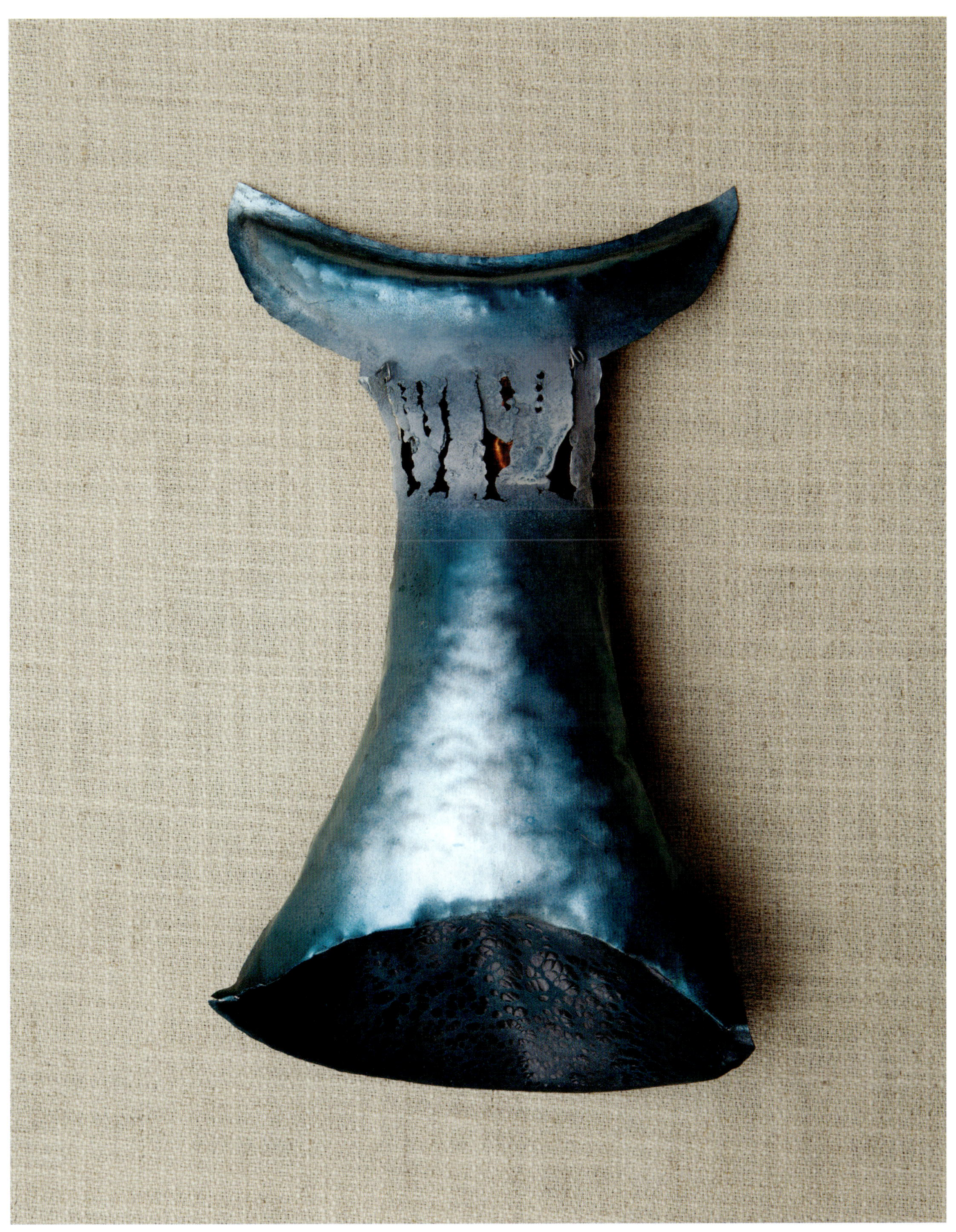

Light of My Life, 1984 (25 × 14 × 5 cm)

D

A, B

> 'There's a GLOBE (A) in her studio on which Shelagh stuck a blob of blutac to every country she had visited. By now that globe looks as though it has got hives.'[13]

The SCHOOLBOY (B) carrying a suitcase is one of her posse of mechanical toys: frogs a-leaping, pandas drumming, zebras jumping, their jaunty suspense adds an optimistic animism to the cabinets – they can't wait to be wound-up. The blue blobs on the globe mark her intrepid itineraries across Asia:

> 'We ventured into the mountains of Nepal, the ruins of Cambodia, the caves of the Toraja, the temples of Thailand, the paddy fields of Vietnam, the beaches of Bali [...] long before it became fashionable, and in most places even comfortable, to do so. All along these trails we sipped arak and local beer, entertained each night by a well-worn traveller's edition of Cluedo (she was always Colonel Mustard).'[14]

From Turkey to Thailand, from the Maldives to Malaysia, from Sri Lanka to Sulawesi, from India[†] to Indonesia, from Java to Japan, from Cambodia to China – en route exploring Burma, Laos, Vietnam, Nepal, Korea as well as occasional diversions to Egypt, Tunisia, New York, Greece, Venezuela and Italy – she neither neglected 'local' trips to France and Scotland nor to her home in Weymouth.

Her itinerary was already global in the early Eighties, due to her research into South East Asian Buddhist sculpture and architecture, but Cluett's travelling became notably ambitious with a request for study-leave to return to Burma in 1987. Her proposal offers concrete reasons behind her fascination with Asian art:

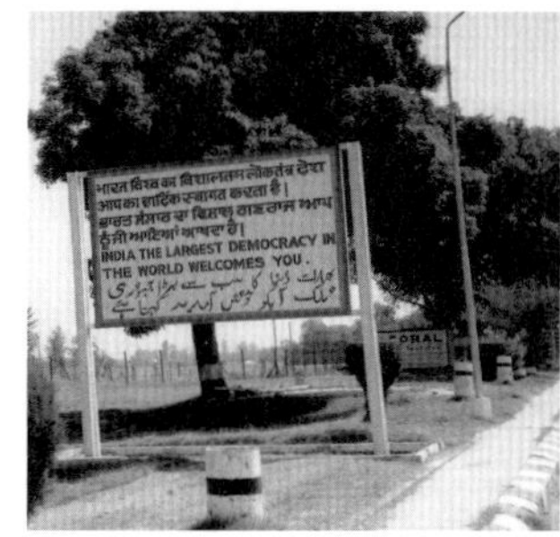

† Welcome to India photograph

13 Charles Garrad.
14 Nirmalo Wilkes.

> 'Past travels have revealed the extraordinary range of sculptural development and its relation to the society in terms of everyday life. The separation and distancing that typifies the western attitude is absent, sculptural objects and images are fundamental to the thinking, not regarded as religious artifacts […] I want to learn from the ingenuity of local craftsmen […] make sculpture in the environment whilst learning new techniques […] to make documentation available to the department and other interested parties.'

This one paragraph contains the triad of characteristics common to her practice: curiosity, displacement, dissemination. Cluett wanted to learn about other cultural practices so she travelled; she wanted to translate her experiences so she made sculptures; she wanted to pass on knowledge so she taught. Possessing both method and madness, a Cagean sense of the 'purpose of purposelessness' accompanied her curiosity as an adventurer.

She was not interested in luxury commodities, or 'authentic' artworks as status symbols of social distinction; rare in her collection are potential 'museum pieces'. She was interested in the power of objects: artifacts, such as votive relics or small carvings, as signs of a particular social system or the trivia of 'small memory'[15]; and everyday things like spices, dyes, cloth or beads as tokens of a cultural history. Like Duchamp, she enjoyed the ritual of bricolage and the idea of the artist as an 'artisan', as somebody who made things:

> 'Shelagh was a 'fabricator' […] the fabricating process can be seen in the finished work but is often quite different, almost perversely so, to established craft practices […] she liked to work intuitively, gradually transforming her materials,

15 Boltanski, C. 1997, p.19. op. cit.

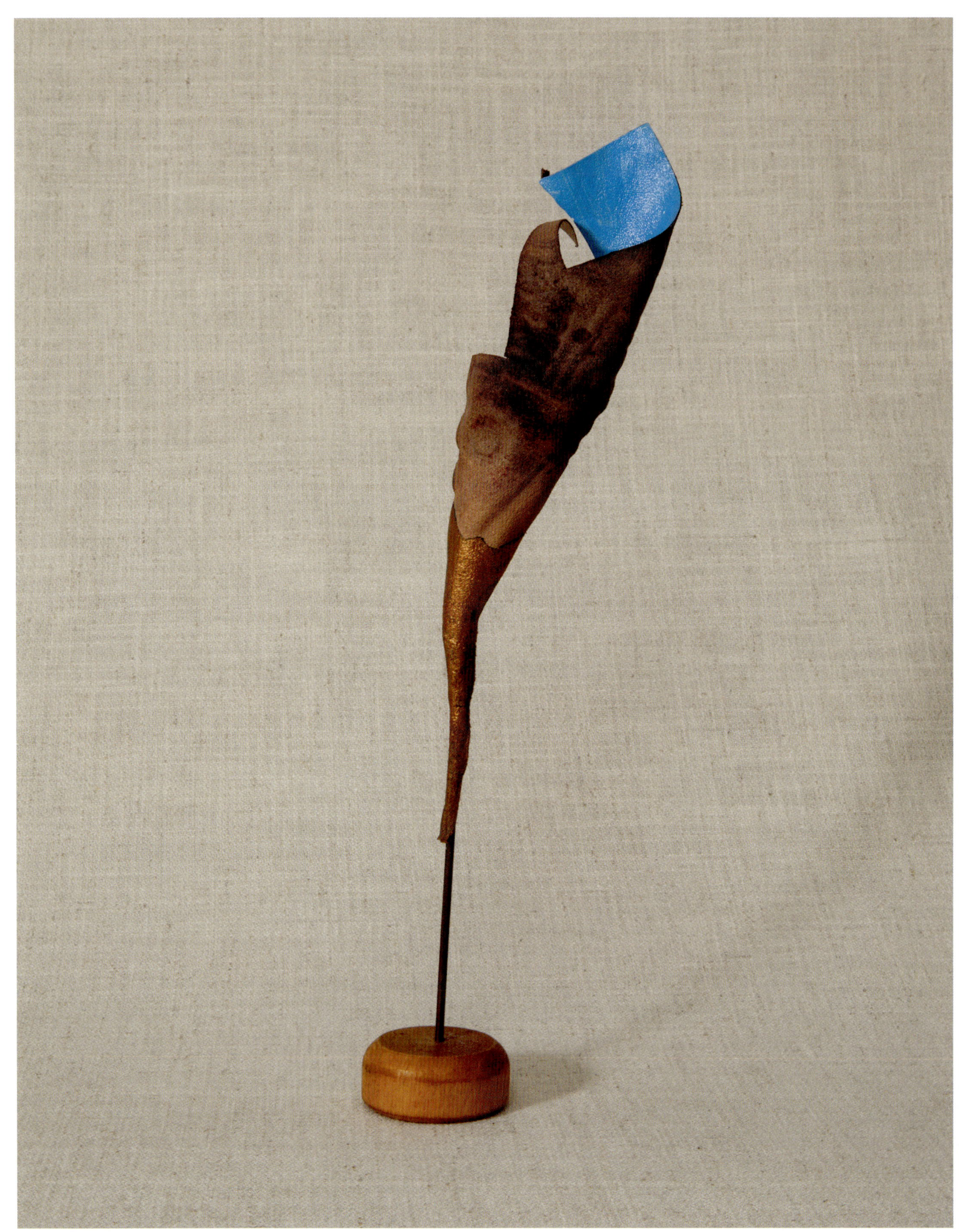

Untitled, c.1985 (38×5×5cm)

E

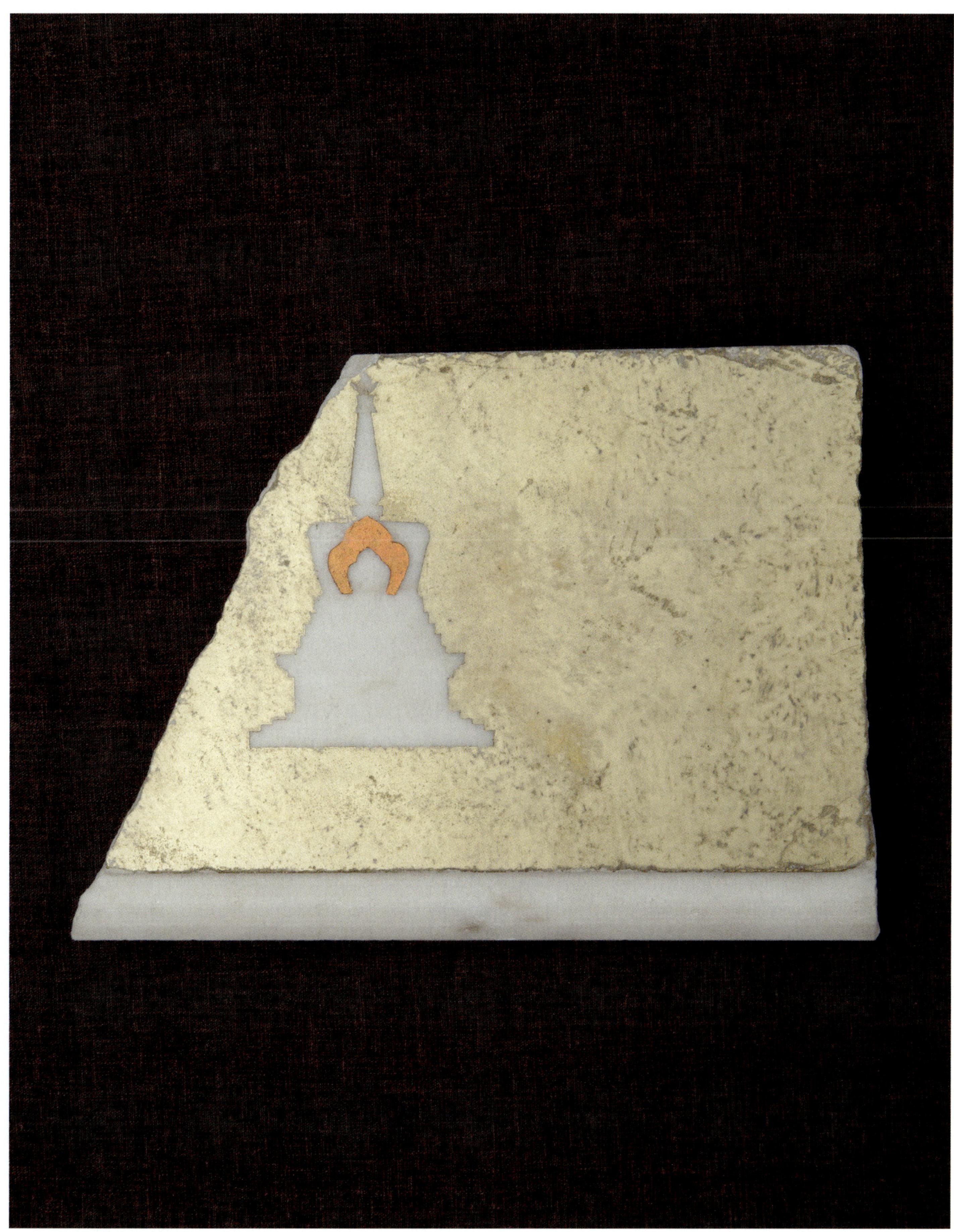

Stupa, c.1993 (16×22×3cm)

F

finding the sculpture via the working process, surprising herself with the finished piece and with a cavalier attitude to working methods'[16]

C, D, E

Her own small SCULPTURES (C, D, E) from the early Eighties zing with colour. In chromatic syncopation, they were described by Fourcade in musical terms as: 'a melody being unfolded in space [...] we can follow the melody in a hundred different ways.'[17] They seem to sustain a promise to dance:

'When Shelagh, in her teenage years, won a Gold Medal as South Coast Foxtrot Champion, it was but an indication of the style and standards that were to be her hallmark.'[18]

The Eighties were the time of her travels in Burma and Thailand with Mick Marshall, 'the rock and roll lighting expert' who was indeed her eternal partner in rock'n'roll and lighting: 'Shelagh was in her element in that world too. There was a memorable occasion, late one night in Paris, when Tom Waits, Elvis Costello[†] and Shelagh Cluett did a raucous impromptu spot together on stage in a little nightclub.'[19]

The exotic representation in *Vogue* (December 1984) of Cluett's shimmering piece in beaten and painted aluminium, *Burmese Nights*,[‡] is somewhat tempered by a realistic description of its production: 'Other artists sharing the large Wapping studio were driven mad by the constant noise of beating.'[20] Cluett always worked hard, yet these pieces manifest a lightness of being which evanesced in later pieces. Her titles illustrate a carefree optimism, for example: *I Must go Down to the Sea Again*, *Light of my Life*, *Tangalle.* Such works[‡] were fittingly described as 'agleam with

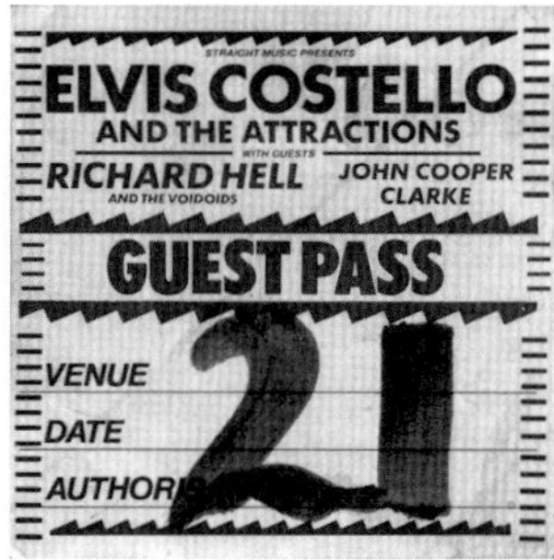

† Guest Pass for Elvis Costello and The Attractions

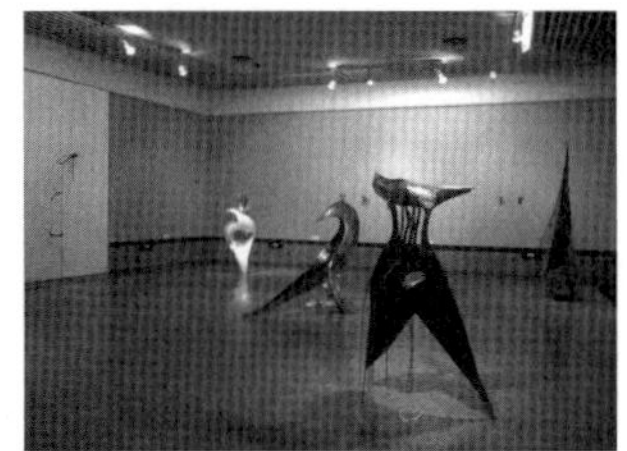

‡ *Shelagh Cluett* at Herbert Art Gallery, 1985. *Burmese Nights* in Foreground

16 Chris Yetton.
17 Dominique Fourcade, Catalogue '*Shelagh Cluett Sculpture*' Nicola Jacobs Gallery, London, 1982.
18 Matt Rugg.
19 Charles Garrad.
20 Chris Yetton.

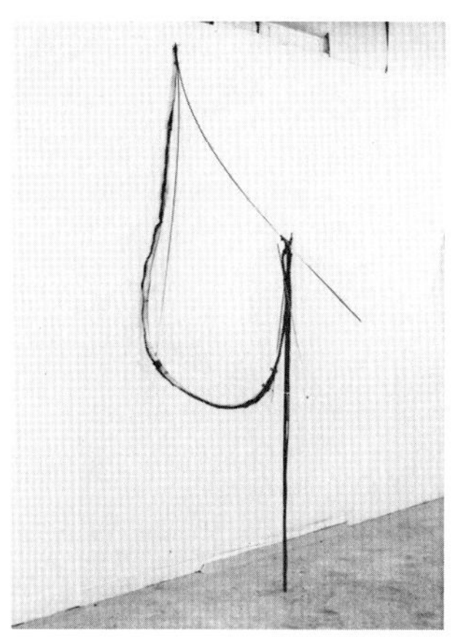

† *Flux I*, Shelagh Cluett, 1979

aluminium, copper, brass, gold and silver [...] these painted sculptures, sculptured paintings [...] are wonderfully enjoyable excursions and explorations, stretching the limits of art into new territories, charted here with high visual intelligence, playfulness and delight.'[21]

One story about her sculpture from this period captures the buoyant mood of the Eighties:

> 'Shelagh had sold a large sculpture (*Flux I,* 1979)† to Dominique Fourcade after the 1982 show at Nicola Jacobs for which Fourcade wrote the catalogue essay. The car was full and we tied the sculpture to the roof-rack. On leaving the ferry and not thinking about anything except the pleasure of being in France on a sunny day, we were stopped by a customs man who, after asking me one or two innocuous questions about what we were doing, suddenly pointed to the roof-rack and said:
>
> "What is that Monsieur?"
>
> I remembered that Gerard Wilson had been stopped at Rotterdam with a van-load of student work which was impounded until the college had paid a very large bond, returnable when the work came back to England. On the spur of the moment I said:
>
> "It's scrap"
> (C'est du bricolage m'sieur).
>
> He smiled and waved us on. I looked at Shelagh wondering what she thought of her work being thus described but she was laughing. When we met Fourcade to hand the work over, he was being rather the French intellectual and we didn't tell him what he had bought in the eyes of the state.'[22]

21 Marina Vaizey, Catalogue '*Colour Constructions*' Curwen Gallery, London, 1985.
22 Chris Yetton.

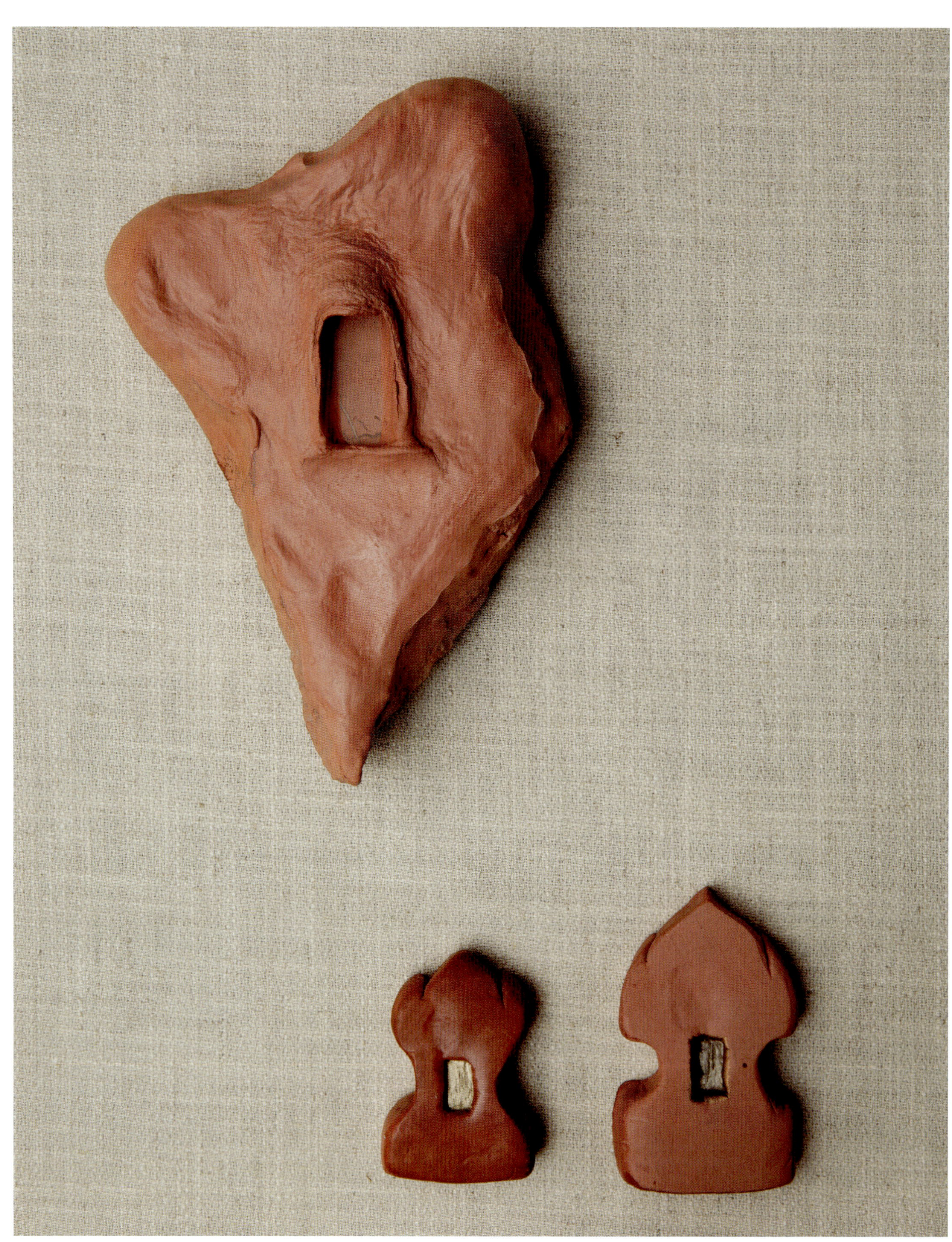

Untitled Works, c.1992
Top (21×14×4cm), bottom left (7×5×2cm),
bottom right (9.5×5×2cm)

G

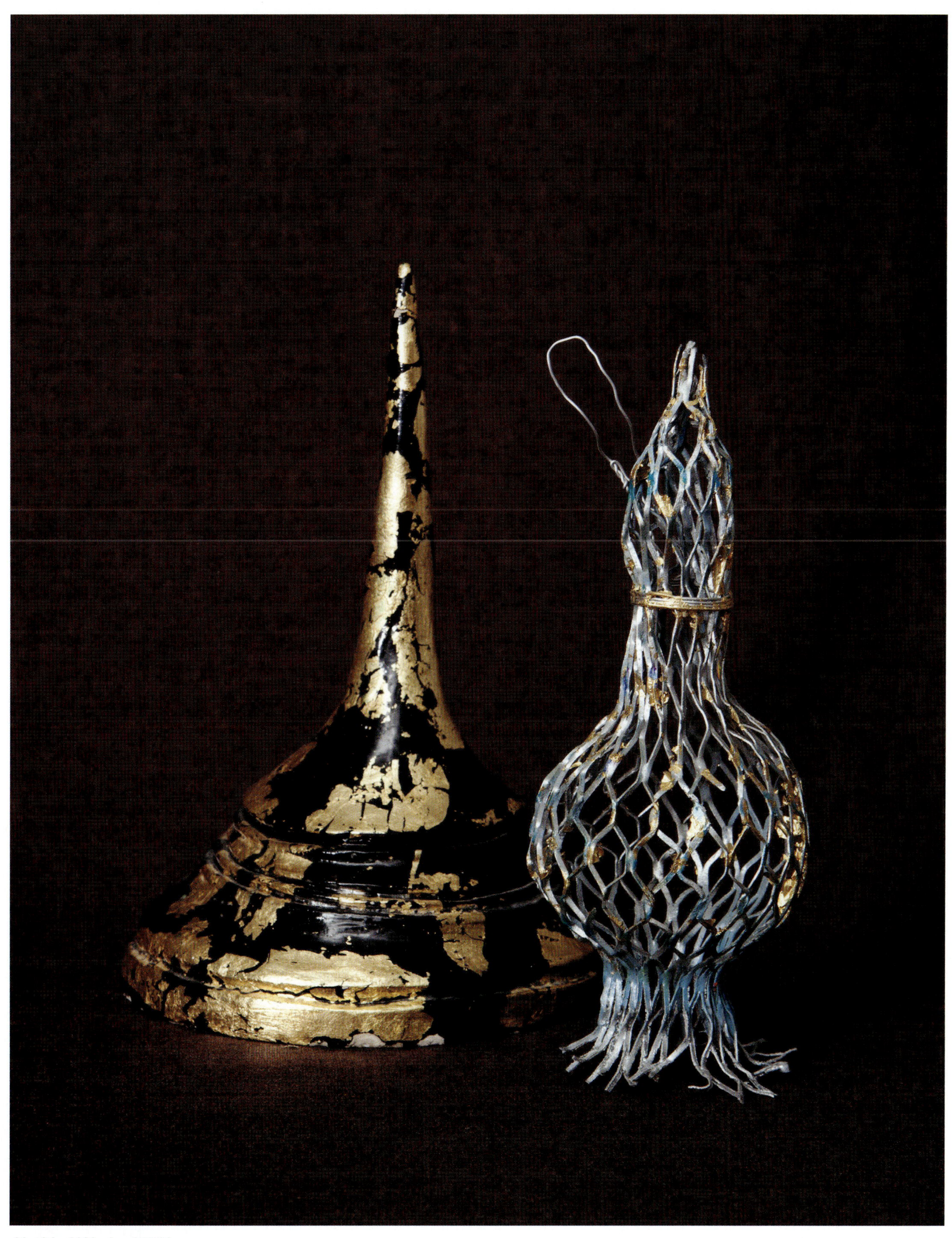

Untitled Works, 1980's
Left (20×13×13cm), right (18×7×7cm)

H

F, G, H

Photos of Stupas † abound in Cluett's copious albums. Their inspiration is evident in the series of sketches and small sculptures visible on the archive website. *Stup* in Sanskrit means to accumulate or to gather together. Originally erected to enshrine the remains of Buddha and his disciples, stupas are imbued with cosmological symbolism and invite the ritual circumambulation performed by Cluett at many such 'Mount Merus' including the great Khmer temple at Angor Wat, Cambodia. Her work was particularly inspired by a visit to the sanctuary of Borobodur in Java. Integrated into a sacred site at the confluence of two rivers, astronomical in conception and scale with layers of concentric terraces and five and a half kilometres of dramatic bas-reliefs recounting the legends of Buddha, its mandala ground-plan is represented in her black granite relief. ‡

One small relief presents a WHITE STUPA (F) whose silhouette is etched against a gold leaf ground on a marble fragment, ascetic yet sensuous. Another set of MINIATURE RELIEFS (G), modelled in red clay, metamorphose into erotic apertures. As portals enfolding memories, or as thresholds of new vistas, they hold a hint of Duchamp's erogenous moulages.[23] A small CLAY STUPA (H) shows peeled off patches of gold leaf, resembling her battered monkey and incorporating the tenderness felt by Cluett for all things in distress – whether temples, toys or animals. In a cabaret performance at Chelsea between students and staff entitled *The Creation of the World*, she instructed: "Everyone must make an animal!" Her colleague Matt Rugg added: "thereby releasing suppressed craft skills of those too long embroiled in abstract thought."

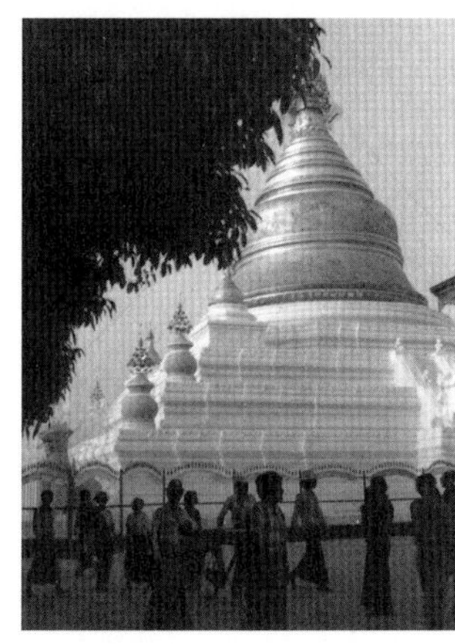

† Stupa, Rangoon Burma

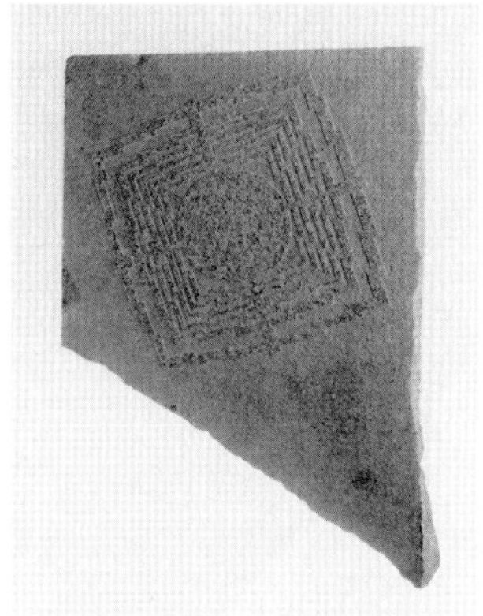

‡ *Borobodur*, Shelagh Cluett, c.1993

23 Duchamp, M. *Feuille de Vigne Femelle,* 1950 and *Coin de Chastete,* 1954.

From Vietnam comes the bold and beautiful WATER PUPPET (I).

> 'Of all the colourful characters that made up the stories in Vietnamese water puppetry theatre, Shelagh found this atypical schoolboy as her 'treasure' from this trip. The incongruity between an ancient Vietnamese art form, and a schoolboy in '50s style uniform was hilarious – and captured Shelagh's delight in the absurd brilliantly. When we went to Vietnam in the early 1990s, the thousand-year-old art of water puppetry had only just been revived. There were only three main troupes in Vietnam and we were fortunate to see one of them perform.
>
> The performances happened on a stage of chest-deep water – which made for lots of splashing and hilarity. The puppets were manipulated underwater by long bamboo rods and string from behind an ornate background curtain. Apparently during the eleventh and twelfth centuries, the puppeteers would lie on their backs underwater and manipulate the puppets while breathing through bamboo straws. Long, the performance had about eighteen scenes ranging from folklore legends complete with fire breathing dragons, to modern fishing and farming scenes, with no obvious logic between them. I remember the accompanying music – complete with bells, vocals, cymbals, flutes and yelling – as being very loud and absolutely intrinsic to the enjoyment of the performance.
>
> We always named the friends we collected on our travels and, if I remember correctly, I think we called this boy Max. Relax with Max.'[24]

From her travels in Sri Lanka, Java, Thailand and Bali, Cluett has a variety of SHADOW PUPPETS (J),

24 Nirmalo Wilkes.

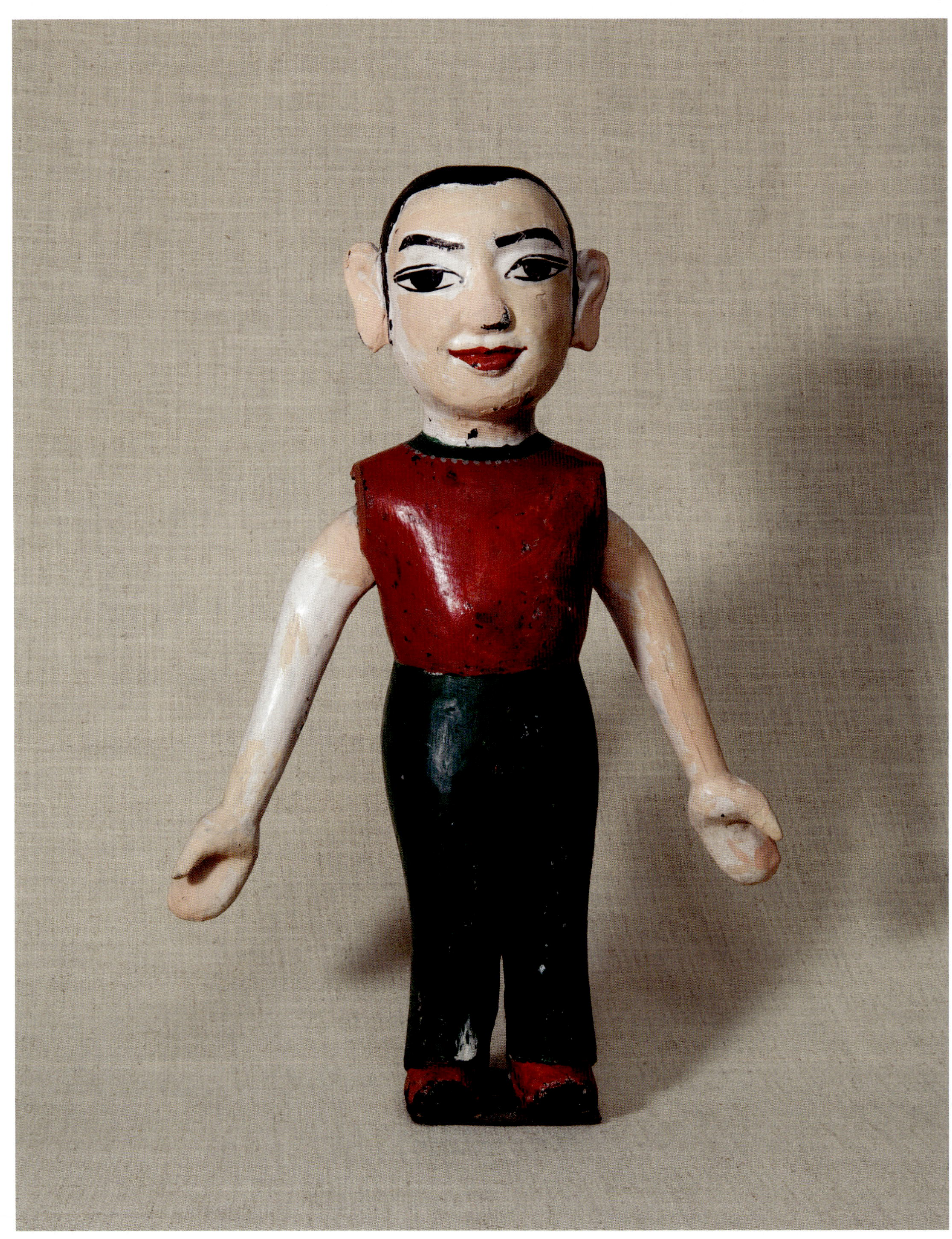

Water Puppet (41 cm)

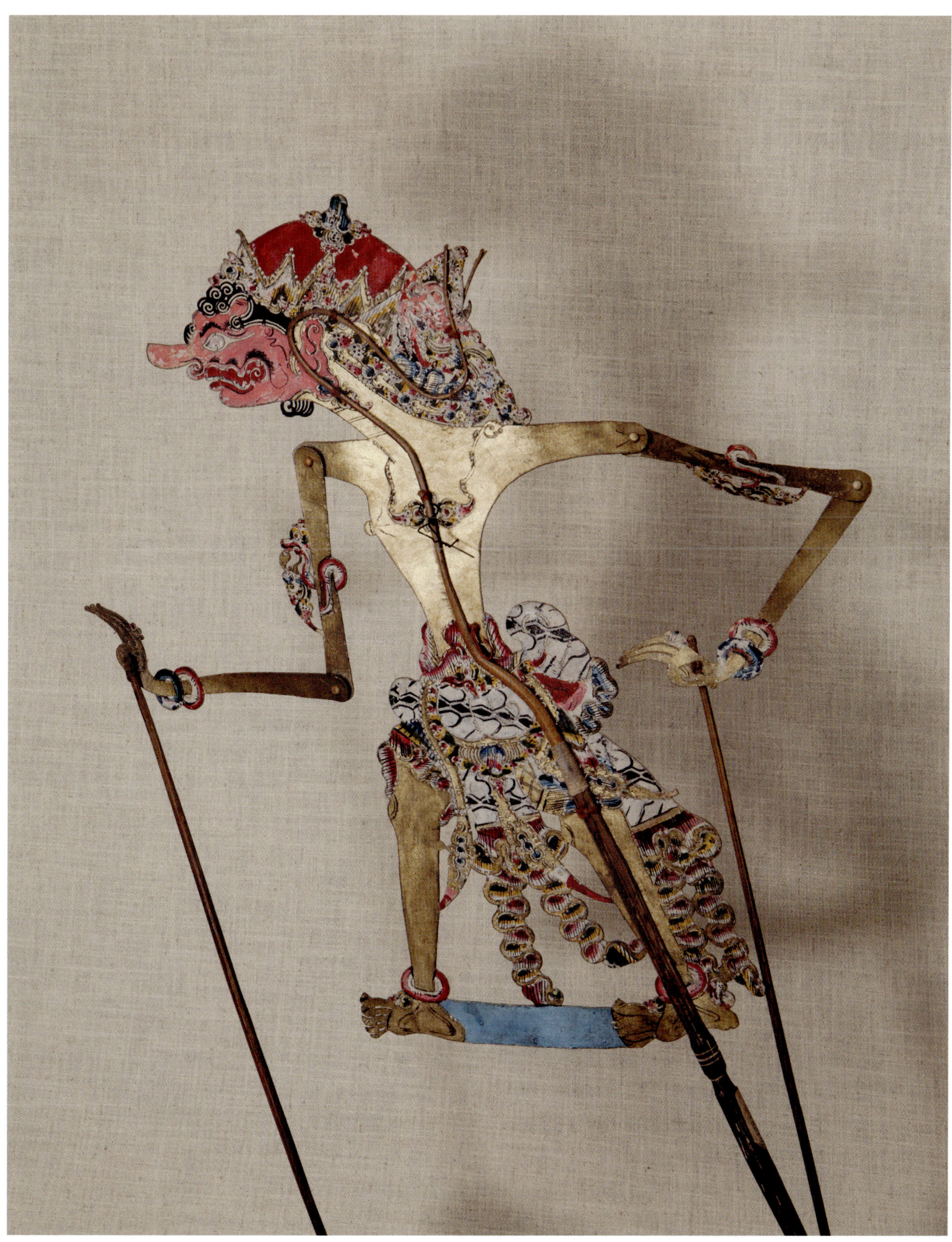

Shadow Puppet (50cm)

J

'preserving through the shadow the presence of the absent person, echoing Pliny's account of the origins of sculpture.'[25] Original themes from the Indian Mahabharata and Ramayana epics were remodelled in the Islamic culture of Indonesia. Like the traditional Indian sculptor of votive icons, the Indonesian *danang* puppeteer acts as a medium between the audience and the ancestral spirits incarnated by the puppets. Yet some performances today dare to infuse a satirical critique of local political leaders, not unlike the practice of contemporary miniature painting in Pakistan.

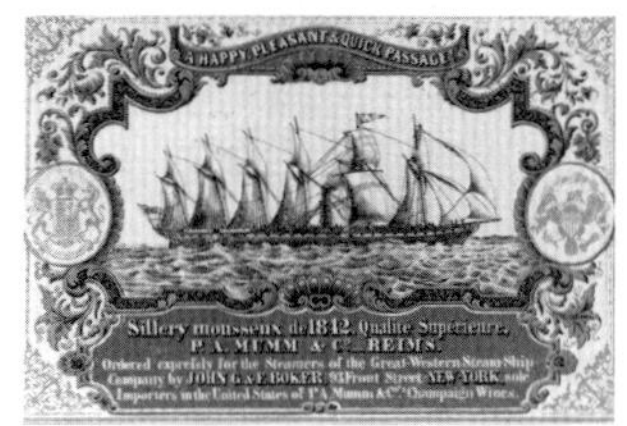

† Postcard from Cluett's collection

Postcards† flood the Cluett Cabinets. As mass-produced, dispersed and disposable objects, by 1900 they had become travellers in their own right: 'a constant reminder of the imperial conditions that establish the basis for modern cosmopolitanism.'[26] The fact that postcard collecting was designated as 'the Cinderella of Collecting' since it was described as both a 'low' cultural form and a 'feminine' vice[27] would only have energized Cluett's hobby, especially since she delighted in scribbling a counter-message to the visual narrative.

K, L

The YELLOW WOODEN TIGER (K) on wheels is of Indian origin and has all three attributes common to her toy collection: it is colourful, mobile and curious. The original India Museum[28] was a typical curiosity cabinet displaying Britannia's colonial acquisitions of miscellaneous and bizarre objects of the world: 'birds with exotic plumage from Java, cases crammed with iridescent insects [...] a fragment of a Roman tessel-lated floor, an Oriental opulence of gold and silver ornaments, pearls and gems, spun and woven silks and woolens [...] a glimpse of some of the plunder from

25 Currell, D. Shadow *Puppets and Shadow Play.* Wiltshire: Crowood Press Ltd, 2007. p.17.
26 Mathur, S. *India by Design*. Berkeley: University of California Press, 2007. p.115.
27 Ibid. p.130.
28 East India House, Leadenhall St.: Redesigned in 1799 by The East India Company as showplace of their successful business and trophies, with museum and library.

the battle of Seringapatam – the golden tiger's head footstool from the throne of Tipu Sultan and, the most popular exhibit of all, his musical mechanical tiger.'[29]

'Curious' was indeed the first adjective applied by British audiences for *Tipu's Tiger*. Construed as a 'childish piece of musical mechanism'[30] this six-foot painted wood effigy shows a voracious tiger devouring a pale-faced man in a red coat. Inside the tiger is an organ with eighteen buttons to musical pipes, when the crank handle is turned the man's left arm goes up, pleading mercy, to the chorus of his feeble groans and the roar of the tiger. Seized by British soldiers from the ruler of Mysore on his defeat in 1799, it soon became a polemical emblem: of resistance for the Indian cause and of triumph for the British, who saw it as a typically crude representation of oriental despotism.

Trophies collected for ethnographic spaces were moved to art museums, whereby not only the spiritual but the 'significant' formal aspects were duly admired. However *Tipu's Tiger* was no religious idol nor did it inspire aesthetic critique, but due to public acclaim, the V&A reluctantly retained it. Today its image still dominates the V&A section in London guidebooks.

The story of this artifact links Cluett with the Indian artist Dhruva Mistry, once a student whom she advised. As an object of 'resonance',[31] *Tipu's Tiger* evokes a network of cultural forces to the viewer with some knowledge of its original context. In the V&A the bloody conflict of British colonialism may well be submerged by its bizarre appeal, but for others with a sense of postcolonial ambivalence it strikes a discordant note. Mistry, whilst a student at the RCA in 1981, spotted the piece and was inspired to make his own version: a painted sculpture of a hunting cheetah in iron, fibreglass and plaster which he called simply, *Tipu*. This sculpture has the same sense of compact

29 Desmond, R. *The India Museum 1801–1879*. London: Her Majesty's Stationery Office, 1982.
30 Davis, R.H. *Lives of Indian Images*. New Jersey: Princeton University Press, 1997. p.145–50.
31 Greenblatt, S. Resonance and Wonder. In *Exhibiting Culture: the Poetics and Politics of Museum Display*. eds. I. Karp & S.D.Lavine. Washington D.C.: Smithsonian Institution Press, 1991. p.42–56.

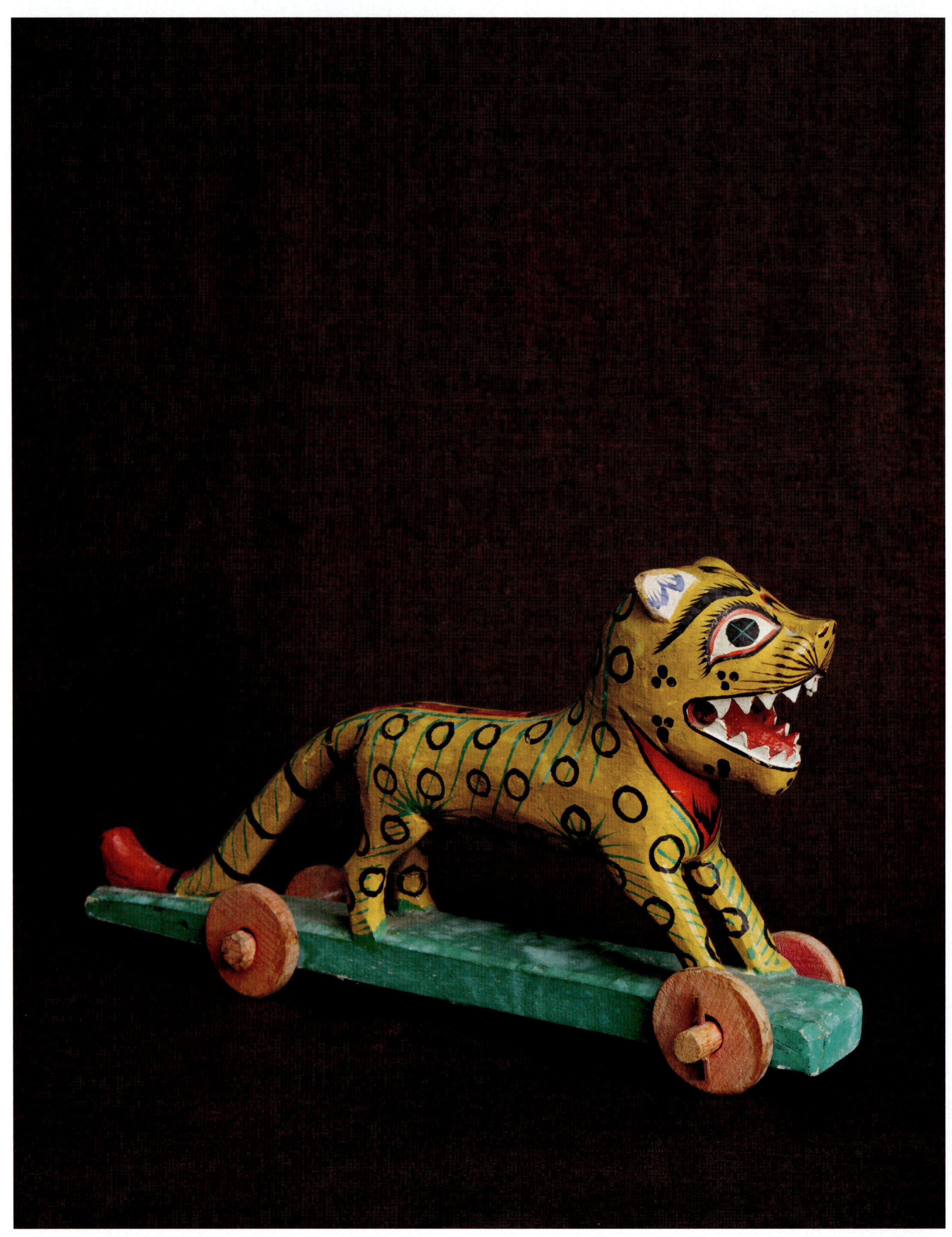

Yellow Wooden Tiger (22 cm)

K

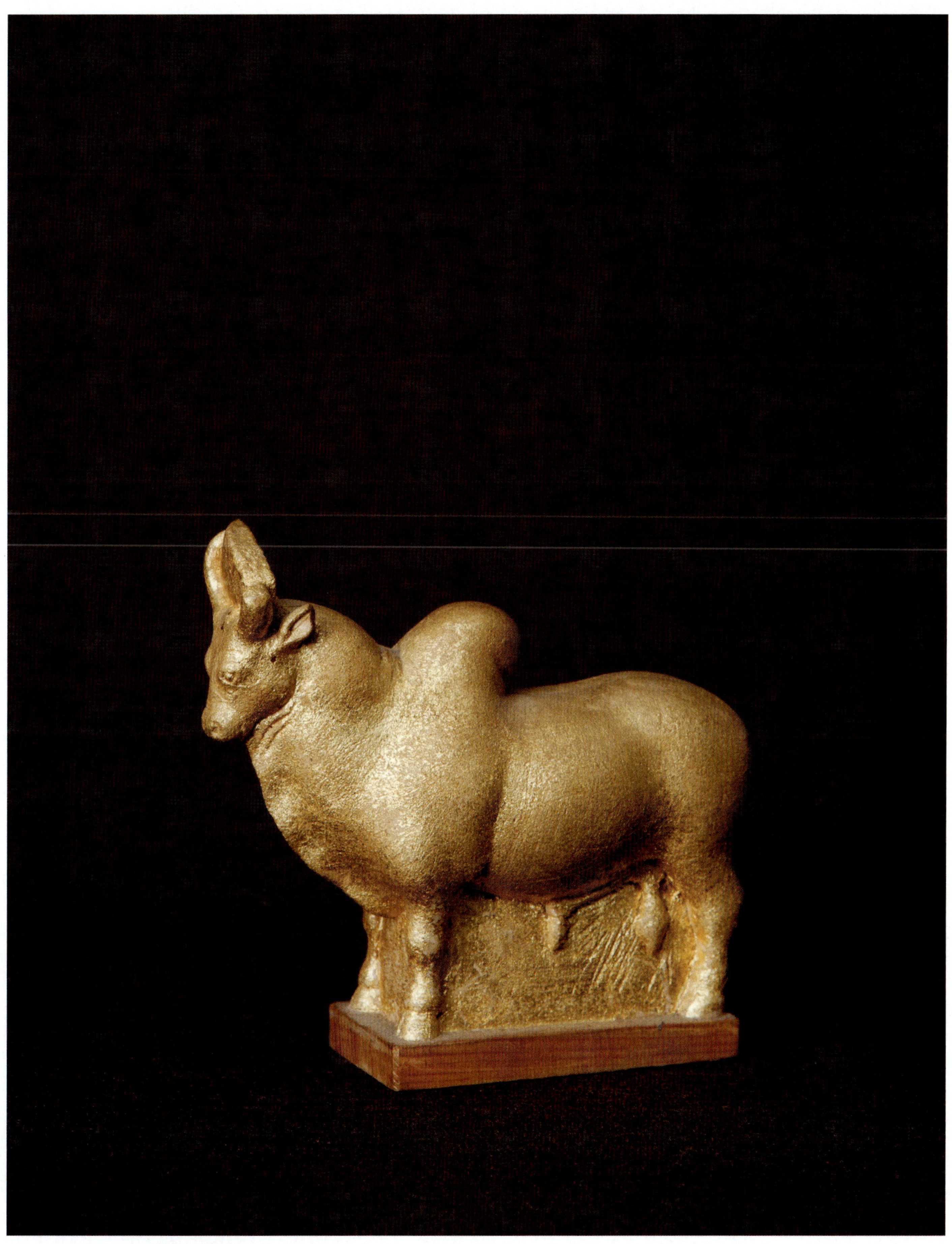

Bullock, Dhruva Mistry, 1983 (9.5×10×4cm)

L

energy as that of the golden BULLOCK (L) (*Nandi*, Joyous One, sacred vehicle of Siva) which he gave to Cluett in the Eighties.[32]

> 'I knew Shelagh as a kind and good humoured tutor among male dominated sculpture when I was at the RCA Sculpture School on my maiden journey from India at the age of 23. I liked her disarmingly gentle, warm and frank demeanor packed with an infectious smile. Following my first tutorial with her she had encouraged, prepared and invited me to visit Chelsea Sculpture School for a slide-lecture and talk in 1982. During Christmas break at the Royal College of Art, I had carved some small and few tiny pieces in chalk, hard plaster and fine-grained sandstone. There was a small sandstone Bull which I offered to Shelagh when she came to teach next.'

M, N, O

Exotic symbols of imperial conquest such as *Tipu's Tiger* are not the stuff of Cluett's collection. The very fact that *Tipu's Tiger* has been transformed into an object of tourist consumption would suit her sense of irony and her evident fascination with the contradictory stories told by objects. For example, a benign HEAD OF A BUDDHA (M) from Cambodia emerges with grace from a stone fragment as if it had awoken from years of meditation. Pick it up, turn it over and inside is the sticker marked $6 [...] she added the found fragment as a base.

Although she had visited China with her dear Aunt Pat, Cluett never went into Chinese occupied Tibet, respecting the Tibetan freedom struggle. Our internet exchanges during my time in Pakistan parodied a neocolonialist scenario: in reply to my email:

32 Dhruva Mistry, Sculptor, former Dean of Baroda College of Art, MSU University.

“Will let you know how our former hill-stations are surviving under the Tibetan inflow into Dharamsala”

Cluett replied:

“Remember to behave yourself madam, keep a low profile and don’t talk to strange men carrying sub-machine guns, have a good trip and give my love to your chum Mr. Lama.”†

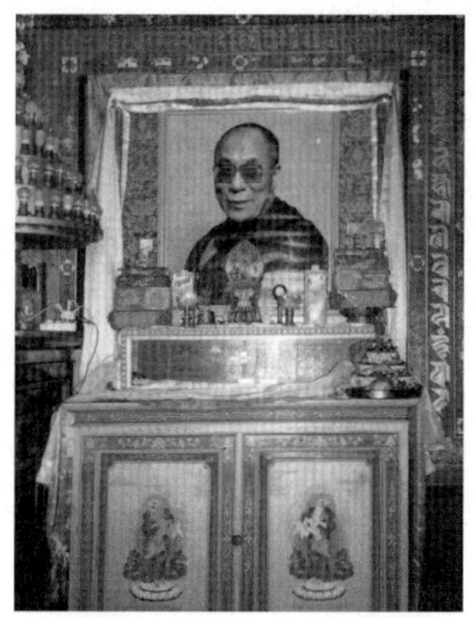

† Shrine to the Dalai Lama

However, she did trek in the Himalayas of Nepal and brought back from Kathmandu a small *t’hanka* mandala painting, an exquisite prayer-wheel and an extraordinary JAR (N) made of wood which served as jug for butter-tea. It has a faintly anthropomorphic aspect, suggested by the cord suspended around its neck. In many of Cluett’s drawings towards sculpture, lines spiral into tendrils or harness in lassos, evoking umbilical cords or the rigging of her beloved boats. For example, a small INDIAN SCULPTURE (O) in Chola style, exquisite in its sinuosity and its modelling of muscles, has a spindly frame of metal on its back. Added by Cluett as a support, this serves as a metaphor for Alfred Gell’s notion that art objects function as human prostheses, ghosting social dialogue.[33] It is a manikin embodying the spirit of Cluett’s teaching: exchange.

As an impassioned activist in Art Accord,[‡, 34] Cluett attended the AGM on both sides of the channel. These were a source of surreal merry-making. At one meeting in Angoulême in 1994, after a desperately dull discussion on intercultural credit-ratings, a group of us played truant from the art school and spent the rest of the day in a bistro on the ramparts of the town. We were outlining plans for a radical new course in Public art auspiciously christened by Cluett as *Ramp Art*.

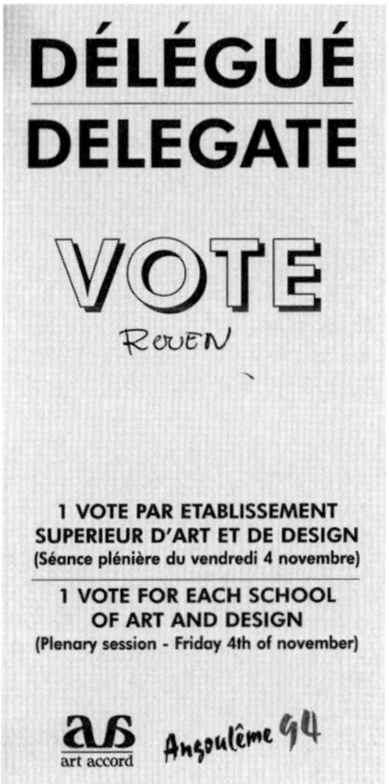

‡ Art Accord

33 Gell, A. *Art and Agency*. Oxford: Clarendon Press, 1998.

34 The first international student exchange programme for art schools set up in 1969 by Maxim Adam Tessier (1920-2000), sculptor teaching at Hornsey and RCA and George Younson, former Head of Hornsey Fine Art (1920–2001): See Younson’s Obituary by Shelagh Cluett (Guardian 18 June 2001) for portrait of Art Accord.

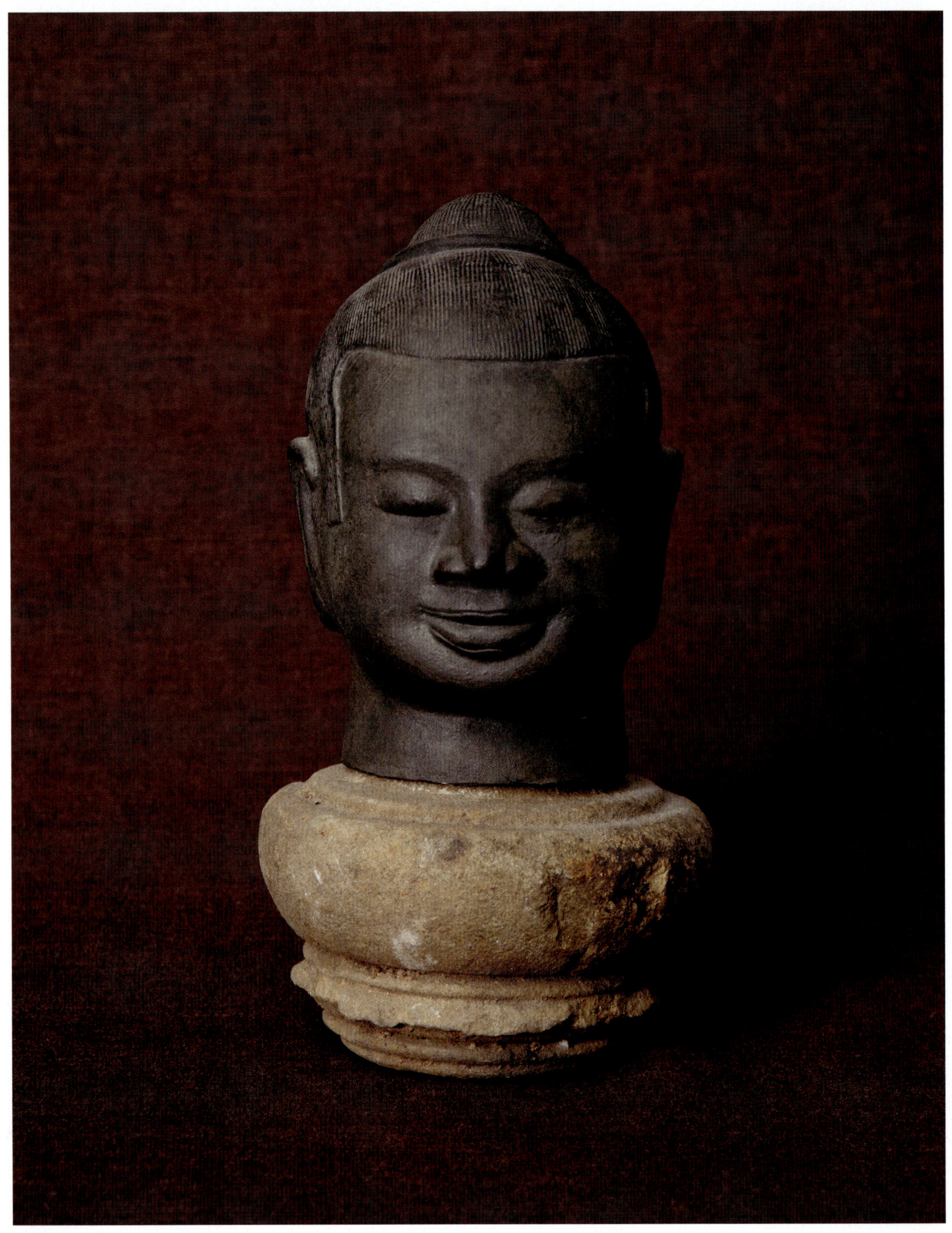

Head of Buddha (20 cm)

M

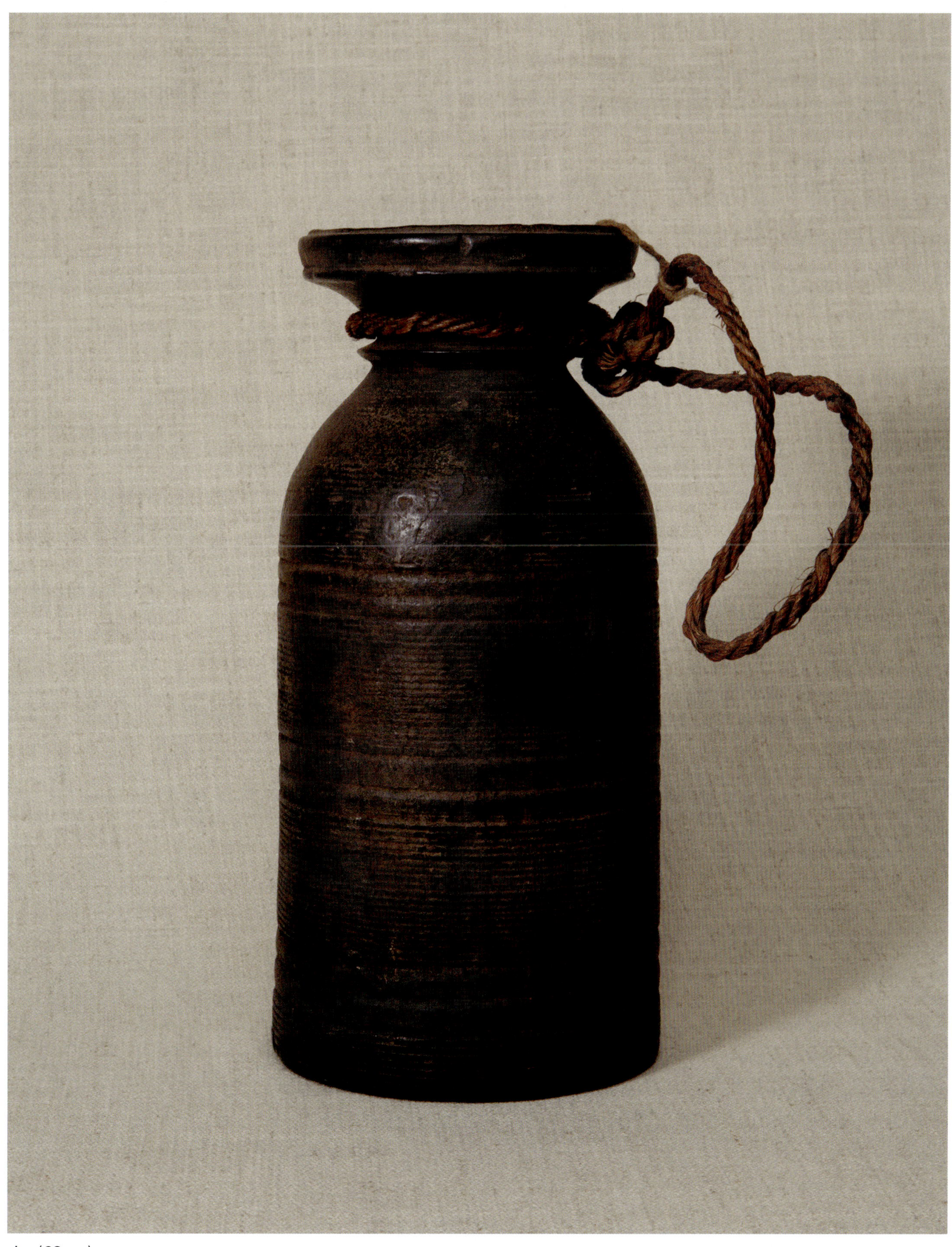

Jar (28cm)

Amongst her contributions to the core curriculum was its modish title: *Art at the Cutting Edge*. This launched the dadaist curriculum:[35] 1st year; Foundation Course. 2nd year; Damp Proof course. 3rd year; Dry Stone Wall building with polyfilla sandwich-courses on structuralism, bricolage, assemblage, collage, barricading, agitprop, hard and soft-core modules, ballast electives, seminars in support systems & flying buttressing with the French group Supports-Surfaces. Theoretical post-structuralist studies would examine globalized grafitti propaganda via Derridean deconstruction. Post-graduate art therapy courses in Dry Rot or Crazy Paving would be offered. An MA in Rampartology would combine ecological contextualization with critical post-colonial studies leading to a PhD in in Rampartautology. Invited artists would be specialists, alive or dead, such as: Rachel Whiteread, Max Wall, Charlotte Rampling, Robert Smithson, Donald Judd, Carl Andre and Daniel Buren, with Diego Rivera on extra-mural technology. Student exchanges would be solely through towns with historical ramparts such as Edinburgh, Elsinore and Cairo (Rampses), Animal studies would be linked to Ramp-Rage with Ms Cluett on the Ganesh module.

P, Q

Unsurprisingly, GANESHES (P,Q) rampage in the Cluett cabinets. As the son of Siva and Parvati, Ganesh was born as a glowing child with a pot belly and the head of an elephant, holding a trident and riding his vehicle: the mouse. Of variegated materials from clay to granite to plastic, she had many models. Originally a folk deity of pre-Vedic Tantric sects, as a Hindu deity Ganesh traversed Asia along with

35 Duly noted in my note book as then Secretary of Art Accord France.

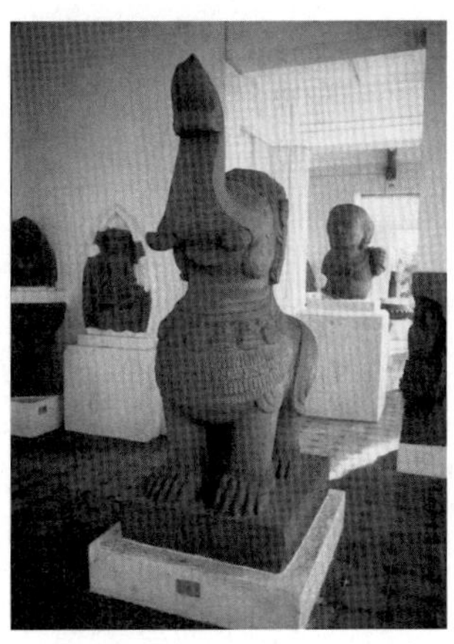

† Champa Lion-Elephant

Buddhism. He travelled south to Sri Lanka, east to Burma and down to Southeast Asia, to Thailand, Cambodia and Vietnam, where the Cham Lion-Elephant † in the Danang Museum was photographed from every angle and described by Cluett as:

“The most wonderful sculpture
I have ever seen.”

Ganesh as the cosmopolitan voyageur, the playful god of the young and great guru of the old, teaching that through wisdom alone can one reach salvation. He was the obvious talisman for Cluett’s journeys and subsequent craft ventures.

R, S

In between her travels, teaching and artwork, Cluett took immense therapeutic pleasure in engaging with COUTURE (R), BIJOUTERIE (S) and making CD compilations from her massive music library. The products became offerings for her friends.

> ‘Inspired by what she saw on our travels, most often the uncommon but everyday treasures the rest of us failed to see the beauty in, Shelagh’s project would evolve throughout the trip as she collected bits and pieces along the way [...] vivid memories of bargaining for paper bags of multi-coloured powders in Tibetan markets – to find them having spilled through our suitcases when we returned. Spurred on by Shelagh’s enthusiasm, we collected everything from buttons, beads, silver, glass, jewels, shells, stones, rice papers and silks. All of which would reappear months later as wonderful pieces of jewelry or works of art.’[36]

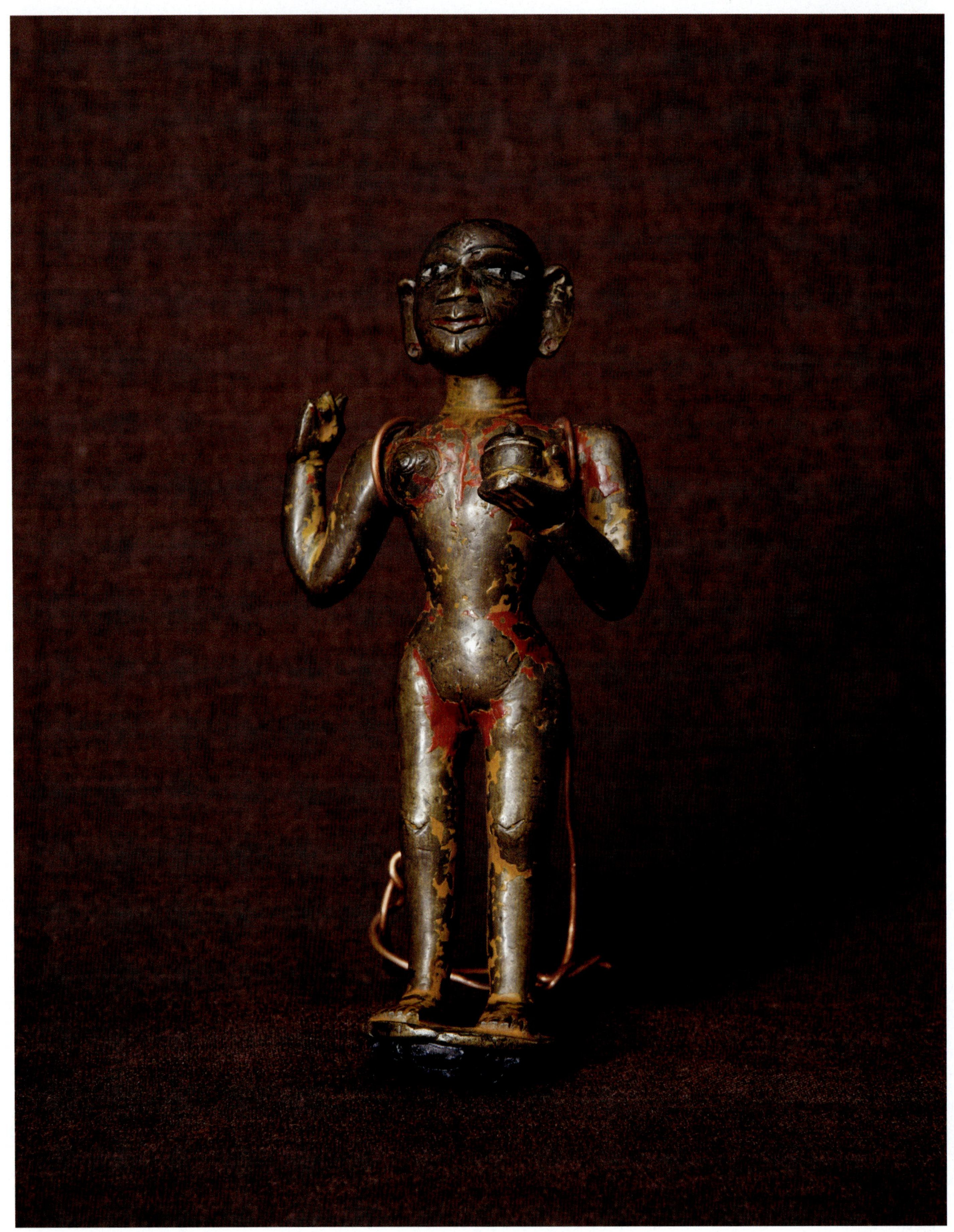

Chola Sculpture (16cm)

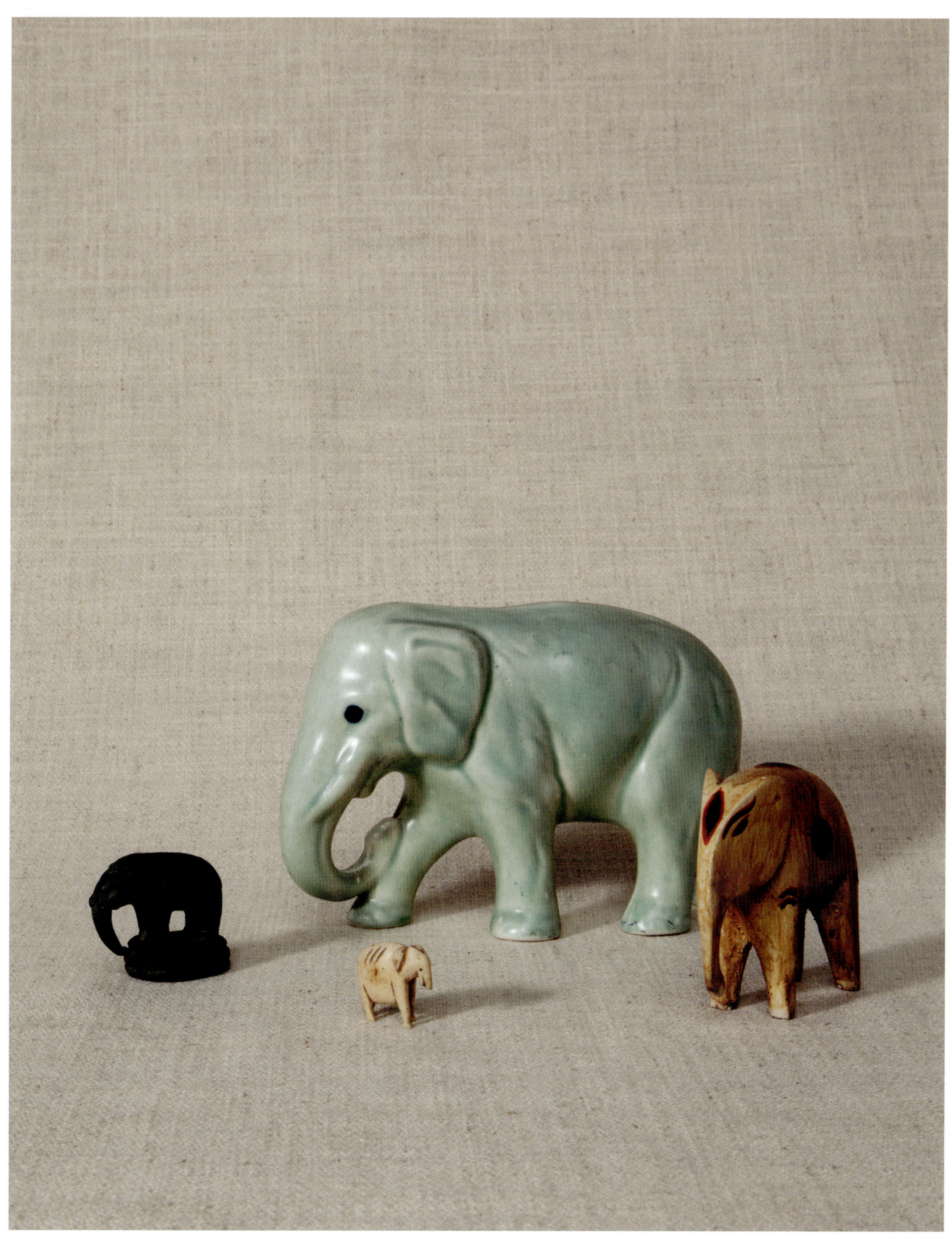

Collection of Elephants (1.5 – 12 cm)

P

Such altruism did not hinder her frank enjoyment of retail therapy, particularly shopping for textiles and beads, whether in Brick Lane or in Charing Cross in Ootacamund:

> 'Ootacamund, better known as Ooty, is situated in the Nilgiri Hills and is the most famous of Southern India's hill-stations first adopted by the British, then by wealthy Maharajas hence the nick name *Snooty Ooty*. We favoured a walk into downtown Ooty for a bit of retail therapy in the aptly named shopping area Charing Cross [...] After much haggling Shelagh and I left with two silver necklaces, one bracelet and a pair of earrings all made by the Nilgiri Hill tribes. We felt set for New Year's Eve party clutching our boxes of jewels eagerly waiting to sport them that evening. [...] After dinner had been served, all wined and dined, an announcement was made that the dancing would take place in the empty pool! [...] we all duly clambered down into the pool and danced the night away careering from the shallow end to the deep end rocking and rolling, partnering Shelagh to the odd foxtrot being thrown in for good measure (always a challenge – having been a South coast champion in her youth).'[37]

T

Whilst in Delhi in 2001, she met up with her oldest friend, Richard Lewis, whose reminiscences on their frequent travelling together somehow puts any 'orientalist' tendencies into a balanced perspective:

> 'We travelled together in Singapore, Bali and India so I had ample opportunities to enjoy her companionship (and astounding range of contacts). On the outskirts of Ubud we weaved

36 Nirmalo Wilkes.
37 Lesley Anne Davies.

among dusty houses to find the studio of an old student of hers. Near Delhi we met up with Virginia Whiles at an exhibition at the end of a bumpy bus ride [...]'

Here she and Richard visited the Khoj International Artists' Association workshop in Modinagar and an exhibition in Delhi[38] where she acquired THE KISS (T), a contemporary miniature painting by Saira Wasim whose witty parodies of the political shenanigans between India and Pakistan were much admired by Cluett.[39]

'[...] But for me the trip which most typified a day's outing with Shelagh was the Poet's day we spent in her beloved Dorset.'[40]

U

If the temple dies out, ritual tradition becomes, in the phrase of Jacob Neusner, a 'map without territories'.[41] Initiation rituals are suspended in space, the practice is transformed into a mental process, it is transferred onto the human body [...] the territory of the map becomes the psychic processes of the individual.

In the Nineties, an orientation towards cartography and installation allowed Cluett to interweave her drawing with formal concerns. *Maps Without Territories,* citing Neusner, is the consequent series in which she sandblasted digital images of Asian temple ground plans onto fragments of stone. Each sombre slab, lit up by lines, was juxtaposed with a small photograph of the temple's inner sanctuary. Collocating the cosmic mandala with a more intimate and direct representation seemed to hint at the ineffable. One of this series was created in 1997 in Rouen titled AITRE ST-MACLOU (U), the former

38 Manoeuvering Miniatures, ICI New Delhi 2001. *The Kiss* was lent by Cluett to 'The American Effect' exhibition in 2003 at the Whitney Museum. N.Y.
39 Shelagh had planned to come to Lahore to arrange exchanges between Chelsea Art College and the NCA (National College of Art) but this was cancelled due to post 9/11 and my enforced exile to India.
40 Richard Lewis.
41 Neusner, J. *History of Religions 19*, 1979, p.103–27.

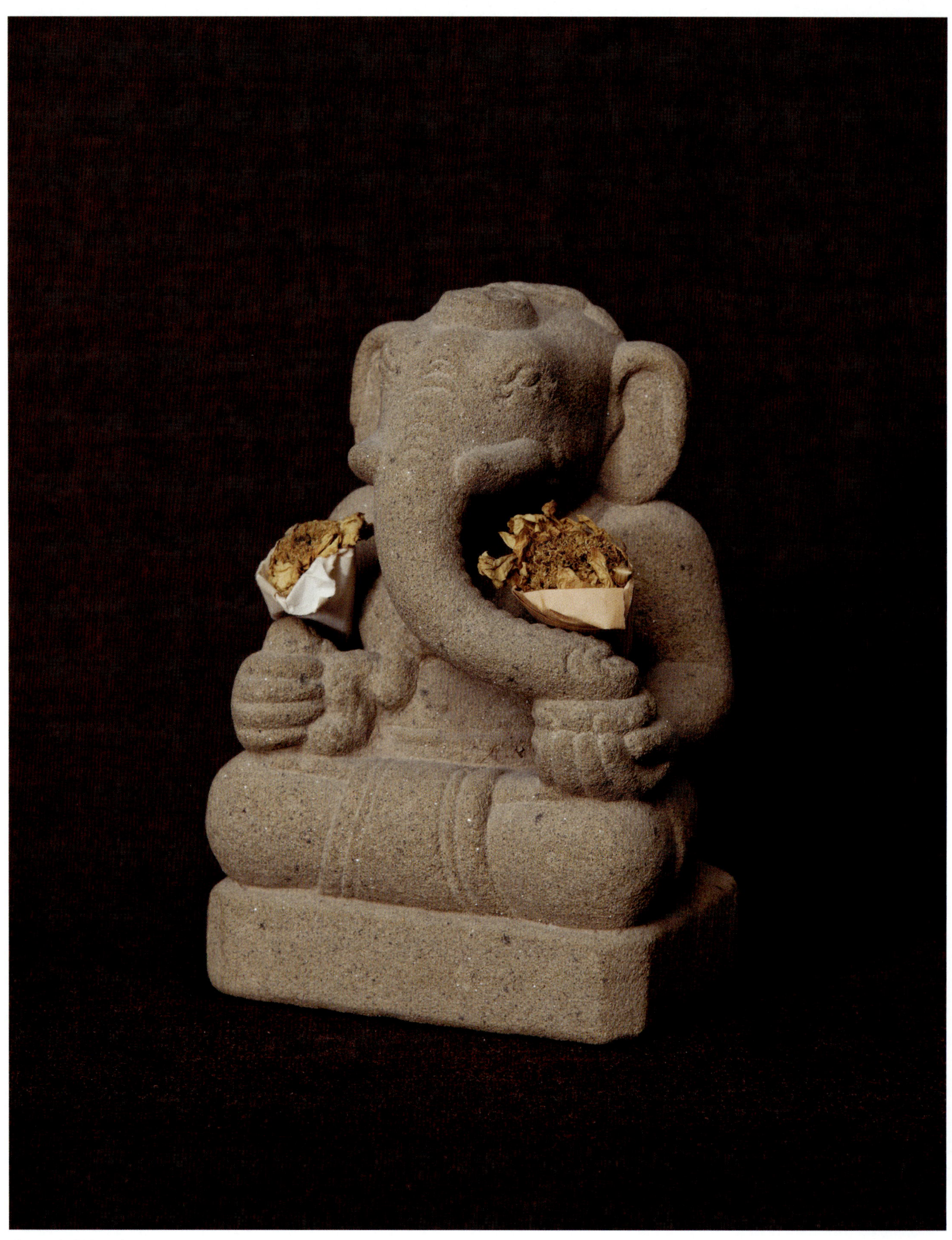

Ganesh (14 cm)

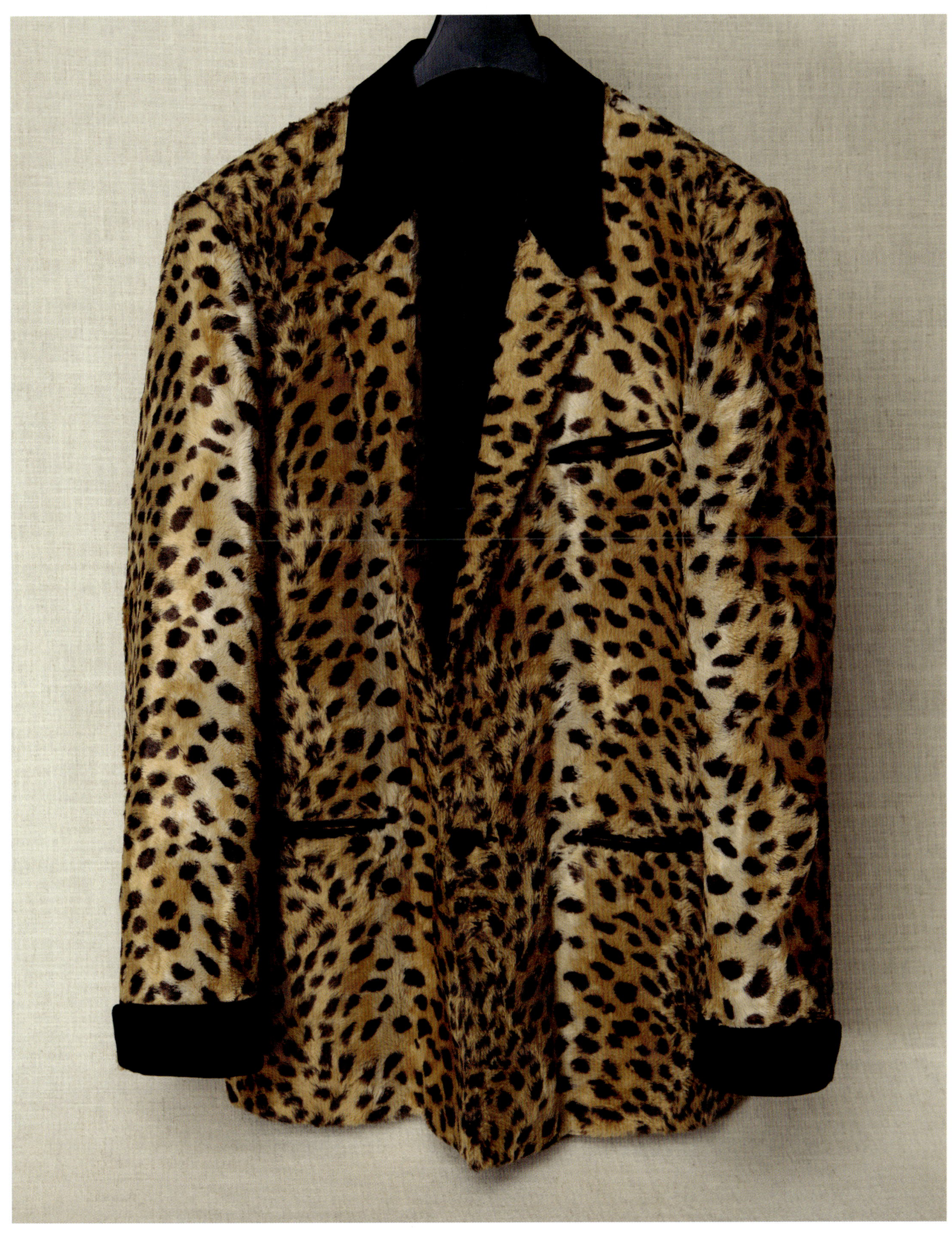

Jacket made by Shelagh Cluett (80 cm)

R

medieval burial ground, now art school, for the exhibition: Terrains Vagues.[42] Cluett wrote:

> 'This recent work searches for an equivalence between a physical and a mental space, and deals with aspects of loss and retrieval [...] I would hope that the works provide a contemplative platform for the viewer and involve them in the search for the pure space.'

Jo Stockham explores the subtlety of the technical experimentation in Cluett's final works:

***

In addition to digital photography and video she used graphics programs to morph the space of ground plans, which were then used, via a plotter, to produce stencils for sandblasting onto stone slabs: 'The plan, the object and the image all have validity, each holding a truth about the sense of place, but each of a very different order.'[43]

Often these marble slabs, hung floating slightly away from the wall, were shown as diptychs, with a small photograph acting as a clue to the site (and sight) of the plan. In sandblasting, the removal of the surrounding surface leaves a 'dry porous vulnerability and a relative lack of focus compared to the polished state.' In this statement, photograph and stone surface become interchangeable, a confusion encouraged by the layering of images and the stretching and folding of plans, often to compose them within the stains and swirls of the mineral impurities which cause the patterning of marble.

V

Footage exists of Cluett experimenting with filmed images (captured on a small handheld DV camera)

42 *Terrains Vagues*. Curated by V. Whiles. Ecole des Beaux Arts de Rouen 1997 and KIAD 1998.

43 All quotes taken from Shelagh's power point presentation notes for *Under the Skin* dated 27/06/03. Presented at the *Digital Surface within Fine Art Practice Conference* at Tate Britain 27/28 June 2003. This work was also presented at conferences in Bangalore and Seoul in 2004.

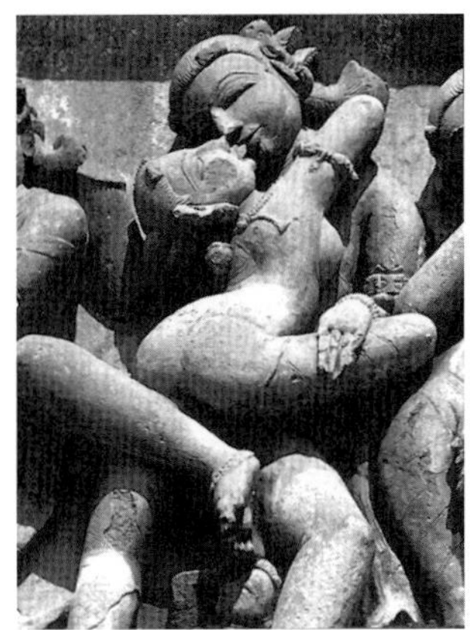

† Postcard from Khajuraho

of the Khajuraho temples she visited in Madhya Pradesh. She had spent a week searching the densely carved walls of the temples containing thousands of figures, to find the particular pair of entwined lovers which had occupied a space on her wall (in postcard form)[†] for many years. Cluett was alive to the nuance of the glitch. An unconventional approach to image capture sees her moving the screen of the computer around to confuse the camera filming it. Simultaneously she is moving through sequences of images, delighting in the side-effects caused by the inability of the camera to read the screen. Passages of what appears to be a digital effect turn out to be an off-screen hairdryer blowing dry a film of water which only moments before had been applied to the marble surface with a soft wide brush.

From a digital collage of these experiments she constructed the video *Under the Skin*, writing: 'It is cut to a track which, although from a different culture, I chose specifically as its use of remixing parallels my approach.'[44] The visuals jump-cut from surface images of the Khajuraho temples to ambiguous, intensely colour-saturated details which are not taken from enlargement (in such small files this would result only in pixelation) but from feeding false information into the images, a remixing which creates density and the illusion of depth rather than disintegration.

This method was also used in the composite digital images from KHAJURAHO (V) which Cluett made to be shown as single Giclée prints. Here the temple plans fall on digital sandstone or marble, not evoking the monumental but rather 'henna [...] tattoos [...] the shadow of an insect.' Using a program called Xara she folded plans around the virtual forms of the photographed sculptures: 'The plan unites the lovers [...]' as it folds across a sculpted body or, half hidden, it glows from beneath a sandstone hand.

44 Nusrat Fateh Ali Khan remixed by Massive Attack.

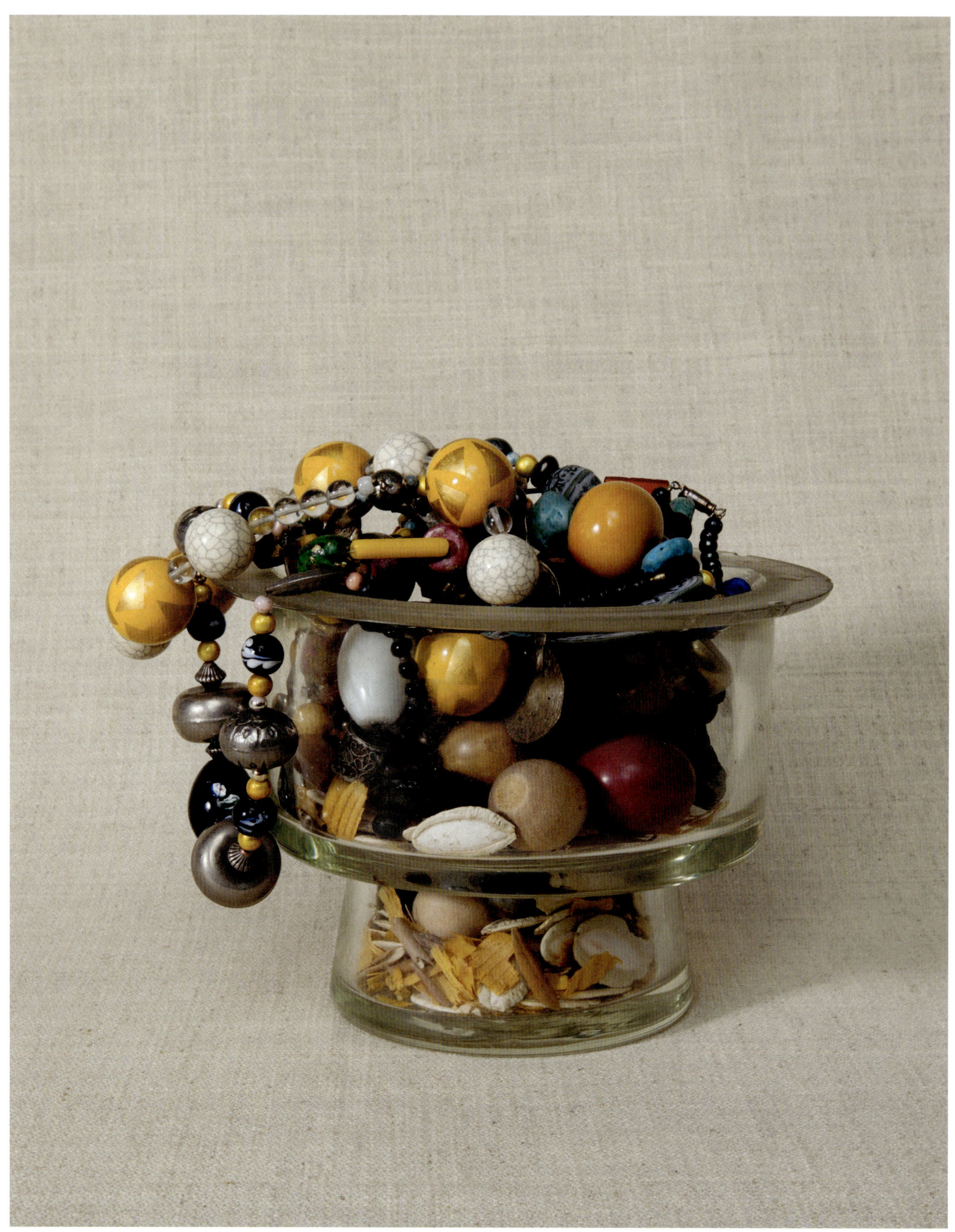

Necklaces made by Shelagh Cluett(17 cm)

S

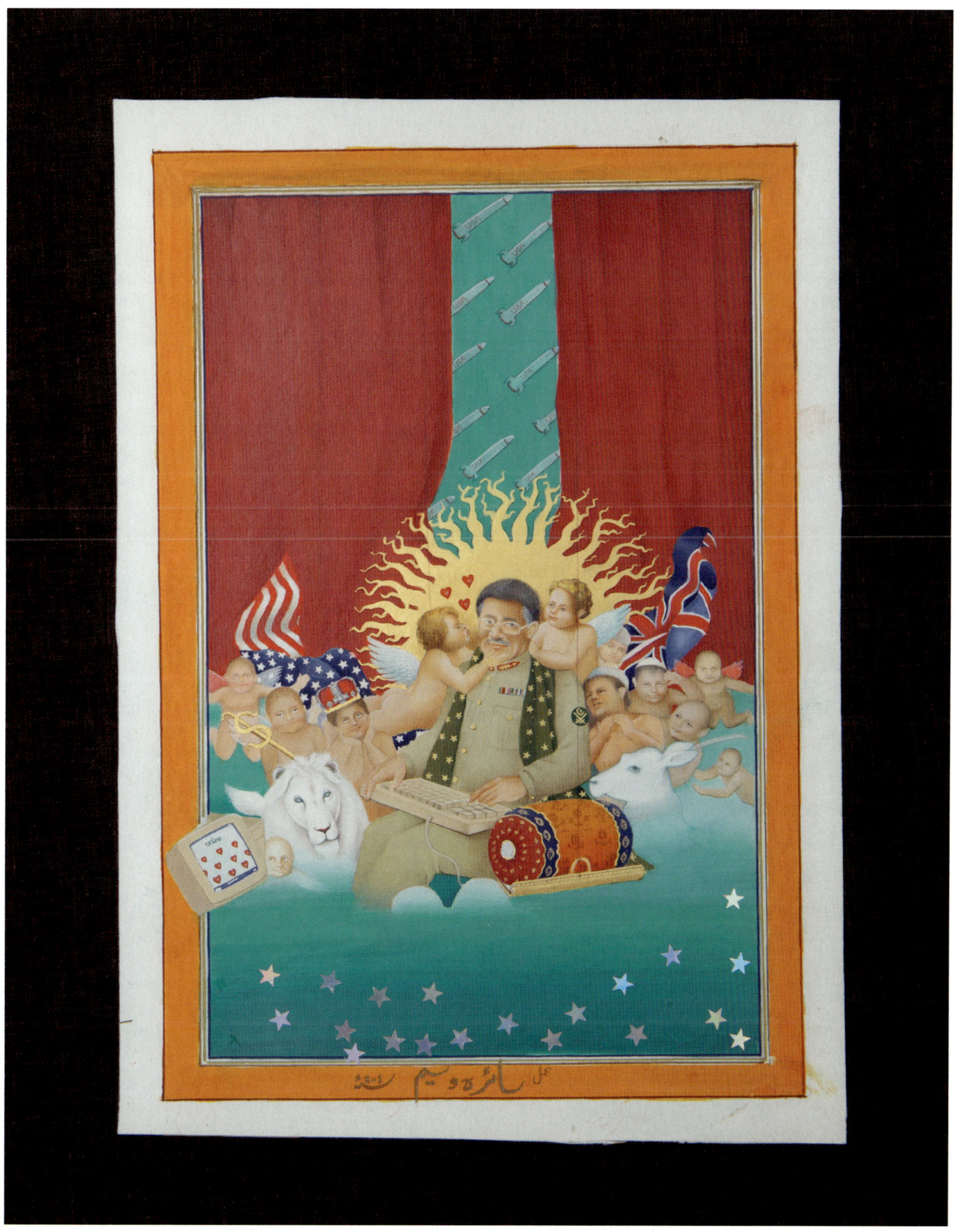

The Kiss, Saira Wasim, 2001 (26×5×16.5 cm)

T

In this investigation into the different temporalities of the digital and the material there is a sculptor's desire to give body to the virtual image. Through this constant oscillating between the material and the immaterial (also present in the subject, in temples themselves) Cluett created a sense of the transience of the viewer or viewpoint. Images on the marble often get lost as the body of the viewer moves, as also happens with many digital screens. The constant shifts of register in the videos seem to me to be a good example of Katherine Hayles's 'flickering signifiers', and her demand that we need to investigate changing experiences of embodiment: 'As we rush to explore the new vistas that cyberspace has made available for colonization, let us also remember the fragility of a material world that cannot be replaced.'[45]

(Jo Stockham)

***

W, X

Cluett picked up many small bronze sculptures in south India. Amongst others, there is a particularly outstanding CHOLA (W) piece of Siva's consort, Parvati (*Uma Parameshvari* in Tamil). Slender and seductive in a graceful *tribhanga* (triple bend) posture, her sensuous pose is matched by the erotic language of a sacred Tamil hymn dedicated to her:

> Fresh as newborn lotus buds
> lustrous as kongu blossoms
> honeyed like young coconuts
> golden kalashas filled
> with the nectar of the gods,
> are the breasts of the resplendent Uma[46]

45 Hayles, K. Essay: *Virtual Bodies and Flickering Signifiers*. October 66. Fall, 1993.

46 Sambandar, Hymn 260 in Dehejia,V. *Slaves of the Lord: The Path of the Tamil Saints*. Delhi, 1988, p.45.

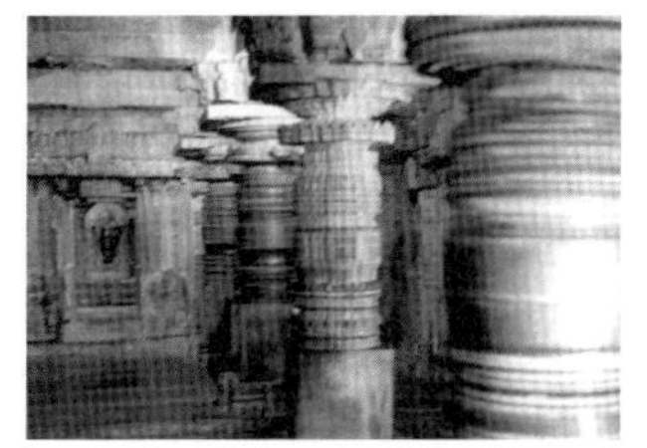
† Photograph taken by Cluett of Somnathpur

This hymn was composed by one of the singing *bhaktas*, Tamil poet-saints who travelled all over south India during the Chola dynasty (850–1250), making up songs in praise of Siva or Vishnu in hundreds of different temples to celebrate the site as a *patal terra talam* (a place sung by saints). Since Cluett was passionate about vocal music, this fact seems significant. Tamil Nadu and Karnataka are the regions where she concentrated her studies of temples, sketching, filming and taking numerous photographs, such as her stunning series on Somnathpur,[†] a temple whose vertiginous dervish swirls evoke a French wedding-cake, *une pièce montée*.

The *utsavamurti* small-scale METAL SCULPTURES (X) which abound in her collection are portable icons paraded on *raths*, or chariots, outside temples on behalf of the immovable images inside, for the purpose of darshan: to see and to be seen, the ritual of worship revisited by Bollywood stars today. 'The exchange of vision that still acts as a focus for *bhakti* [...] the passionate devotion of the devotee [...] a devotee can tell a *murti* (idol/icon) secrets they can't tell even to their wife or children.'[47] Often embellished with garlands, jewels and golden silks, these processional images are bathed during the festivals in temple tanks or sacred rivers. Cluett was intrigued by the rituals of production which she recounted to me when visiting the superb exhibition of Chola bronzes at the Royal Academy in February 2007, not long before her last journey to India. Their ornamentation hints at the amorous powers of the gods in the Hindu Tantric tradition where the *sringara rasa* (erotic flavour) is perceived as a metaphor for seeking union with the divine. Shrines are built around phallic forms worshipped as attributes of deities; *yab-yums* abound among the dancing figures of Tantric temples,

47 Dalrymple, W. *Nine Lives*. London: Bloomsbury, 2009, p.183, 191.

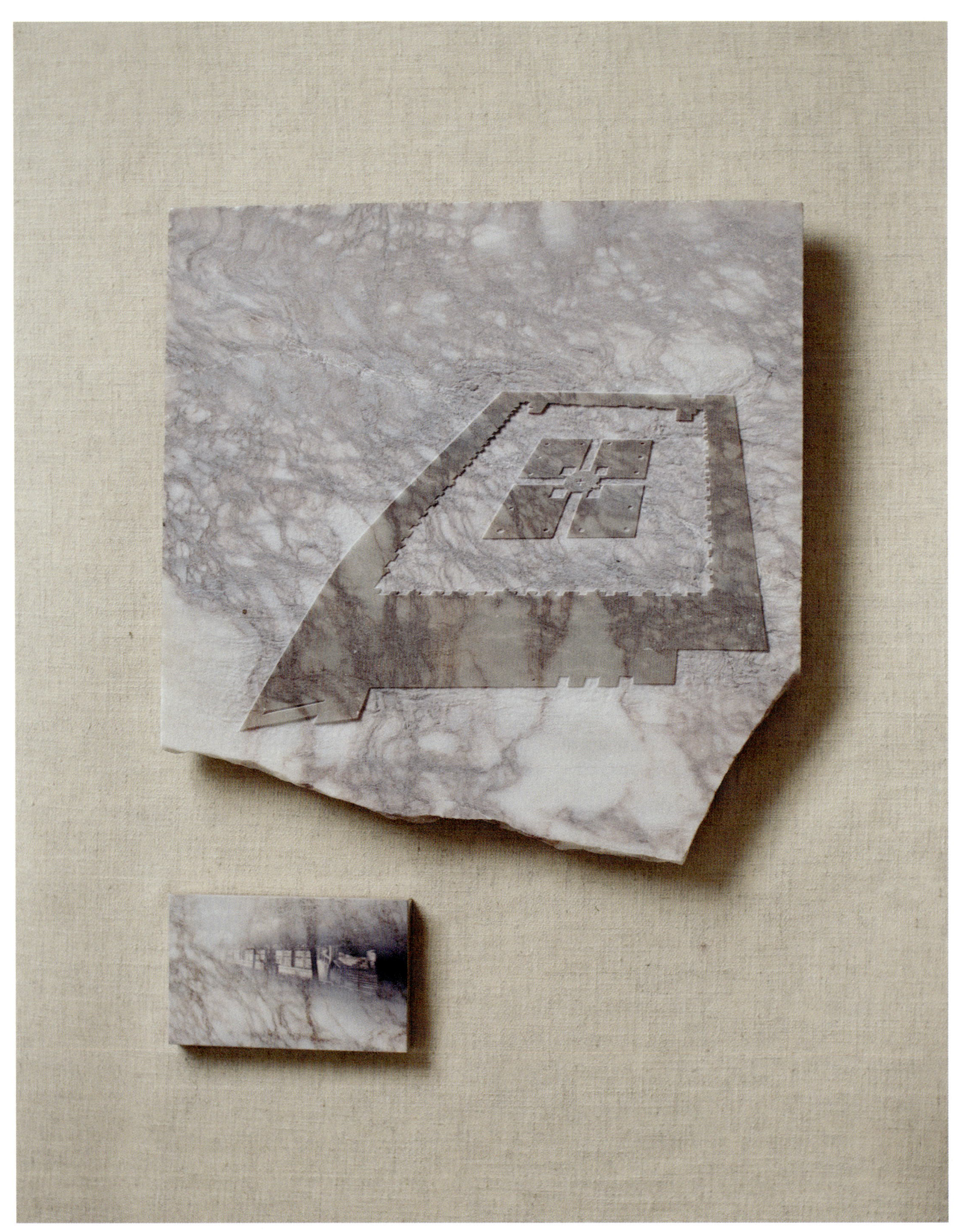

Aitre St. Maclou, 1997 (47×44.5×3.5 cm)

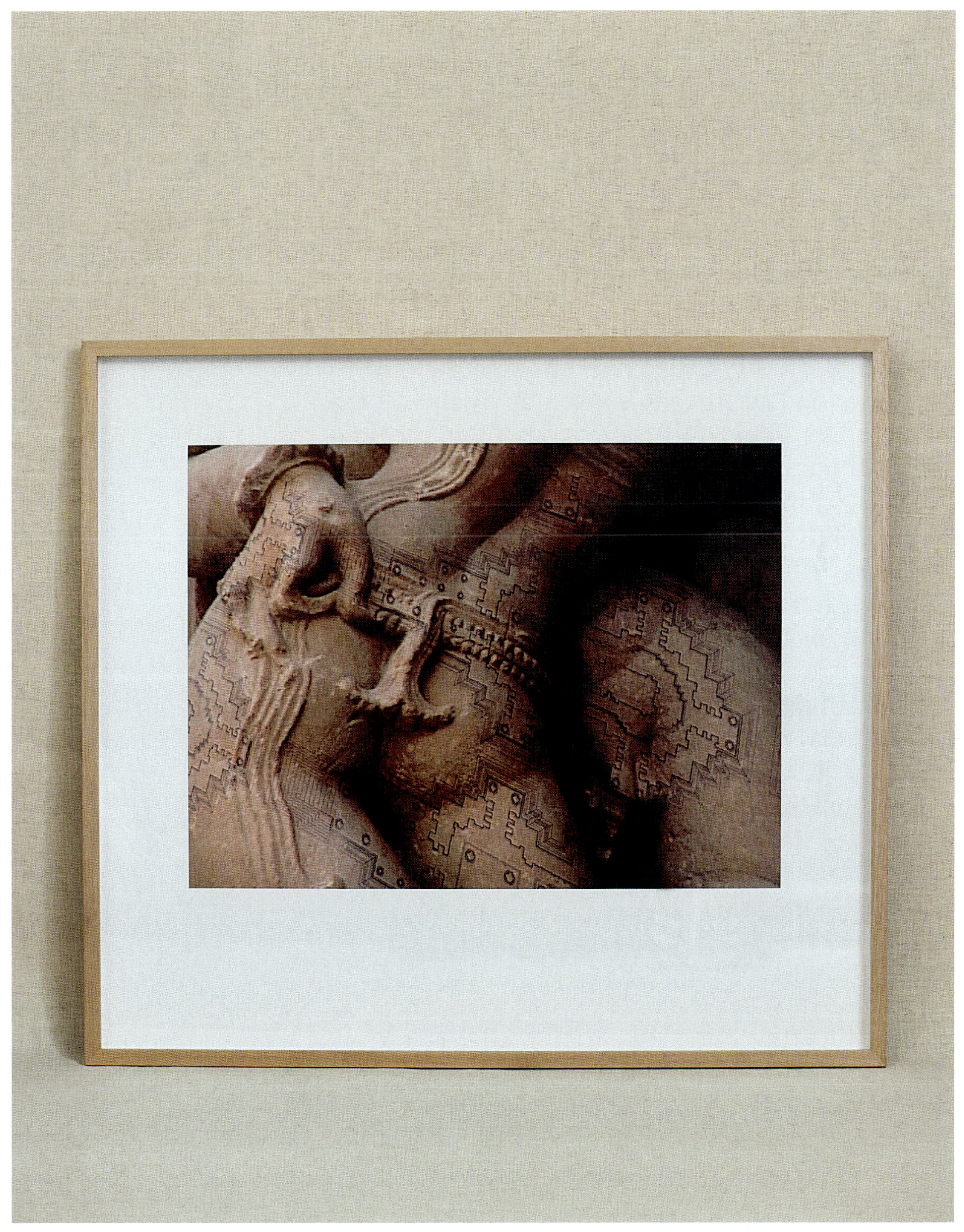

Khajuraho, 2002 (96.5×88 cm)

celebrating the union of male and female forms (vulgarised in popular jargon as 'longing lingams' and 'yawning yonis'). This is spectacularly visible in the temple friezes of Khajuraho and Konarak, where such couples are carved in this particular *rasa* which inspired *Under the Skin*.

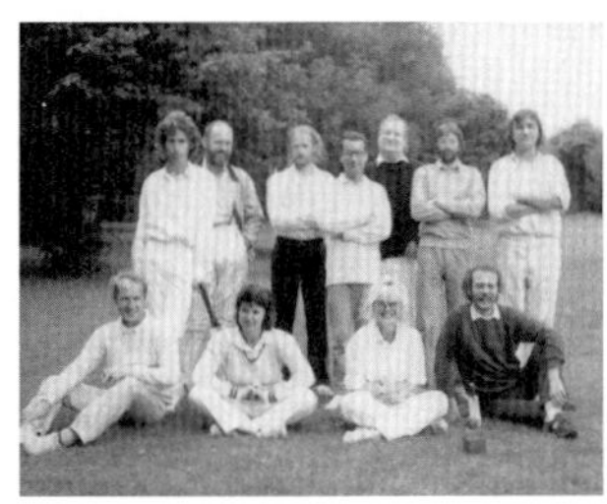

† Chelsea School of Art Cricket team

***

Trophies of Conversion was the title given to the nineteenth century display in the Missionary Museum and described as: 'the idols given up by their former worshippers from a full conviction of the folly and sin of idolatry.'[48]

This exhibition celebrates the formidable folly and sin of idolatry bestowed on her cabinets by the Golden Goddess: Mlle. Clouette, sadly missed by all her colleagues and friends.

> 'I was just thinking – with a glass in my hand – what a very shared world it was, that we all did everything (work and play) together,[†] the central gang that made Chelsea (sort of tolerating the rest), and Shelagh was a quintessential gang-member/player/conspirator.'[49]

48 The London Missionary Society: 'Missionary Museum' on Blomfield Street. Davis, R. op. cit. p.168.
49 Nick Wadley.

Epilogue

Opening the gates to the yard at 7 Ezra St and finding Shelagh sitting in the sun on the bench or on her balcony making drawings for her next pieces of work, it was lovely to sit, chat, have coffee and travel in her world. The joy of opening the front door at the bottom of the stairs and hearing the sounds of Tina Turner or some other music belting out from Shelagh's studio and filling the stairwell with energy and making me smile and feel alive, it was fabulous.

(Sarah Ainslie)

[...] rolling, rolling, rolling rolling on the river.

(Tina Turner)

[...] She'd be out in the yard sipping tea from a yellow cup whilst listening to the Archers or the cricket on one of her tiny radios, then she'd disappear into the studio and work away for days turning base metals into gold, first with her hands and then on the computer.

During that period (the Seventies) there was a vogue for big-framed glasses in bold colors and I remember Shelagh sporting pairs in both her trademark co-lours of turquoise blue and yellow. Years into our teaching partnership it dawned on me that she didn't wear the glasses for tutorials or when hanging student shows. One day I idly picked up a pair of Shelagh's glasses from the desk in the staff room and tried them on.

I had perfect eyesight at the time, but with the glasses on I could only see shapes and blurry fields of colour, so I asked her how she managed to absorb and assess the students' work without being able to see it properly. She replied to the effect that the work looked better like that, and she found it much easier to understand the fundamental relationships between physical elements and colours of a piece without being bogged down by unnecessary detail.

(Charles Garrad)

I imagine her opening her door and walking past the empty steel stalls of Columbia Flower market. I can see her strolling down the Hackney Road, late at night, after visiting an ex-student's private view. I see her riding her bicycle across the Old Ford Canal towpath. Or catching the number 26 along the Strand, leaning up against the frame and just simply watching the world go by. In Weymouth, striding through the sea and the sand, up to her knees in it, filling herself with yellow sun.

(John Hughes:
extract from his text: Study in Yellow 2010)

Golden hair and eyes of blue.
How those eyes could flash at you!

(Johnny Cash:
Ballad of a Teenage Queen)

We had lunch in the Wise Man at West Stafford near Dorchester before setting off across the meadows of the Frome to Puddletown Forest on a glorious summer day. After a steady uphill walk we arrived at Thomas Hardy's Cottage. Shelagh was a great admirer of the poet-novelist but not content with a visit to his birthplace, we set off to his family's graves at St Michael's churchyard, Stinsford, where his heart was buried. His ashes lie in Poets' Corner in Westminster Abbey. To complete the Hardy episode we visited his home at Max Gate, a rather dull house she thought, considering Hardy had trained as an architect.

But one poet was not enough for Shelagh. Leaving Max Gate behind us we set off across fields for Winter-borne Came, the rectory home of the great Dorset vernacular poet William Barnes. We found his grave in St. Peter's Churchyard, an exquisitely English location in the rolling hills of her home county.

So while I have mental images of Shelagh riding on a bum-boat across Singapore harbour and hanging on for dear life while a tuk-tuk driver skilfully broke every traffic law in order to take a short cut to her Delhi hotel, it is that summer day in Dorset which best sums up the joy of times spent in

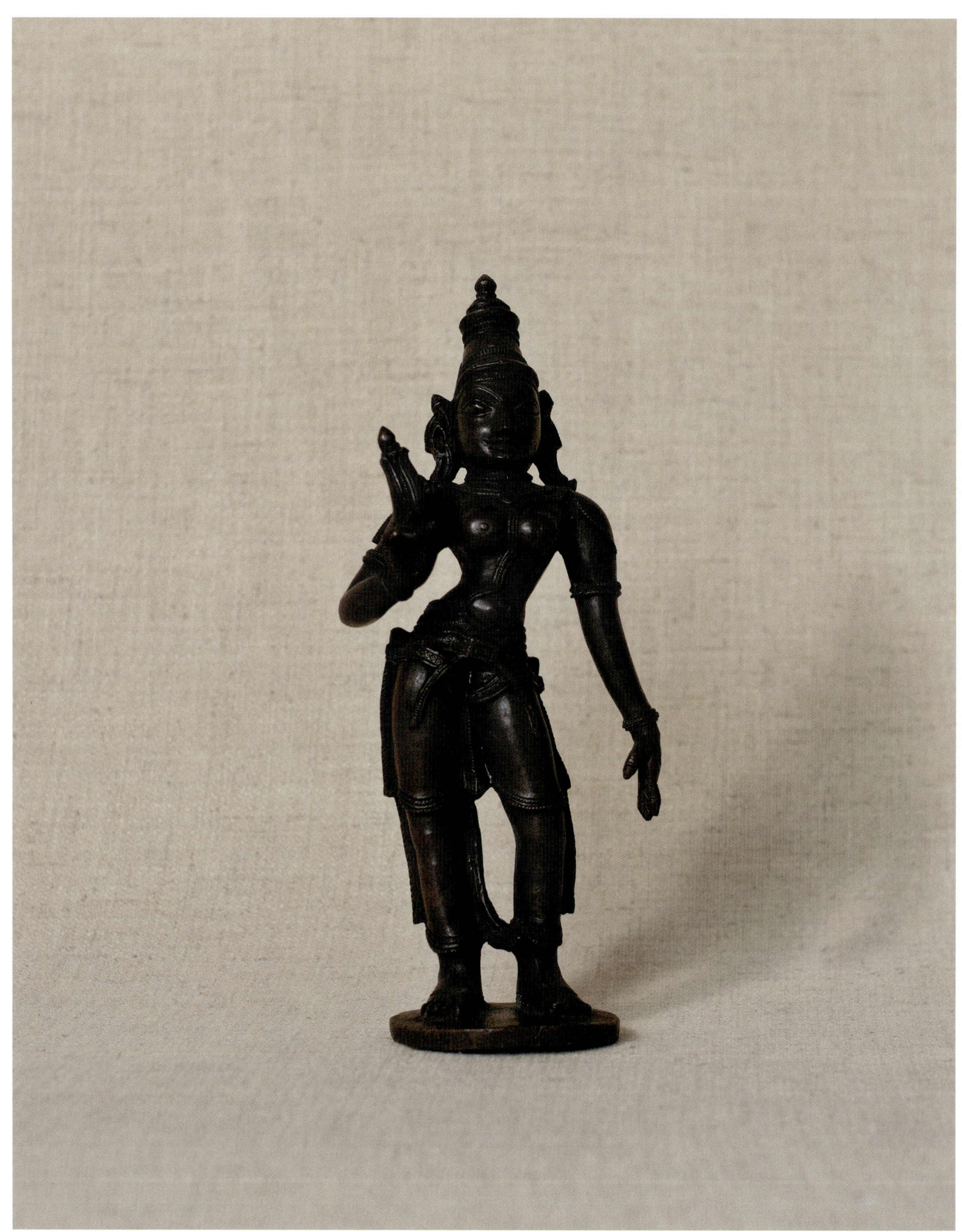

Parati (22 cm)

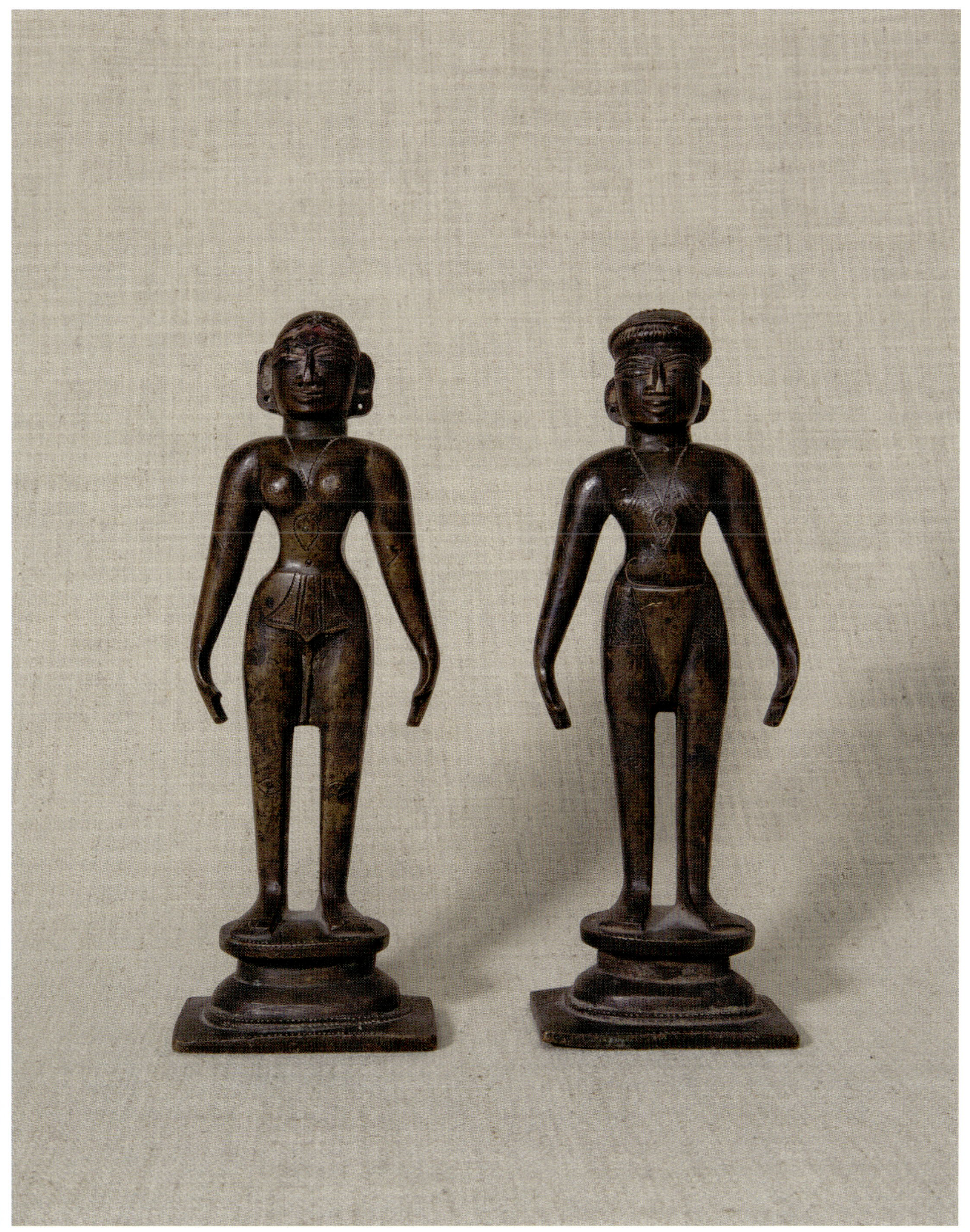

Utsavamurti (23 cm)

her company. She would combine thoughtful planning with carefree spontaneity and her boundless energy and sense of fun made her the ideal companion.
(Richard Lewis)

Working with Shelagh at Chelsea was to experience an ever-renewed under-standing of what sculpture might be. The line of thought ranged from the philosophical to the ridiculous, encompassing the traditions of Dada and beyond, finding expression in fun and games as much as measured critique. To this end cabaret featured as an annual event, although cabaret was ever the spirit of all the parties that Shelagh and the Sculpture School hosted. Songs of celebration, valediction and general criticism, mostly with edge, were standard tariff. We progressed from the extended critique of British Sculpture 'Don't Make Any More Henry Moore' to the New Jerusalem in Pimlico: 'On Millbanks' Brash Reclaimed Land'. All was NOT forgiven [...] Shelagh was the mistress of misrule on these occasions. 'I feel pretty' sung in her best Dorset accent was her theme tune.
(Matt Rugg)

So many student-related events like the banquets she used to arrange with the students each year. This is when Shelagh really came into her element and you realized just how much the students loved her.
(John Cussans)

Topical, incisive, and sometimes with a measured acerbity, Shelagh demanded rigour in her humour as in her teaching and her art. For the sculpture department, these cabarets – with Shelagh as a driving force – were truly a 'world turned upside down' where the power structures of the department, school and, ultimately, university could be held up to a strict debunking and stripping of any pomposity or bullshit. This was also a counter-balance to the absolute focus Shelagh demanded from herself, students and colleagues in the studio. Many is the time that after one of these sessions – perhaps in some godforsaken bar somewhere – I would hear from nowhere "Mr.Ryaaannn" and there would be Shelagh grinning. I never quite knew what the mischievous smile meant, apart from the obvious amusement that someone in art history had made it so far into the long boozy night!
(Dave Ryan)

Shelagh seemed to have the measure of each and every student, to treat each of them with a rare and subtle understanding of capacity and capability. So, for this, she was an exceptional teacher; people simply didn't realise, in the fullness of such attention and touch that she was actually teaching. She was funny and fair, but remained, in all that sociability, strikingly independent.
(Sacha Craddock)

They say behind every teacher is another teacher, Shelagh is that teacher. A way of being perhaps that stayed with many of us, especially the women – who it seems are all making work and all teaching. There was quiet strength as well as vulnerability to Shelagh, a booming laugh, intelligence, integrity and a real understanding of the private exchange between the work and the artist. We knew she fought battles on all our behalfs, though it was only a few things she let fall. It was a time in British university education when colleges were being forced to take fee-paying international students, so there was occasionally unspoken prejudice against us, regardless of the financial reality of individuals. Shelagh always saw individuals rather than generalities and stereotypes, and that in itself makes her hard to replace in the world.
(Maryam Hussain)

I'm sure that if I went into another board meeting I would be moved to commit violence, and do we really want to exhaust ourselves trying to teach rich kids for a pittance so the university can continue to grow rich at our expense, no is the answer, enough is enough.
(Email from Cluett to author April 2007)

[...] Let the train blow the whistle when I go!
(Johnny Cash)

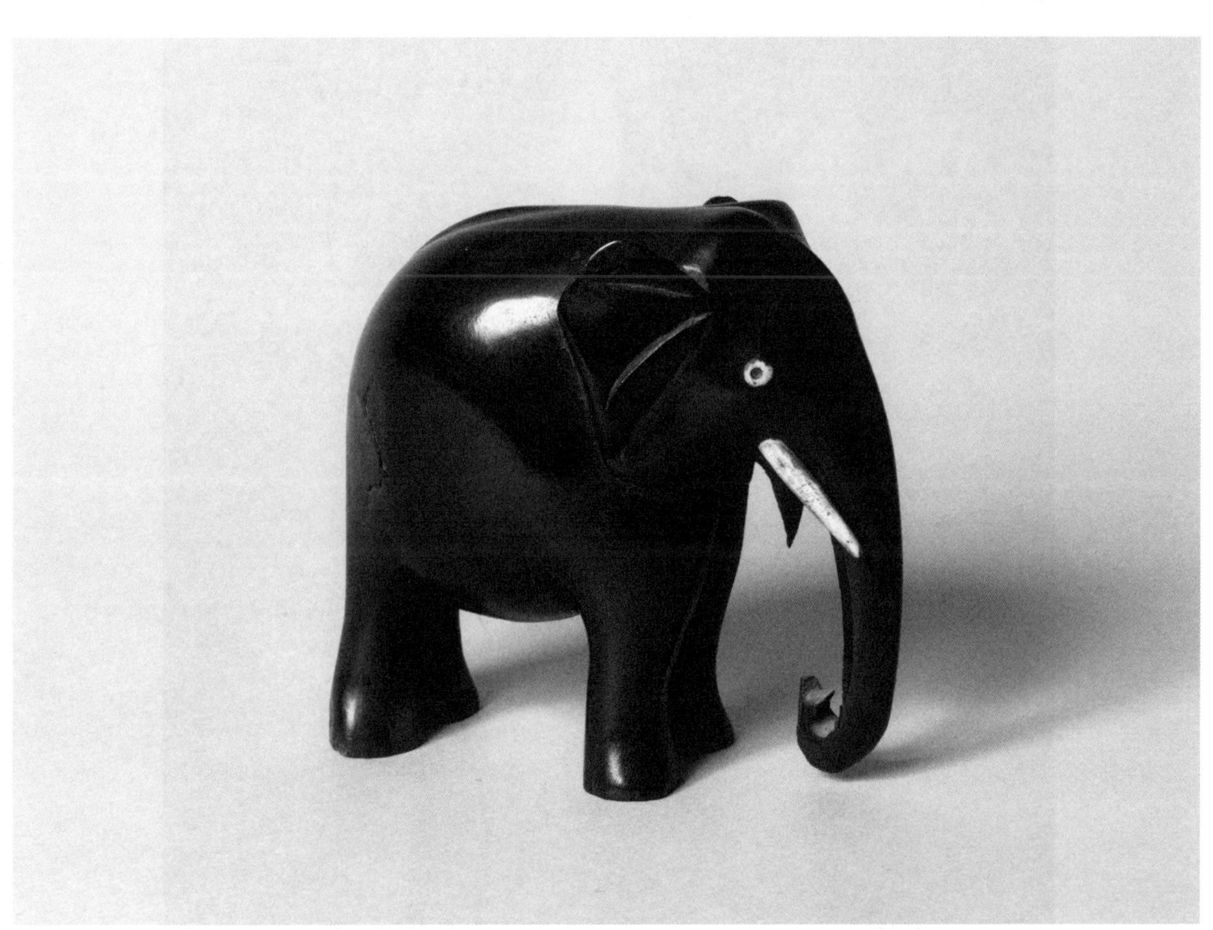

Mahogany Elephant (11.5 cm)

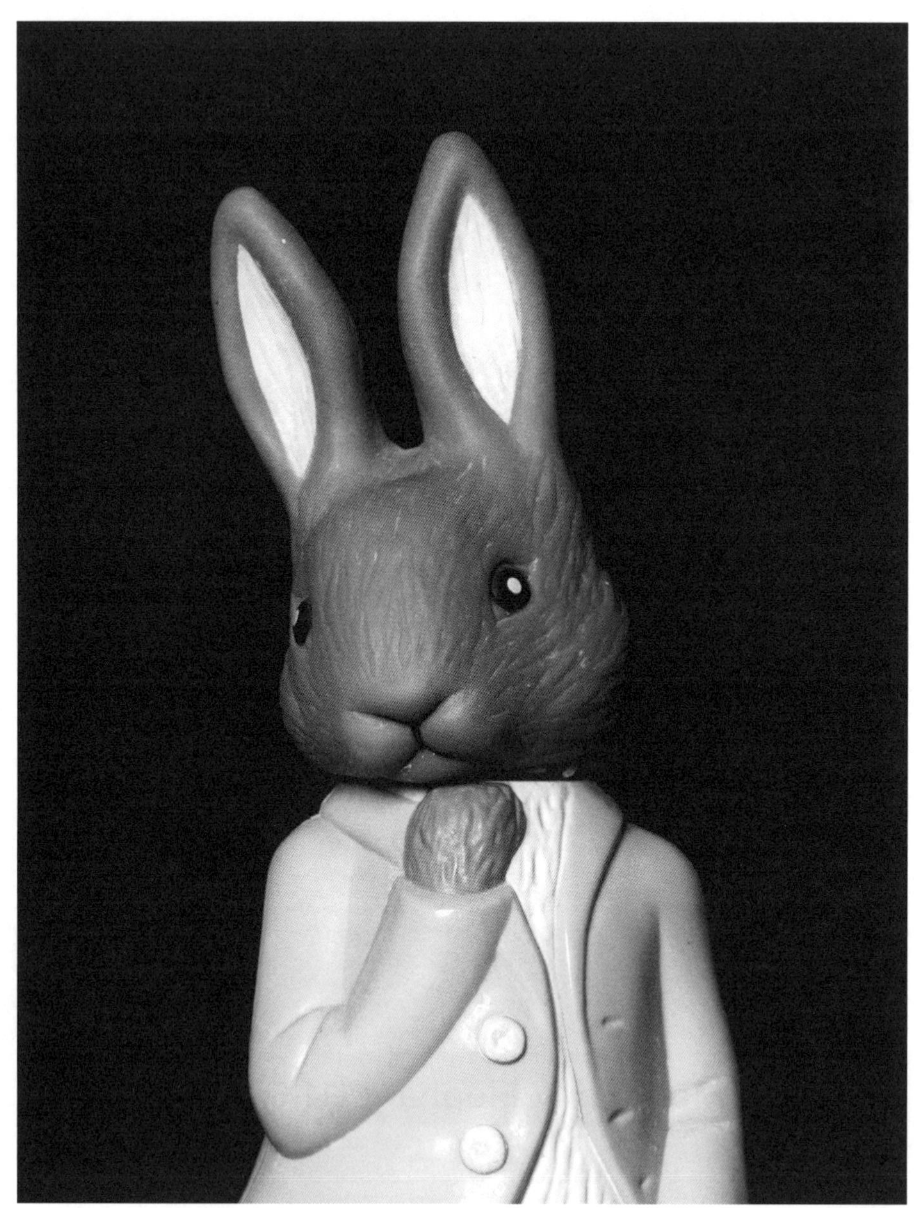

Plastic Rabbit (20 cm)

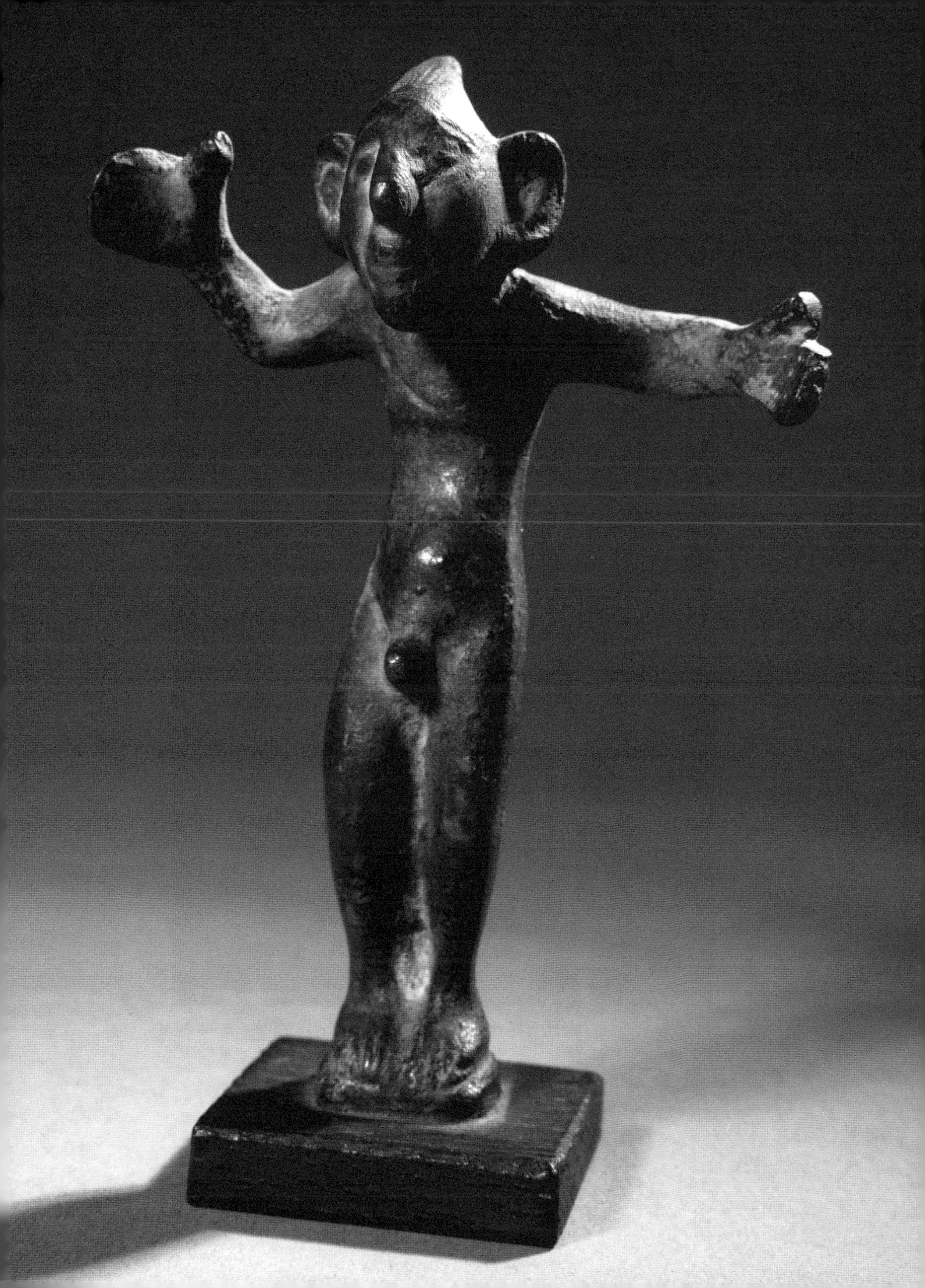

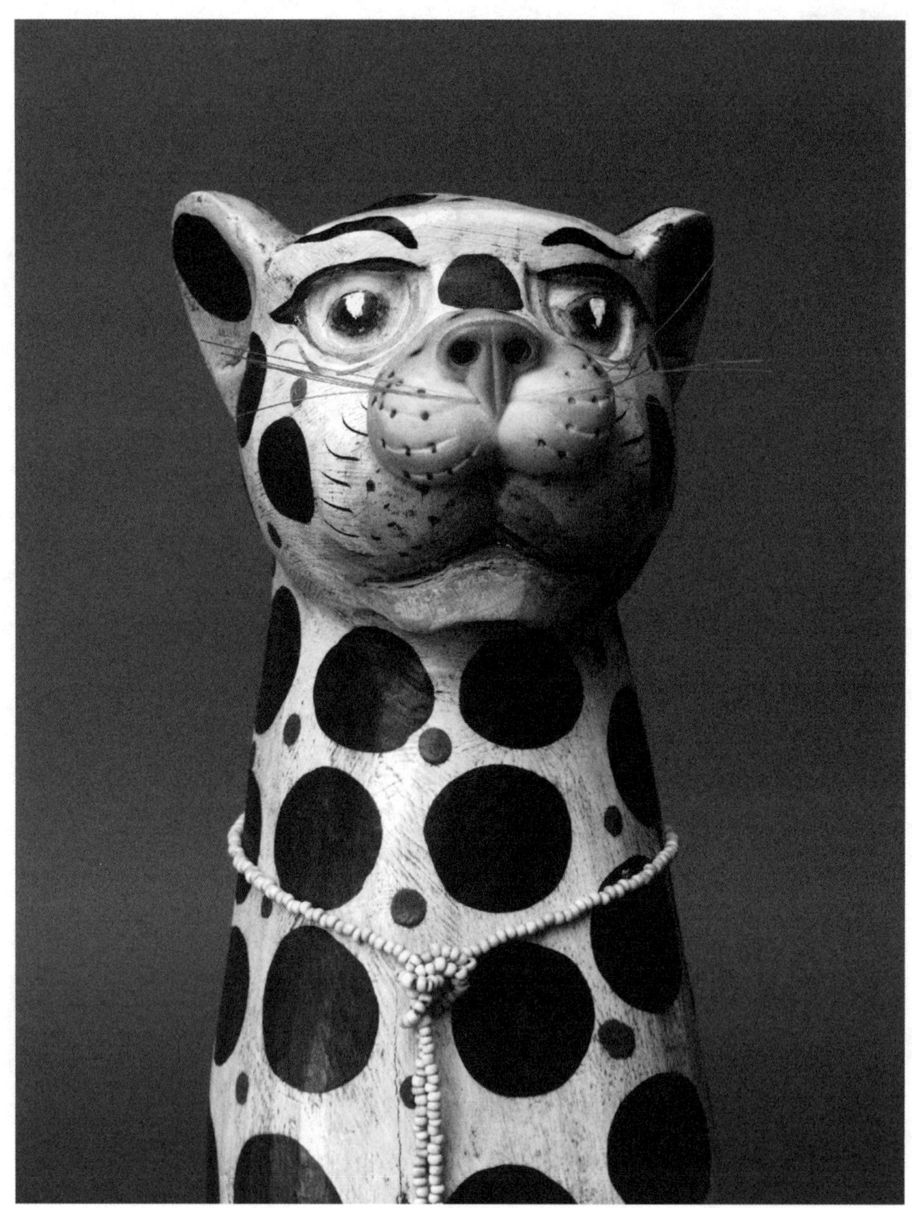

Wooden Leopard (96 cm)

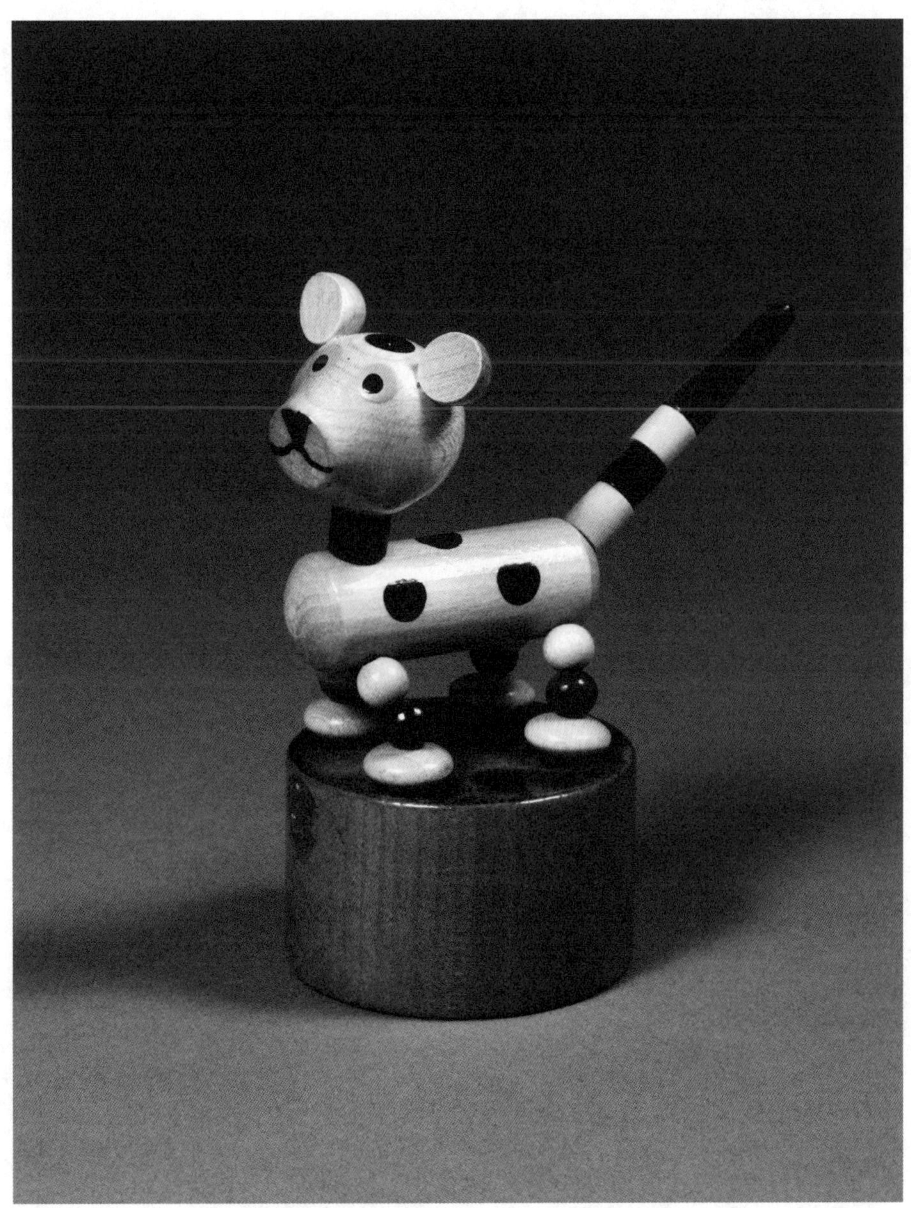

Wooden Cat (10 cm)

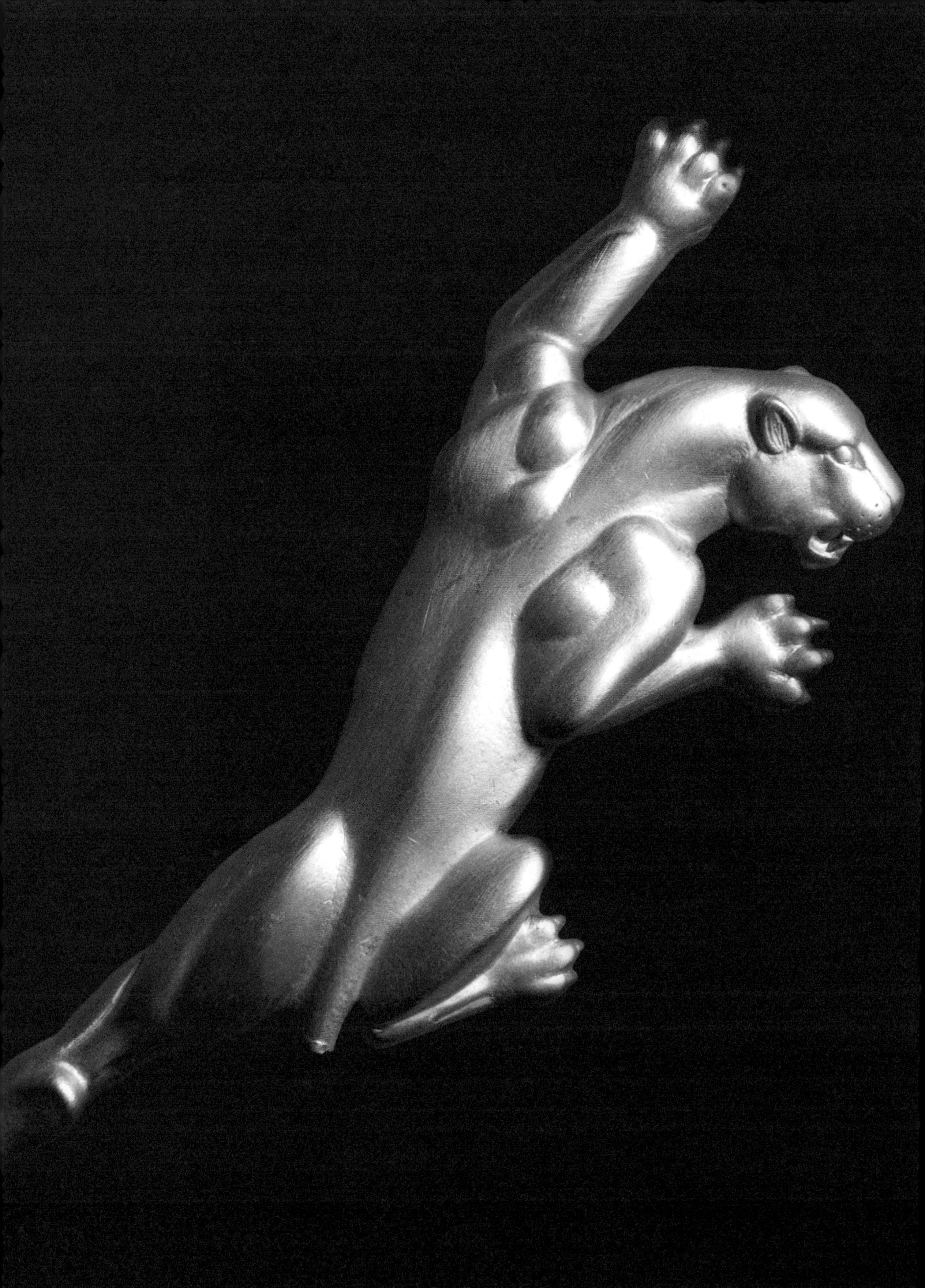

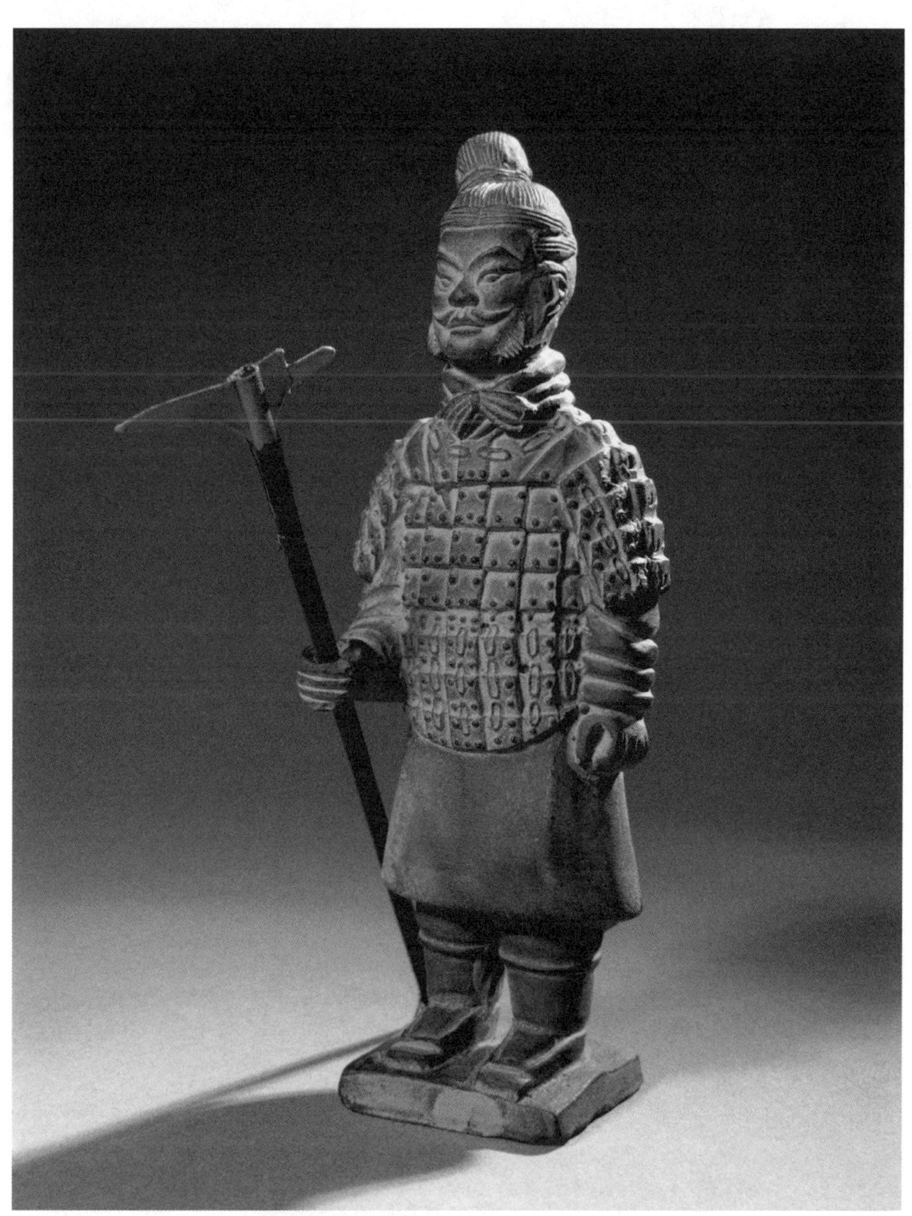

Plaster Warrior (12 cm)

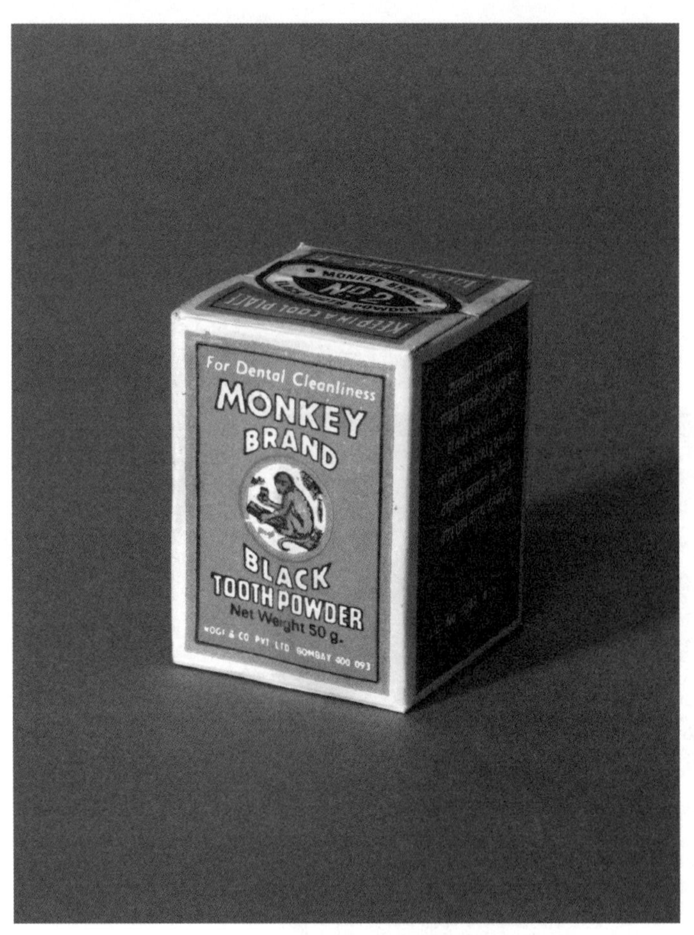

Monkey Tooth Powder (6.5 cm)

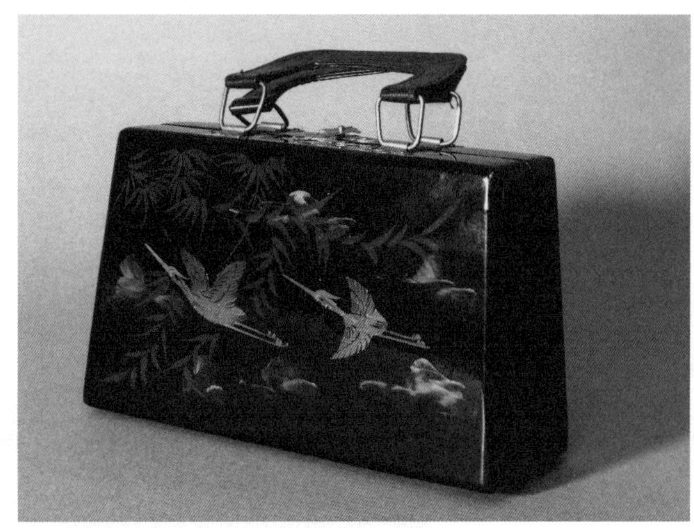

Handbag (19 cm)

Monkey (18 cm) & Prayer Wheel (26 cm)

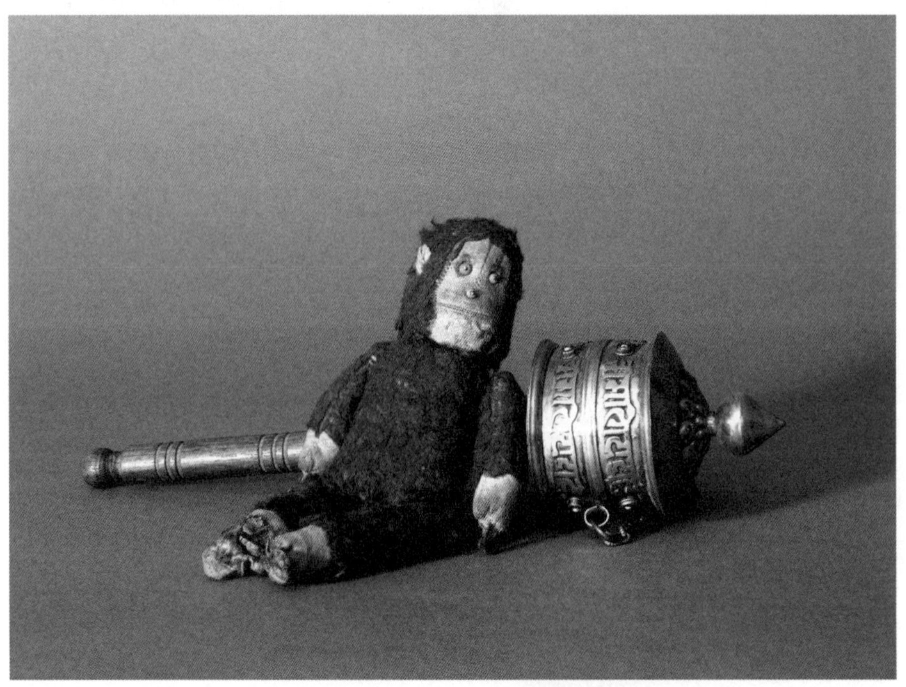

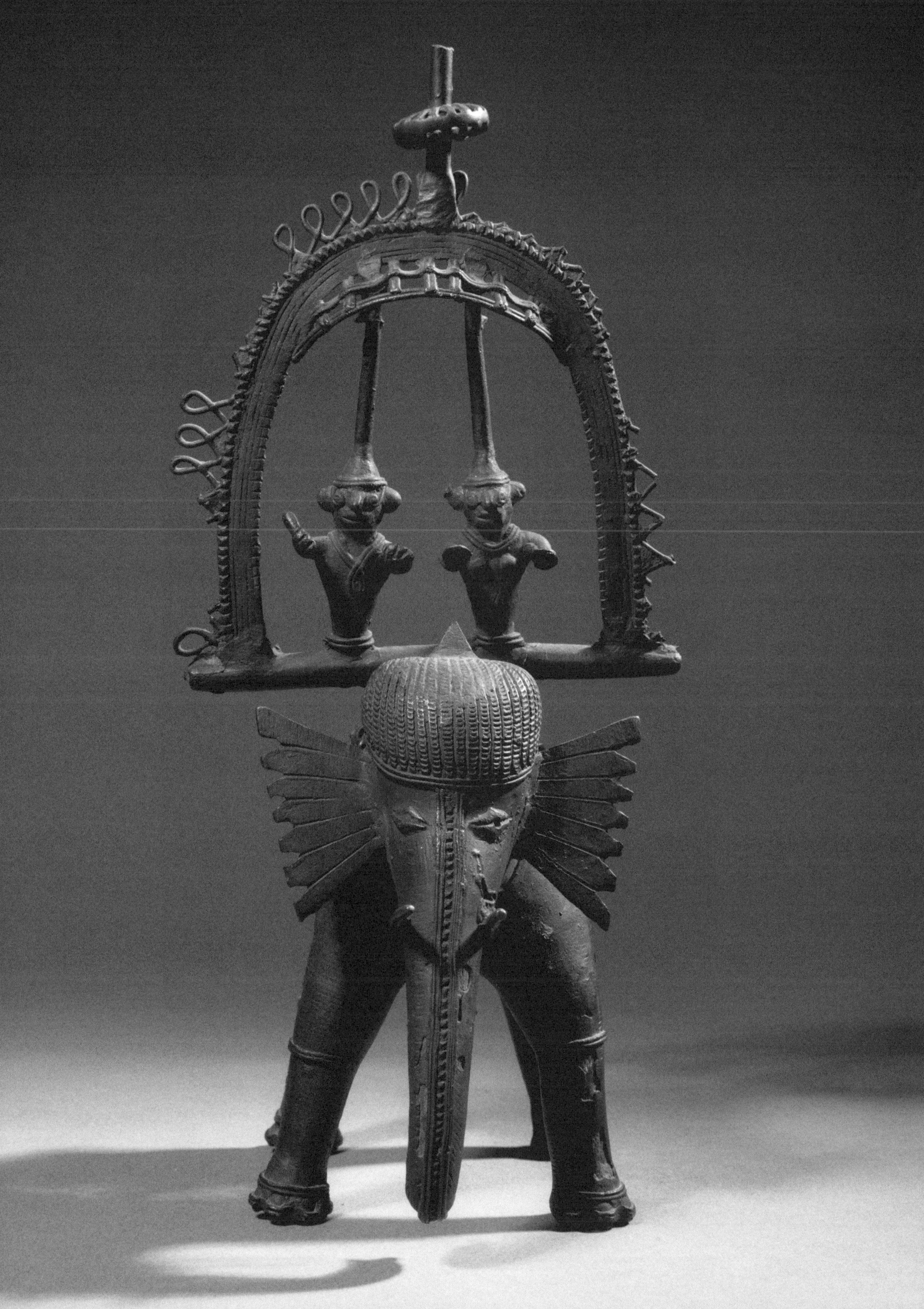

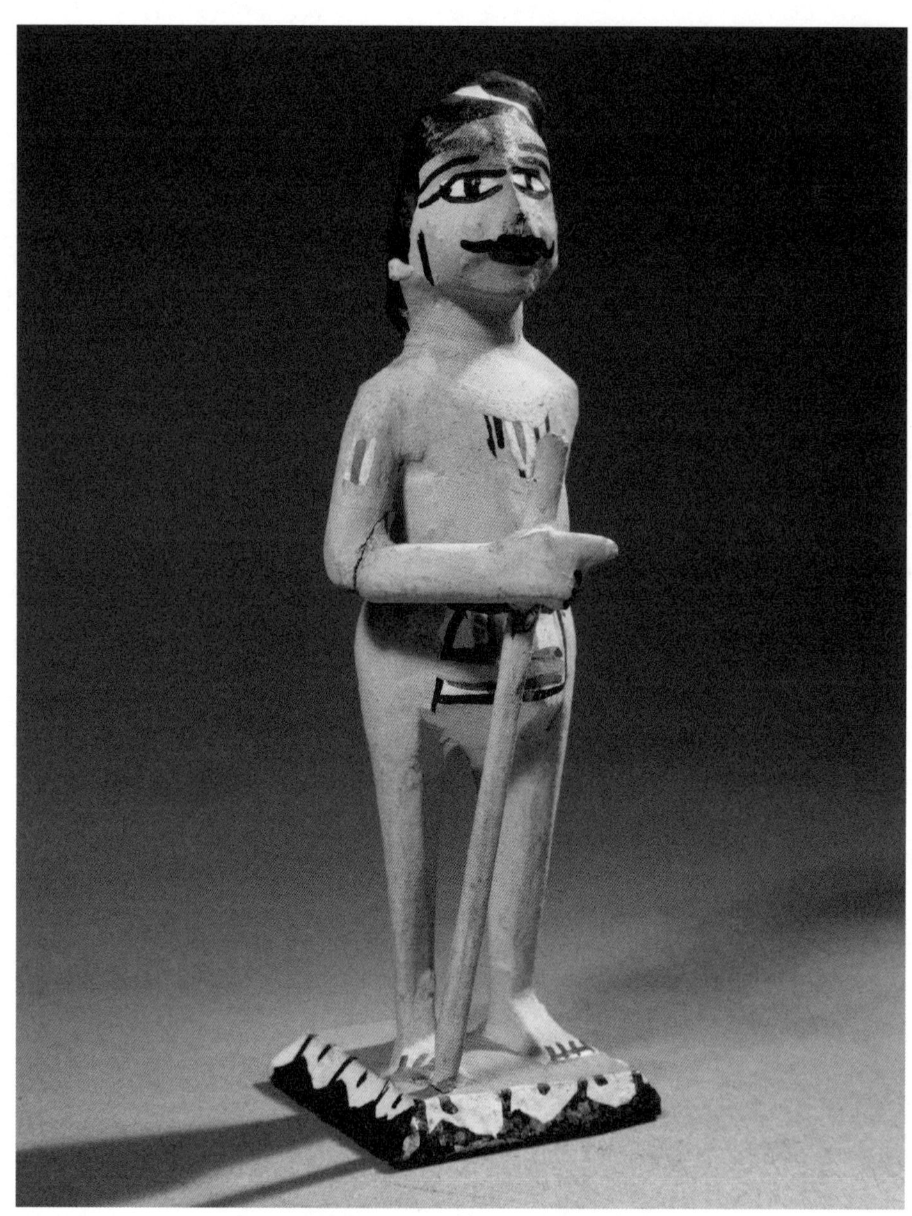

Wooden Figure (9.5 cm)

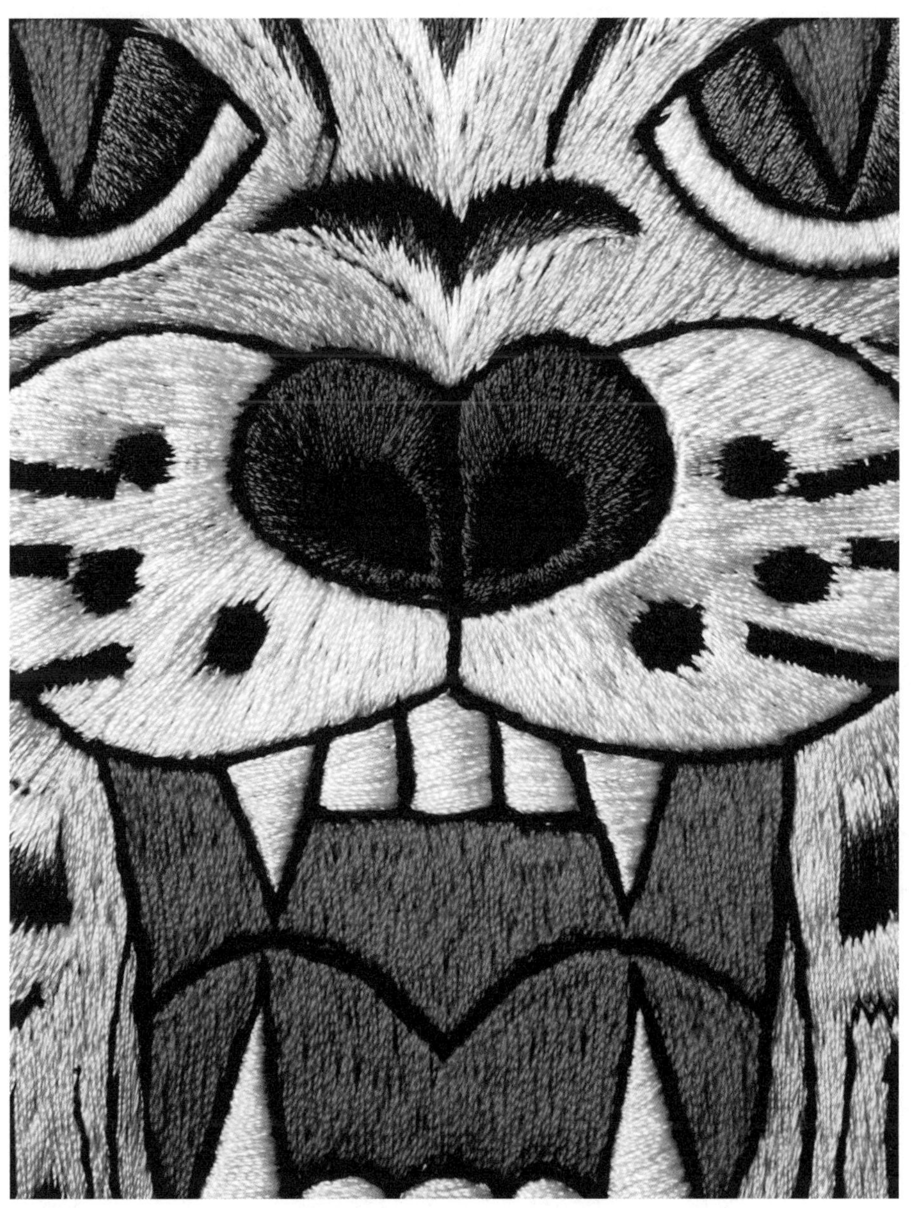

Tiger Patch (17 cm)

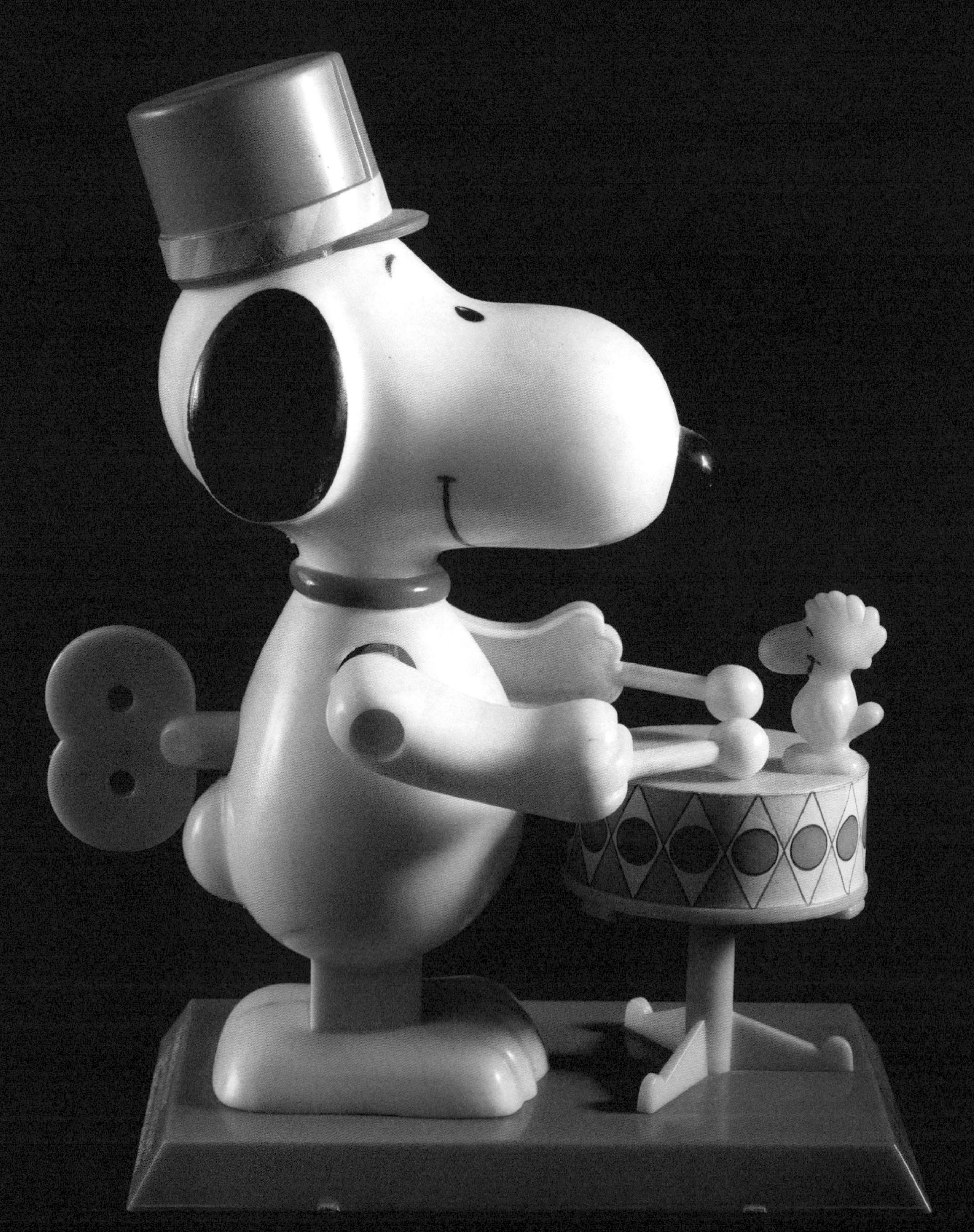

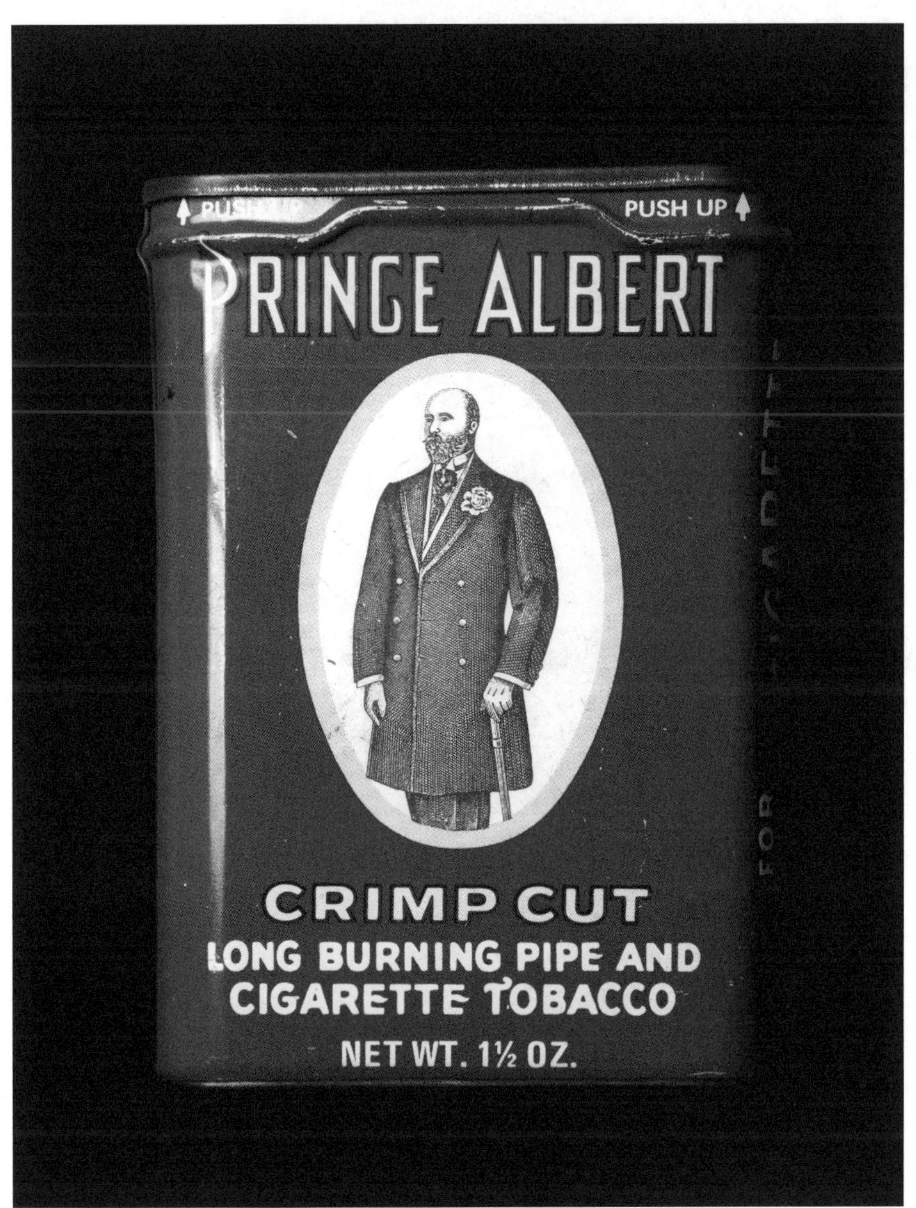

Tobacco Tin (11 cm)

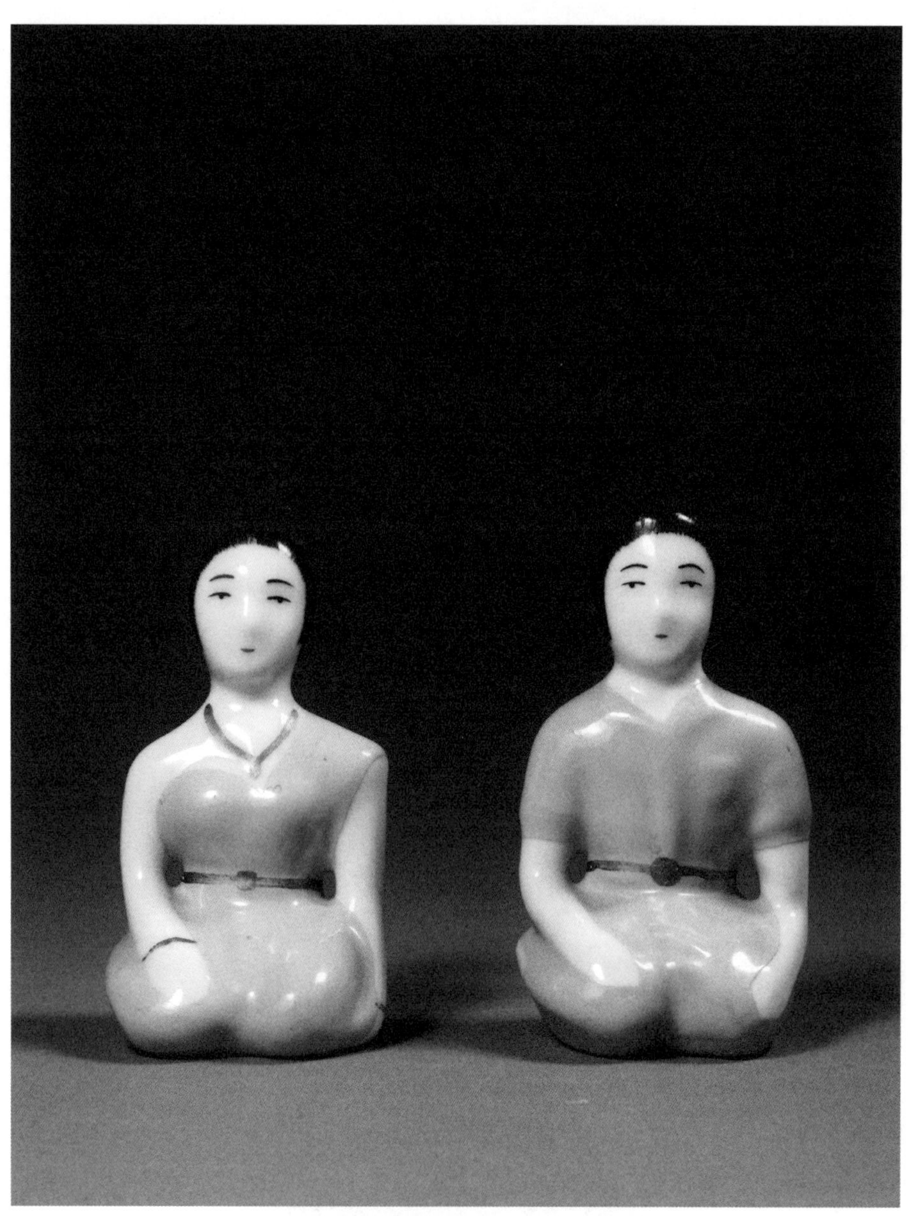

Ceramic Figures (8.5 cm)

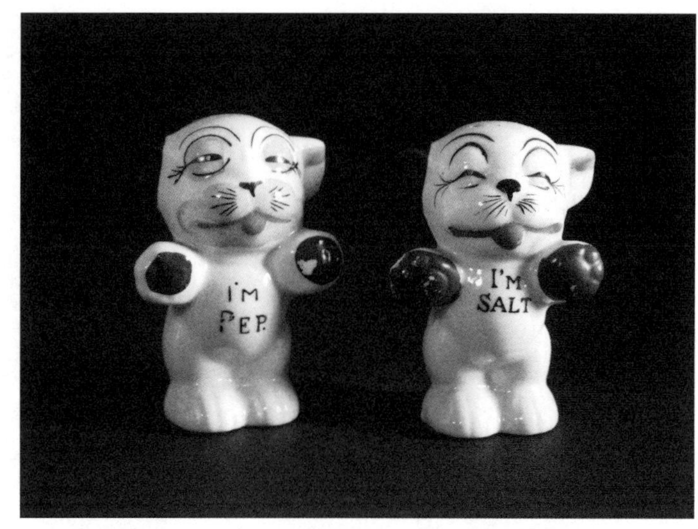

Salt & Pepper (7.5 cm)

Ceramic Elephant (7 cm) & Horse (9 cm)

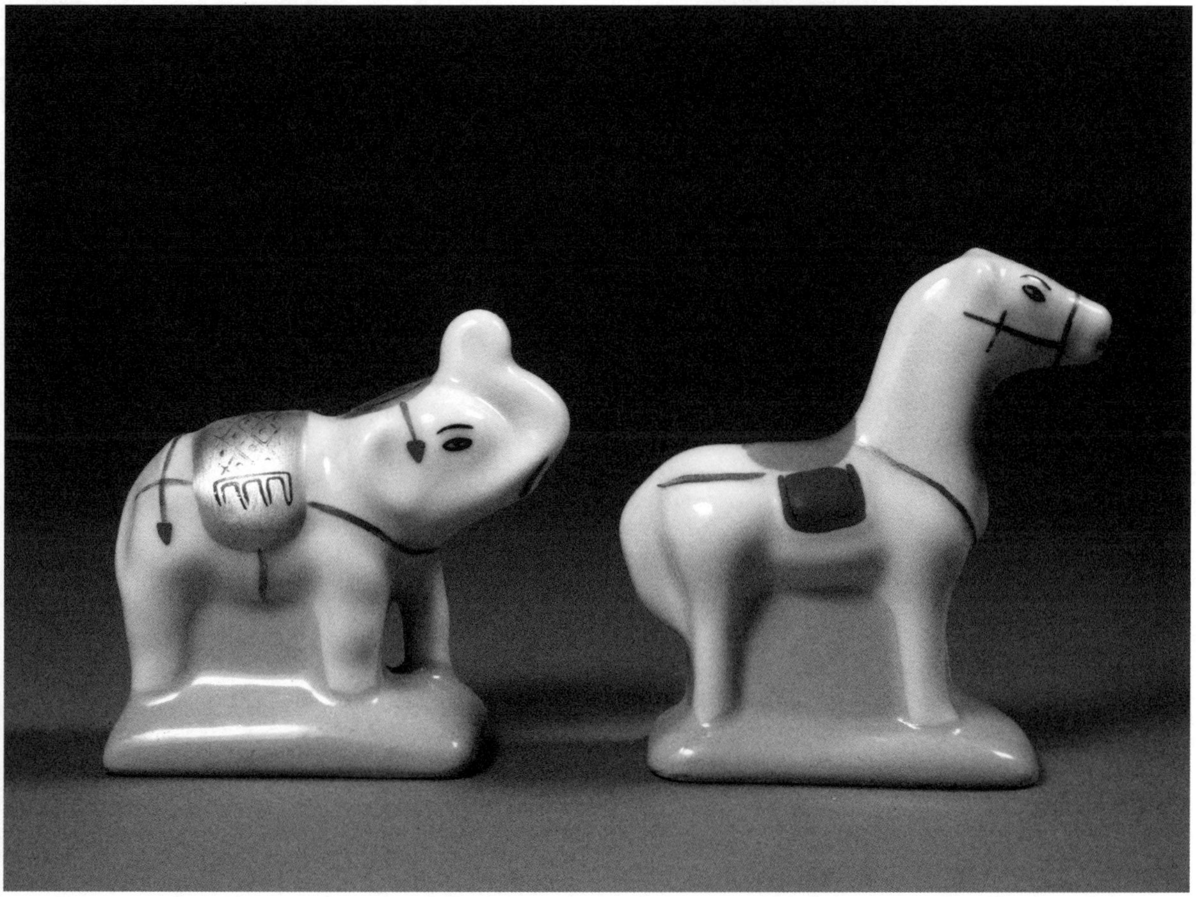

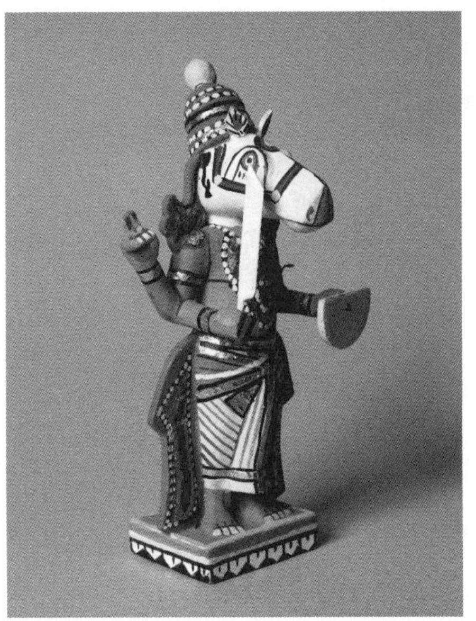

Wood Carving (17 cm)

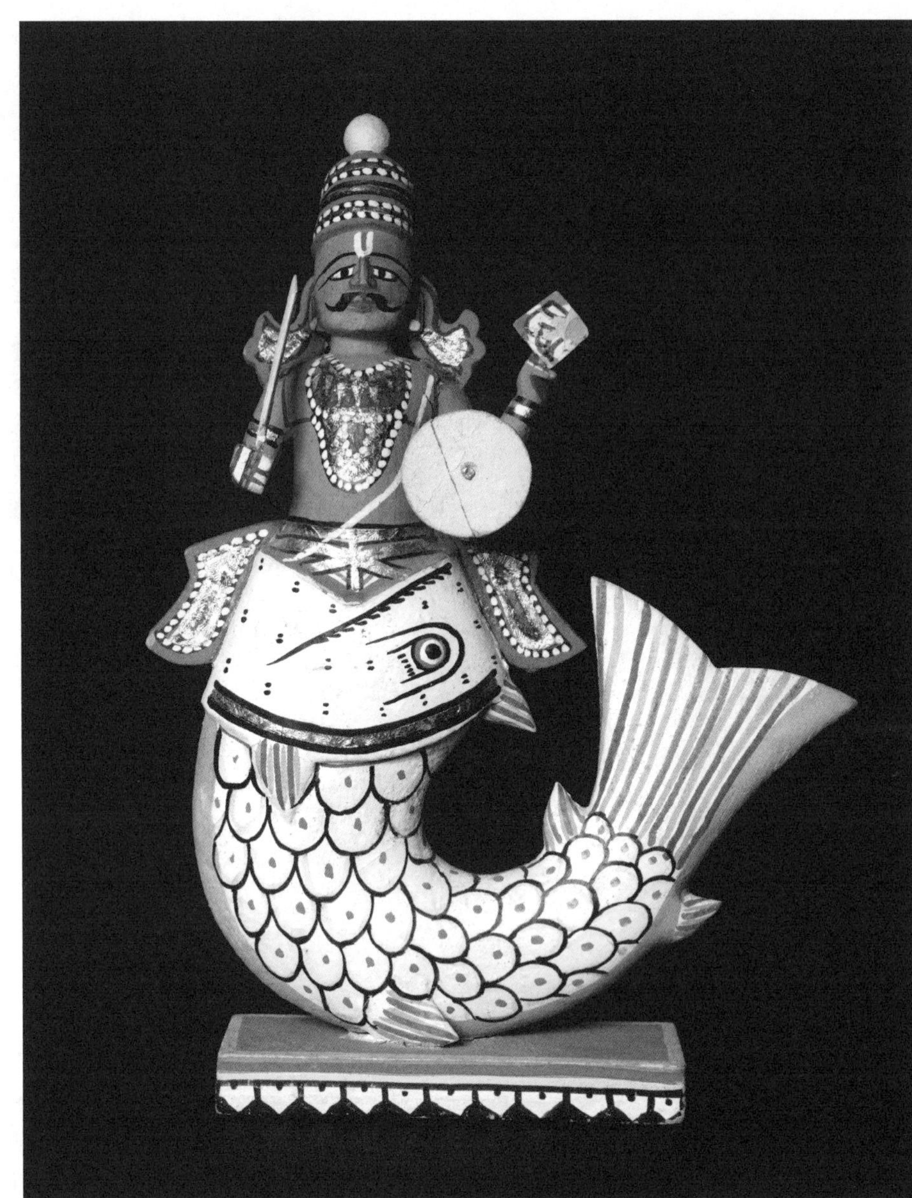

Wood Carving (15.5 cm)

Clay Horse (19 cm)

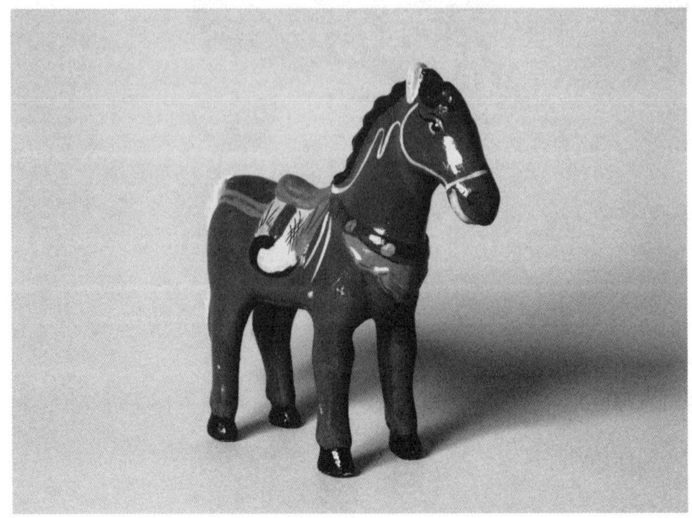

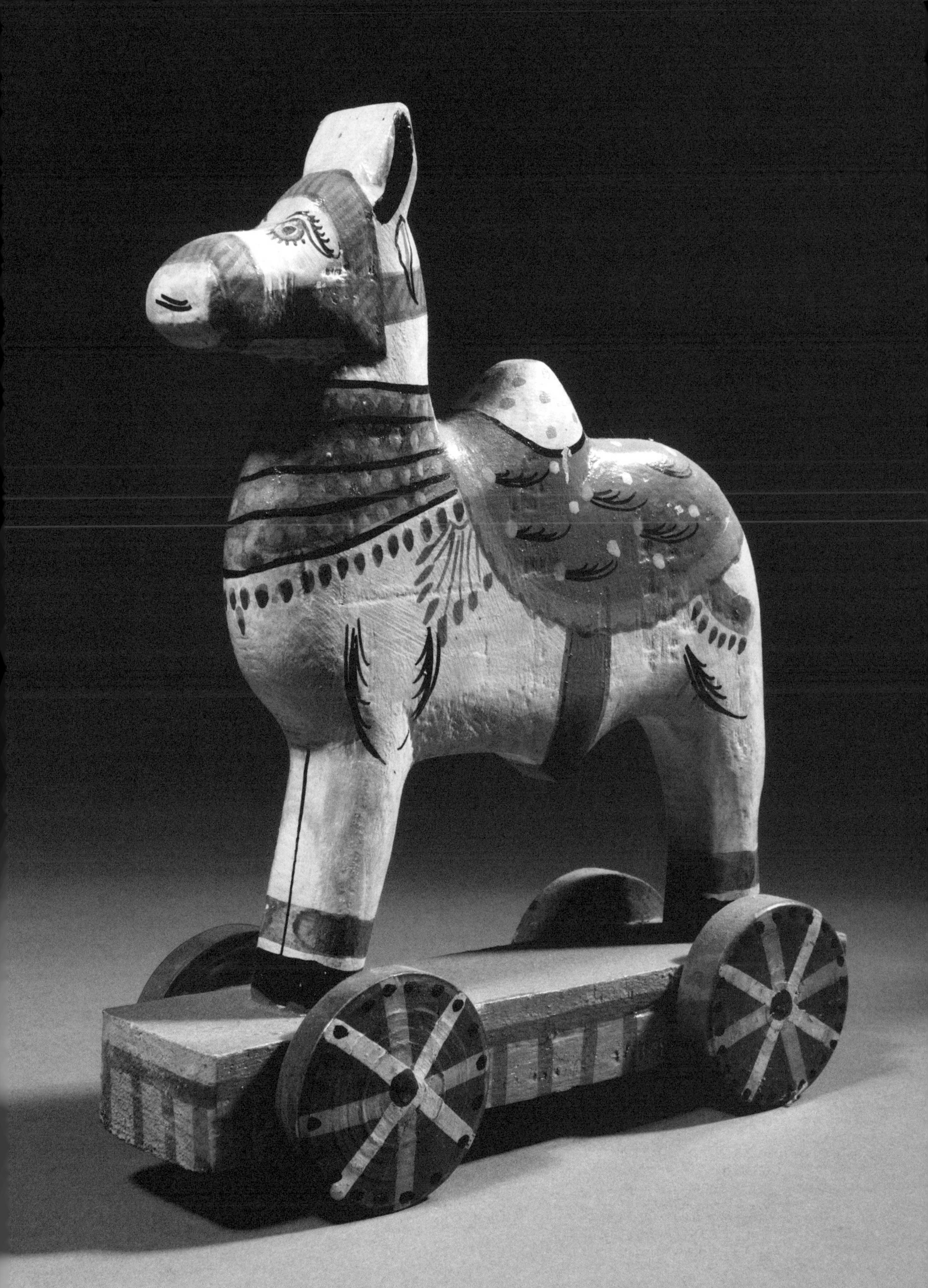

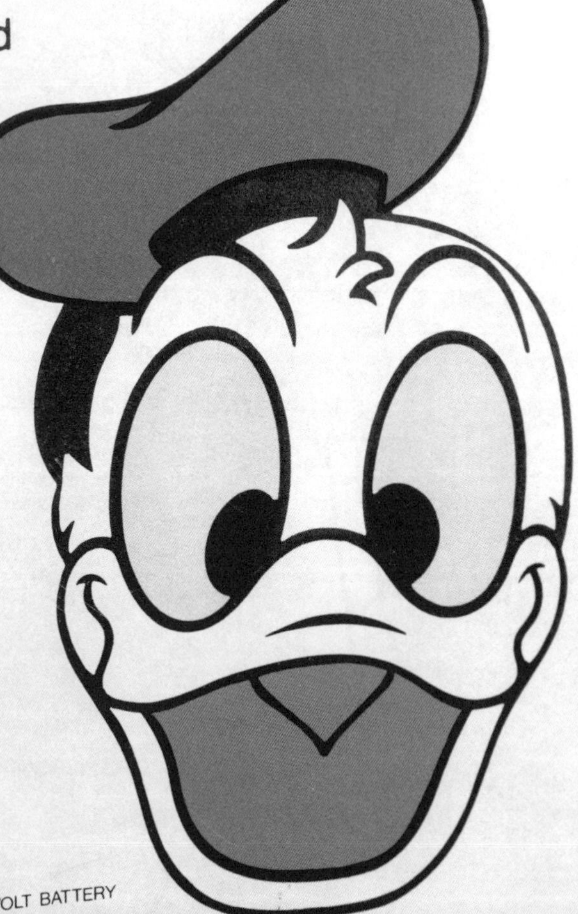
Donald Duck
Radio
Transistorized
Includes
Carry strap
Earphone
• USES STANDARD 9 VOLT BATTERY
(NOT INCLUDED)
MADE IN HONG KONG
©WALT DISNEY PRODUCTIONS
DIST. INTOPORT DEVELOPMENT CO. INC. NEW YORK 10010
Donald
Duck
Radio

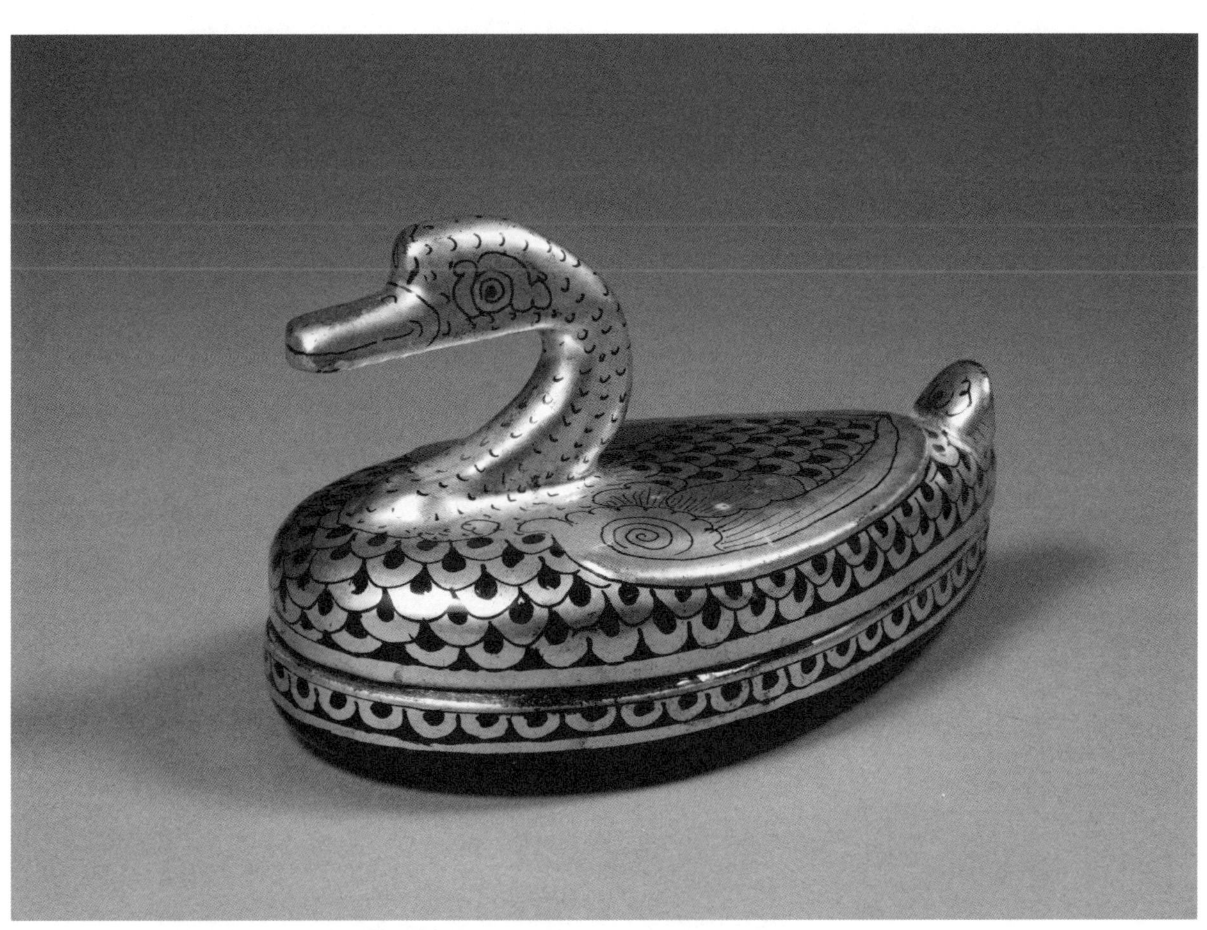

Duck Box (8 cm)

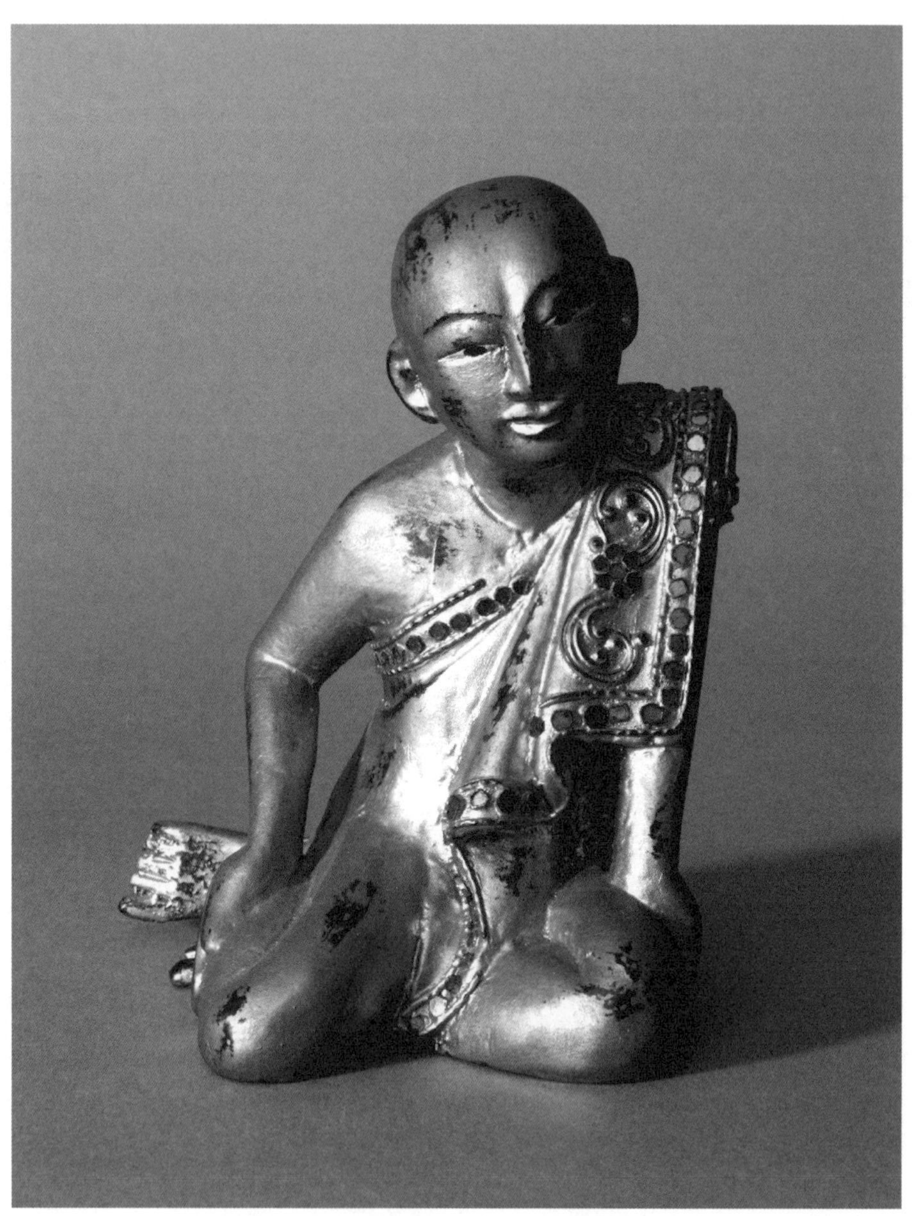

Wooden Figure (16.5 cm)

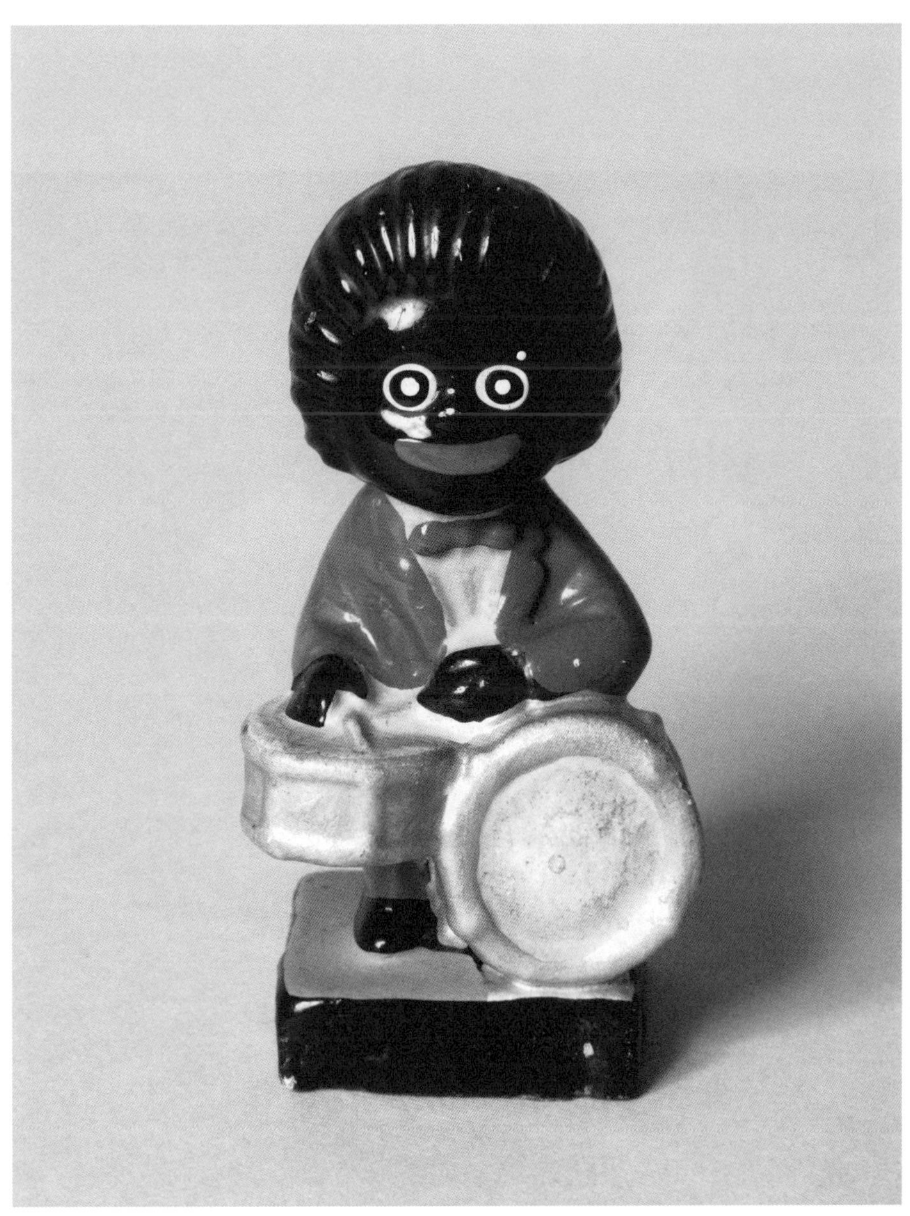

Plastic Gollywog (7 cm)

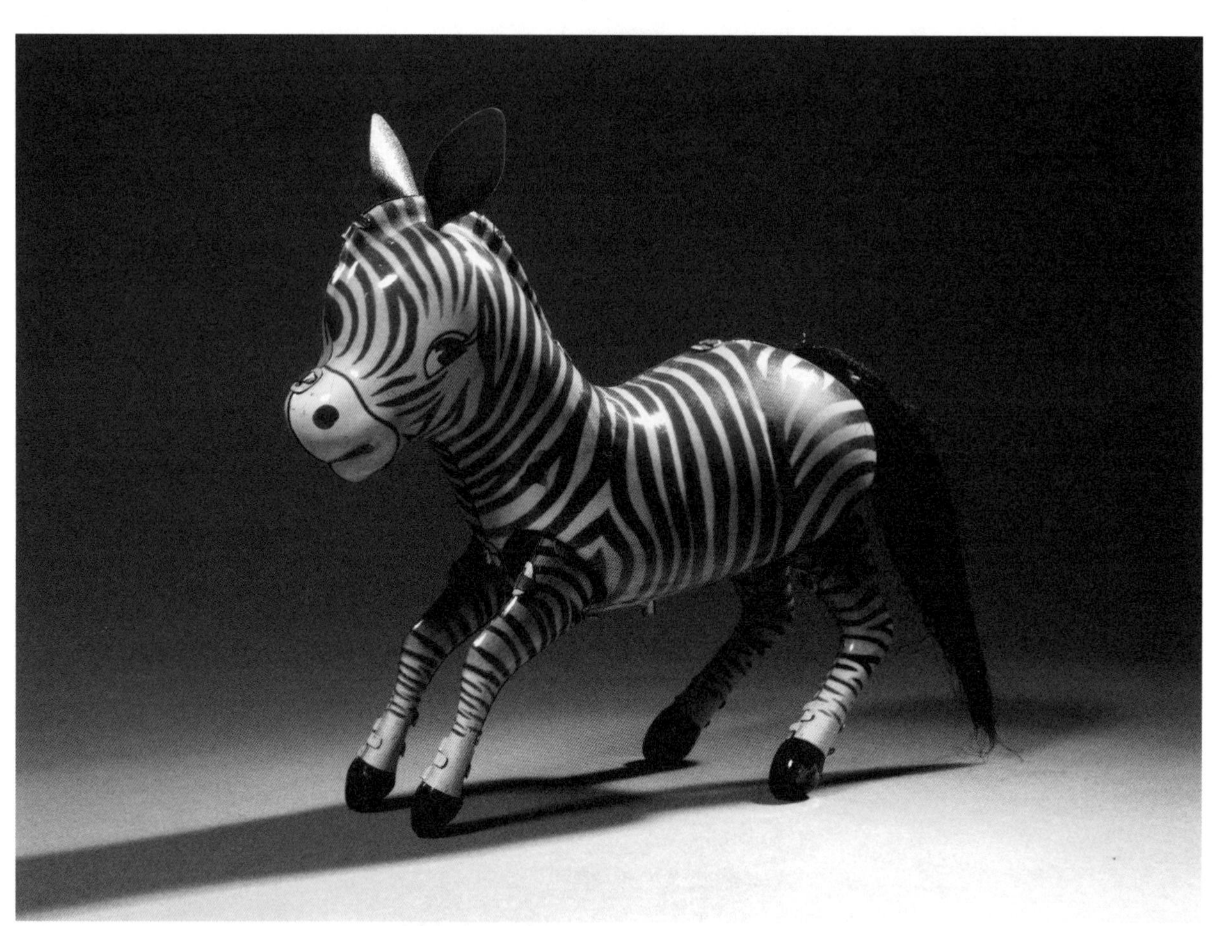

Wind-up Zebra (14 cm)

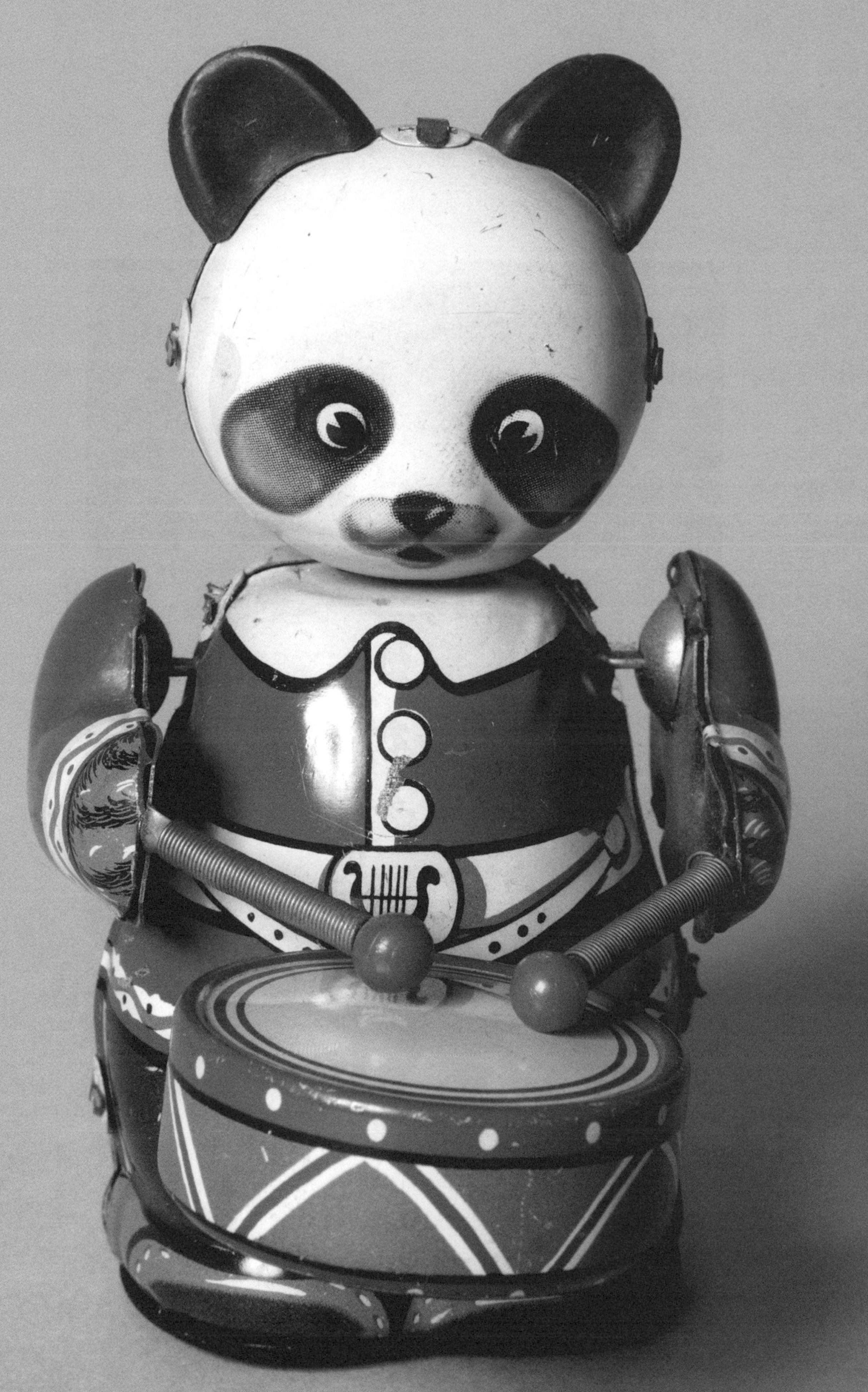

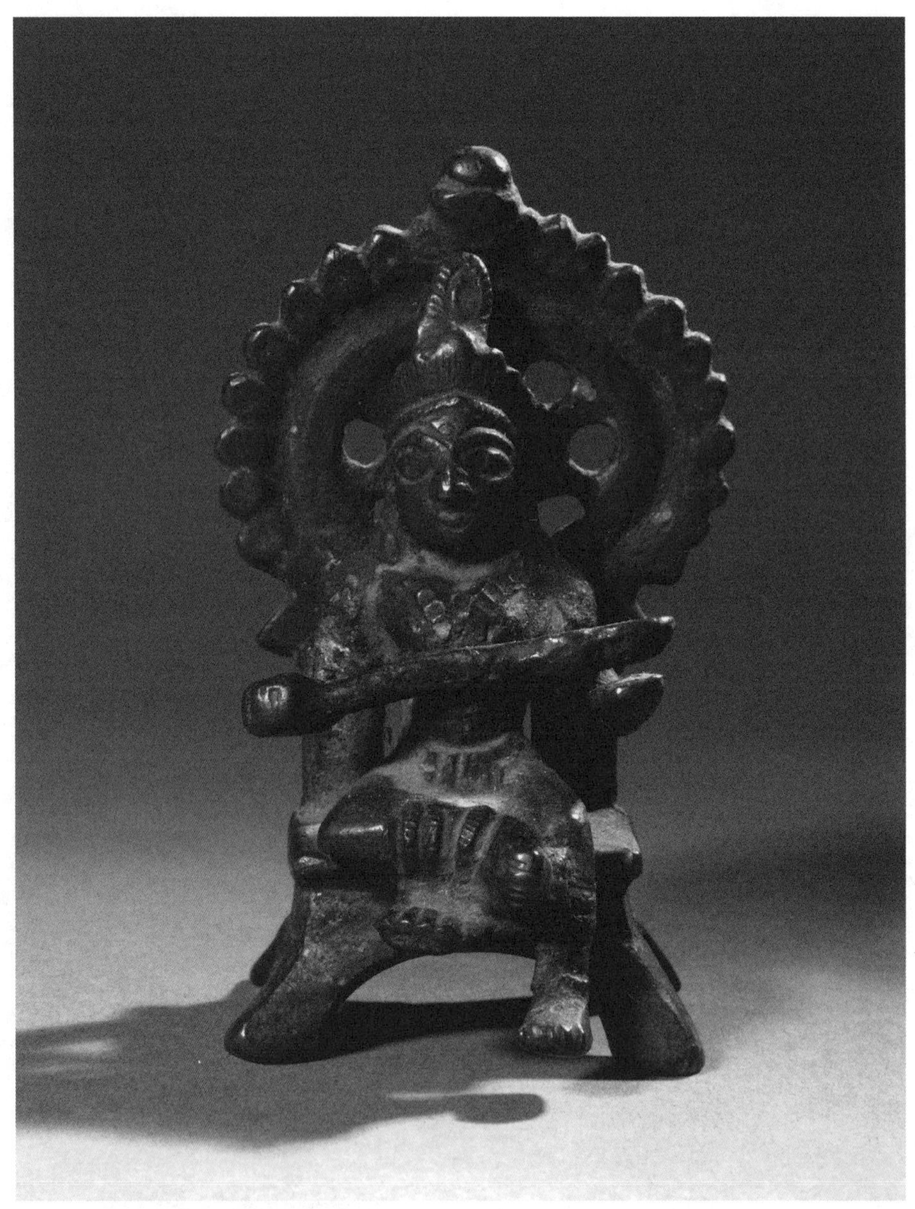

Seated Bronze Figure (8 cm)

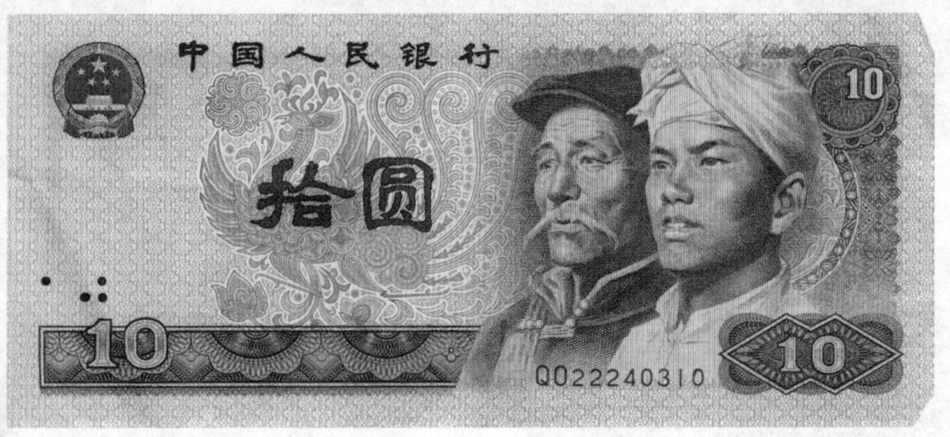
中国人民银行
拾圆
10
QO22240310

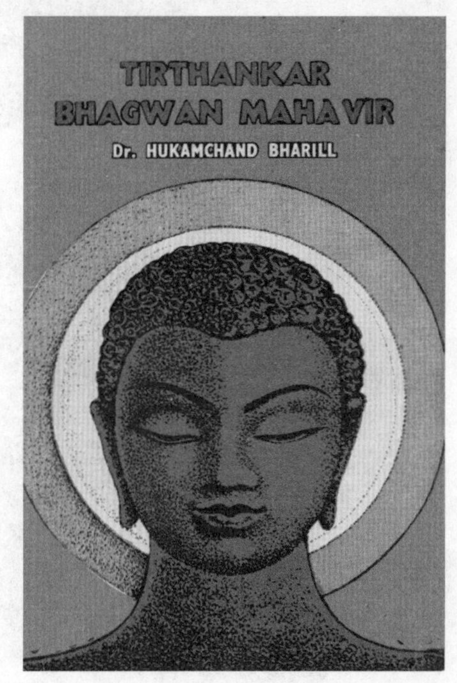
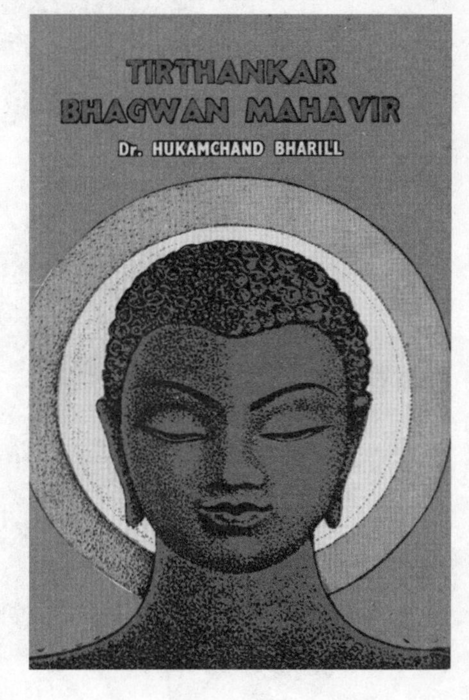
TIRTHANKAR
BHAGWAN MAHAVIR
Dr. HUKAMCHAND BHARILL

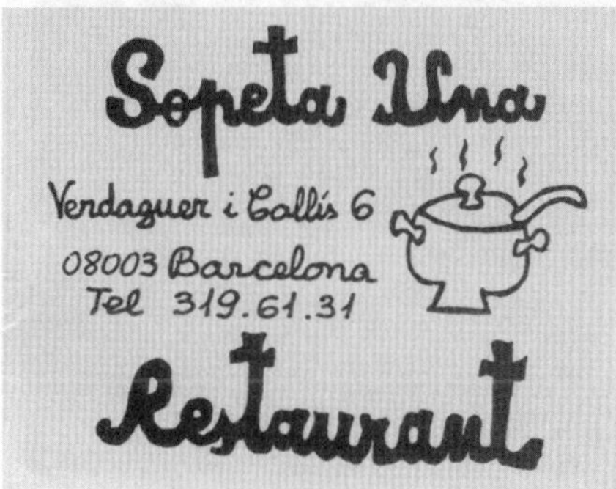
Sopeta Una
Verdaguer i Callís 6
08003 Barcelona
Tel 319.61.31
Restaurant

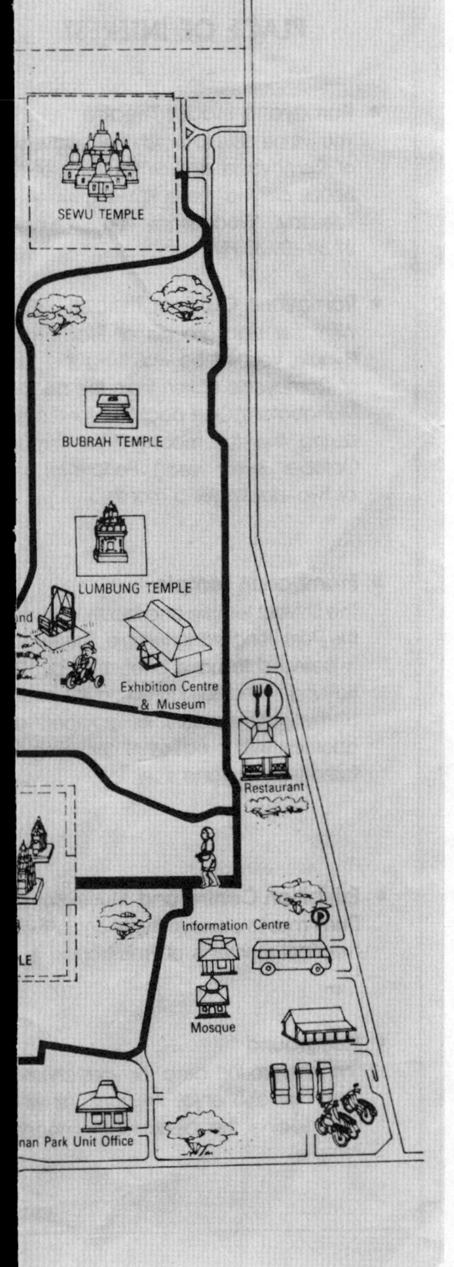
SEWU TEMPLE
BUBRAH TEMPLE
LUMBUNG TEMPLE
Exhibition Centre & Museum
Restaurant
Information Centre
Mosque
nan Park Unit Office

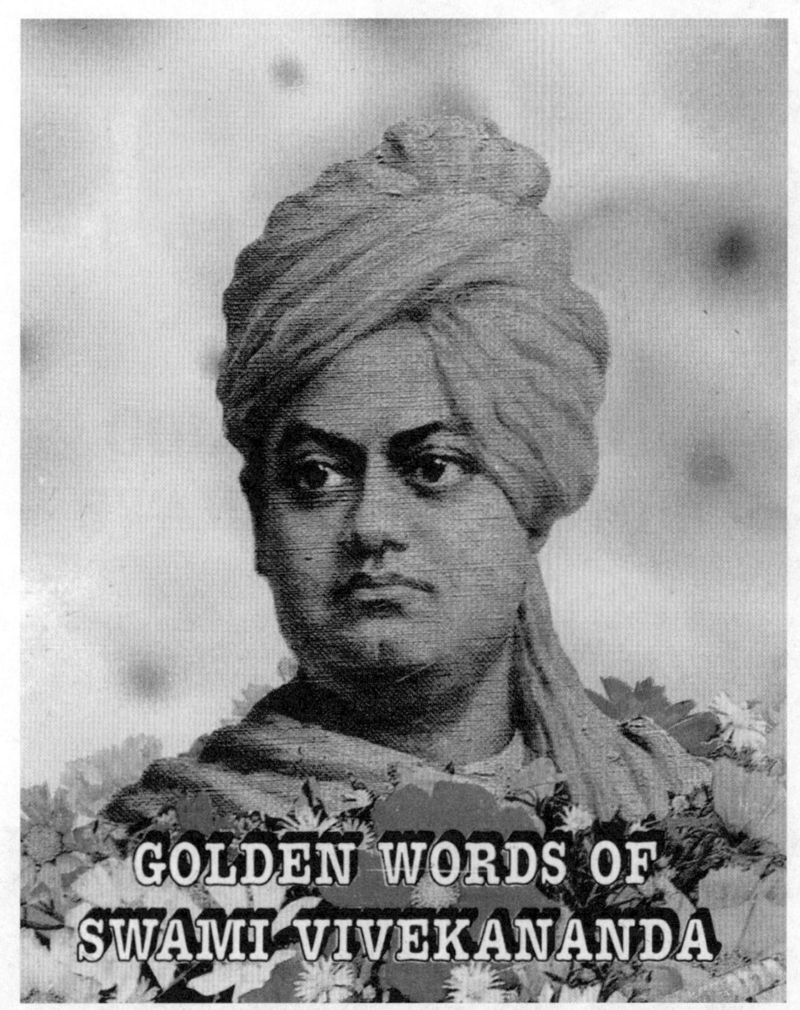
GOLDEN WORDS OF
SWAMI VIVEKANANDA

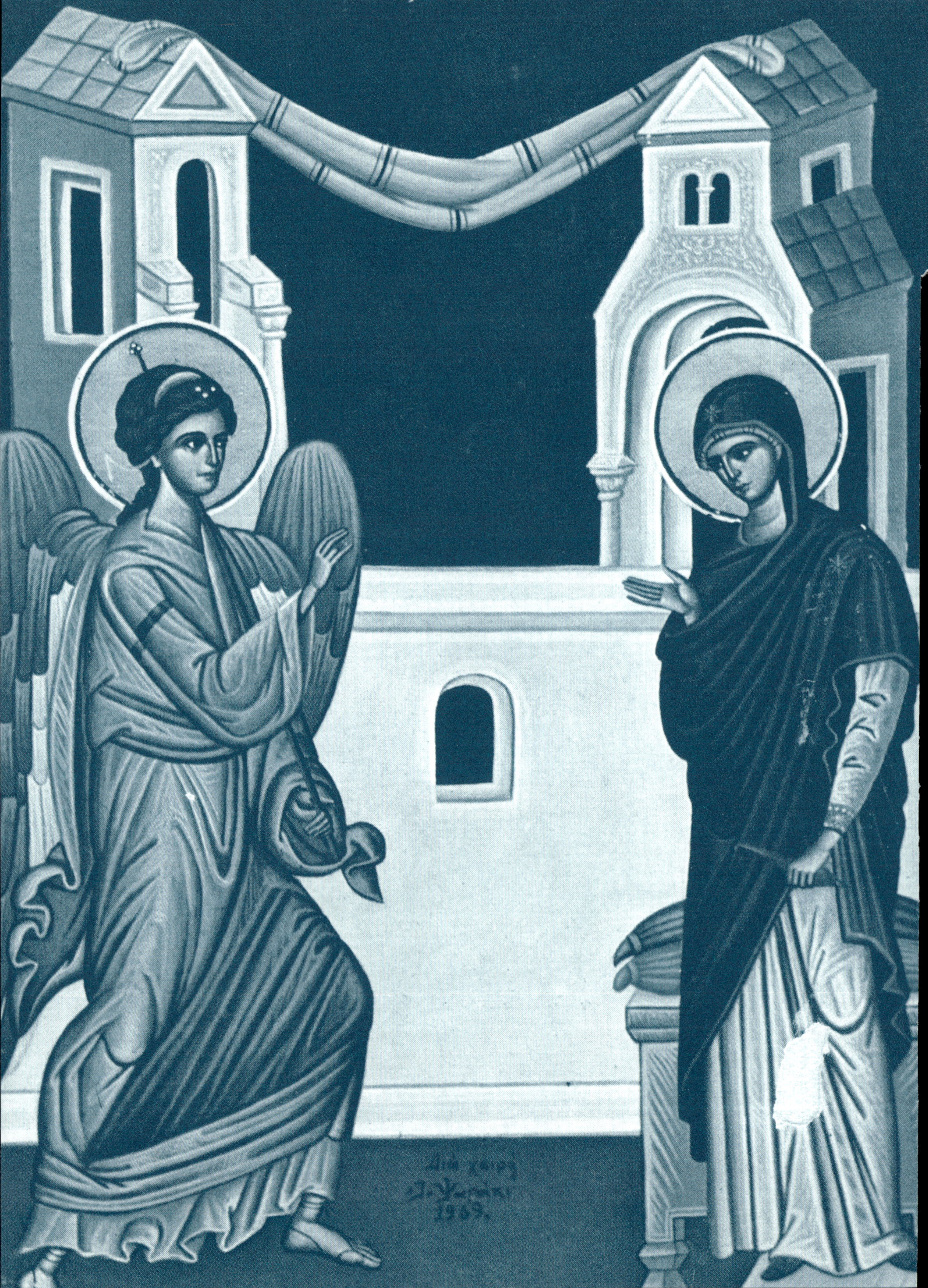

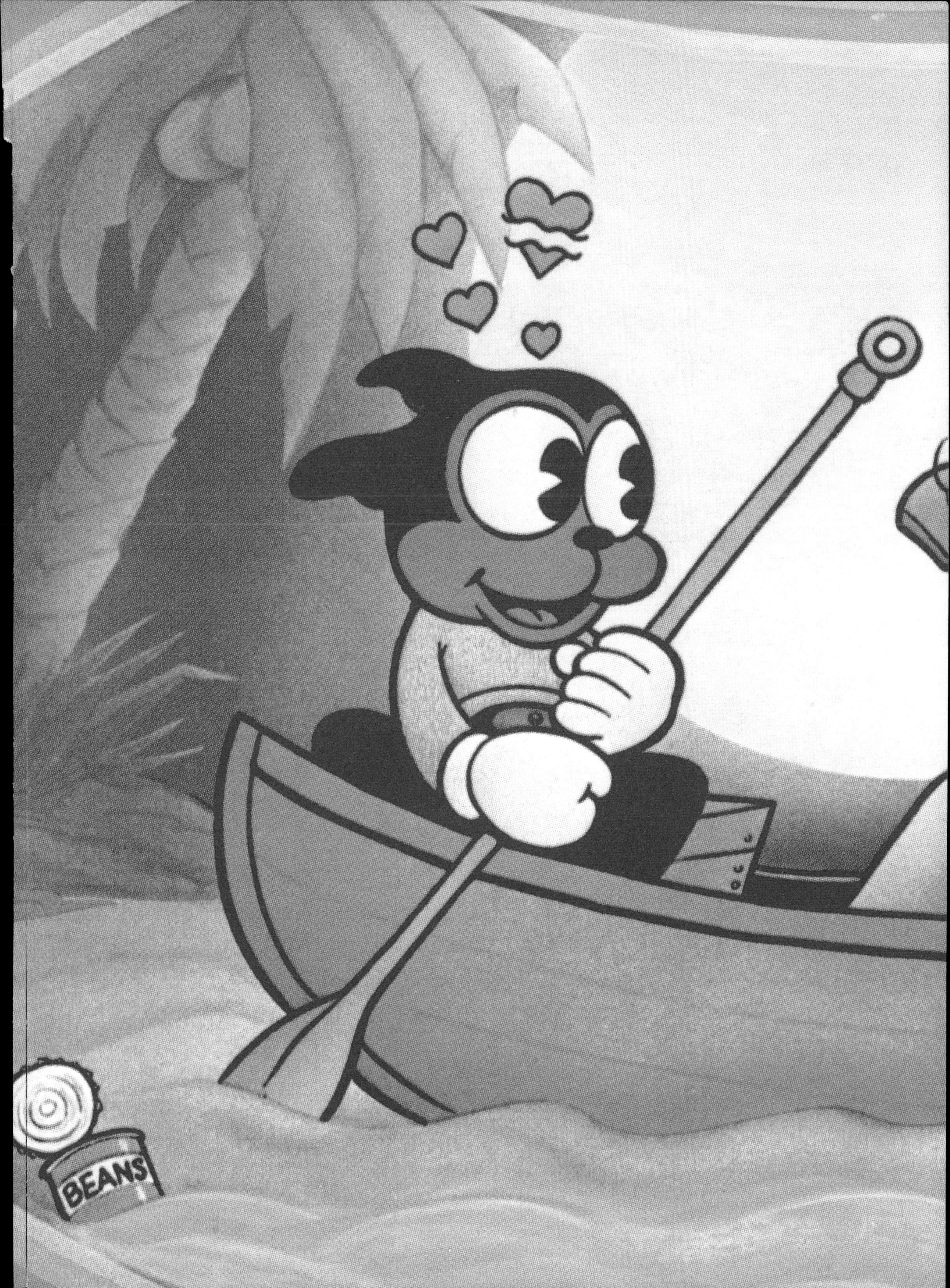
BEANS

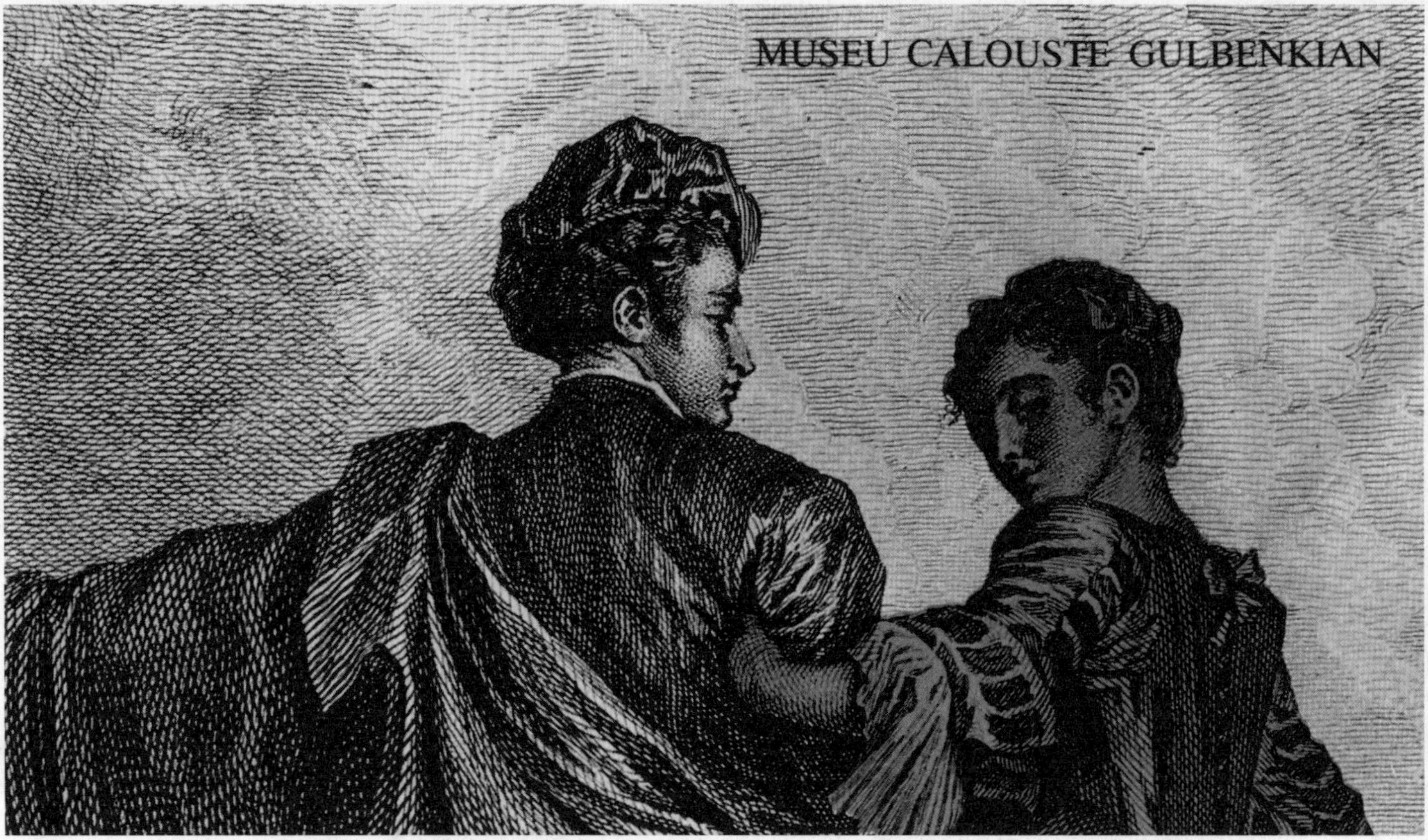

MUSEU CALOUSTE GULBENKIAN

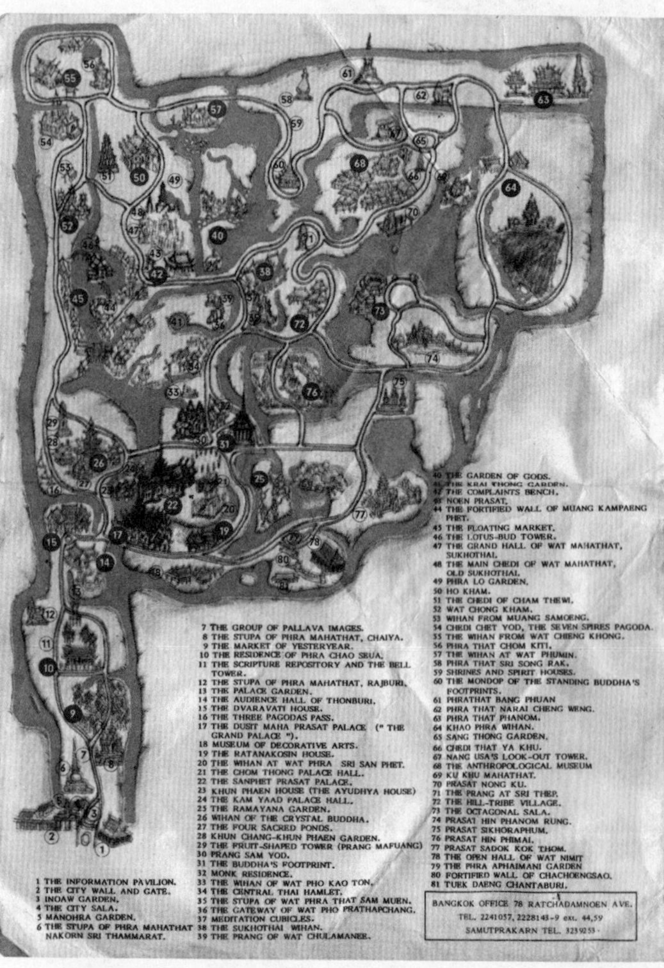

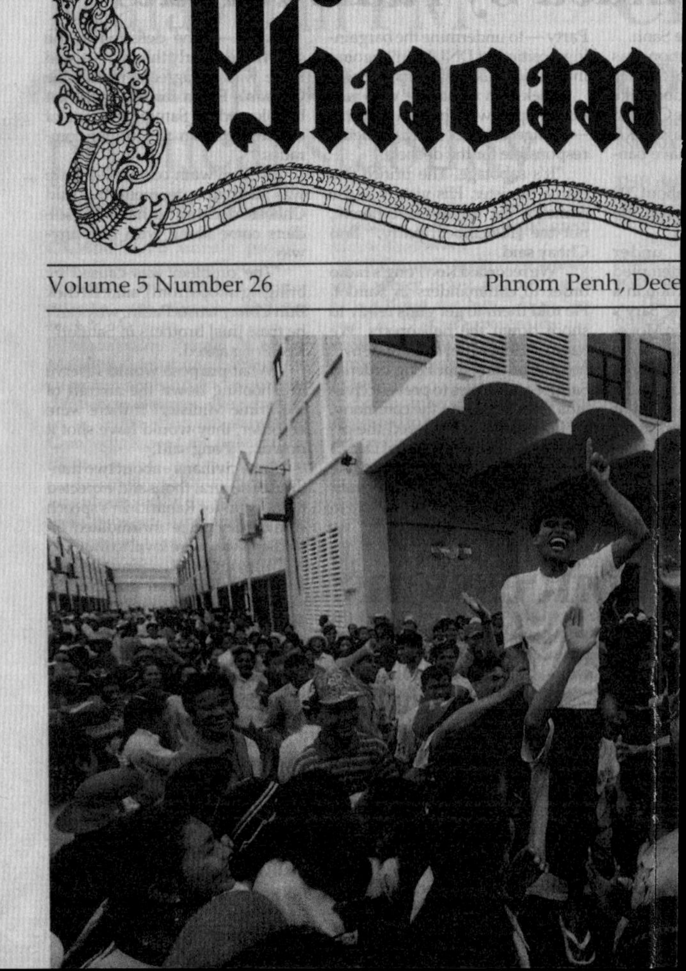

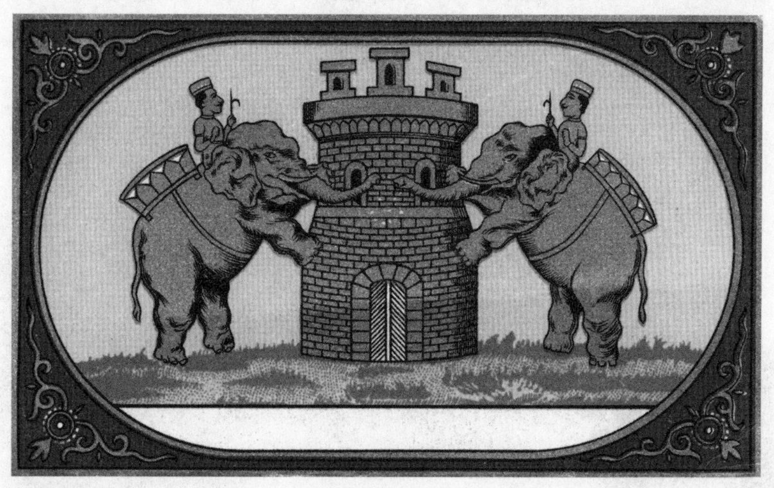

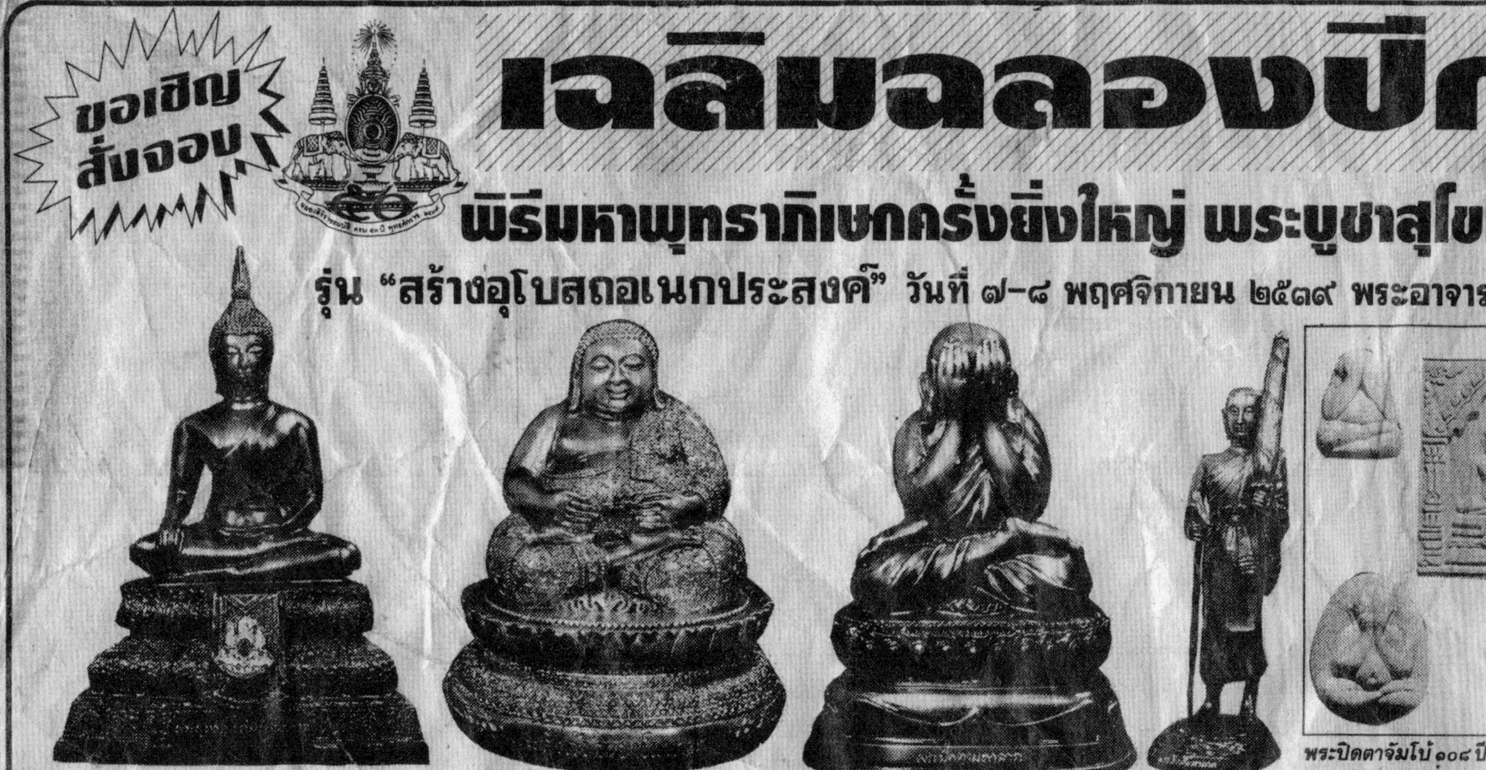

พระปิดตาจัมโบ้ ๑๐๘ ปี

พระพุทธสุโขทัยรัตนมงคล ๕ นิ้ว ๙ นิ้ว (รายการ ๑,๒) พระสังกัจจายน์ ๕ นิ้ว (รายการ ๓) พระปิดตามหาลาภ ๕ นิ้ว (รายการ ๔) พระสิวลีมหาลาภ สูง ๑๒"

ในวโรกาสมหามงคลสมัย เฉลิมฉลองปีกาญจนาภิเษก ฉลองสิริราชสมบัติครบ ๕๐ ปี ปวงชนชาวไทยต่างชื่นชมยินดีที่ได้มีโอกาสอันหาได้ยากยิ่ง ทางวัดนกโดย พระครูสุจิตตาภรณ์ เจ้าอาวาส ได้ดำเนินการสร้างอุโบสถหลังใหม่แทนหลังเก่าที่ชำรุดทรุดโทรม ยากที่จะบูรณะให้ดีดังสภาพเดิมได้ เนื่องจากอุโบสถหลังเก่าสร้างมานานกว่า ๑๐๘ ปี อุโบสถหลังใหม่ที่สร้างเป็นอุโบสถจตุรมุข อเนกประสงค์ ๒ ชั้น ดำเนินการสร้างมาแล้ว ๑ ปี ๖ เดือน ชั้นล่างใช้บำเพ็ญกุศลได้แล้ว ตัวอุโบสถมุงหลังคาแล้ว กำลังปั้นลวดลายอยู่ งบประมาณการสร้าง ๓๐ ล้านบาทเศษ

นับเป็นมหามงคลยิ่ง ที่ได้รับพระมหากรุณาธิคุณให้เชิญตราสัญลักษณ์งานฉลองสิริราชสมบัติครบ ๕๐ ปี ประดิษฐานหน้าบันอุโบสถหลังใหม่ ผ้าทิพย์พระบูชาพระพุทธสุโขทัยรัตนมงคล และด้านหลังเหรียญพระบูชาดังกล่าวซึ่งเป็นการจำลองสร้างเป็นครั้งแรกใน ๑๐๘ ปี ทั้งนี้เพื่อหารายได้สร้างอุโบสถเพื่อถวายพระราชกุศล ในวโรกาสฉลองสิริราชสมบัติครบ ๕๐ ปี โอกาสพิเศษมาถึงแล้วและมีครั้งเดียว สำหรับผู้สนใจวัตถุมงคลพระบูชา-พระเครื่องไว้สักการะบูชา เก็บสะสมไว้เป็นที่ระลึก เพื่อความเป็นสิริมงคลในปีกาญจนาภิเษกสืบไป

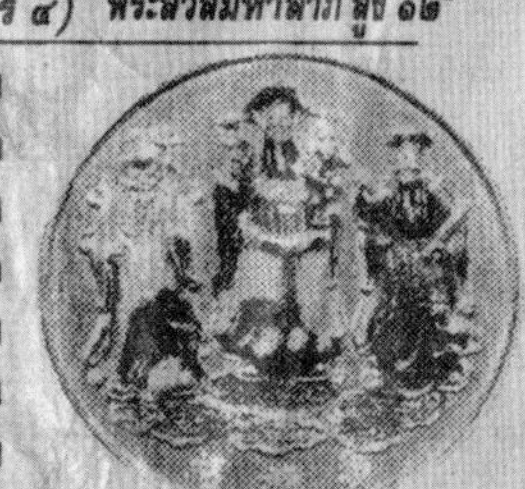

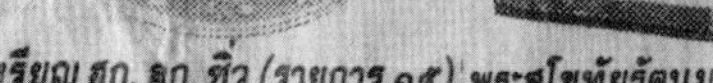
เหรียญ ฮก, ลก, ซิ่ว (รายการ ๑๕) พระสุโขทัยรัตนมง

ลำดับ	รายการ	จำนวนเงิน
๑.	**พระพุทธสุโขทัยรัตนมงคล ๙ นิ้ว รุ่นแรก เนื้อโลหะผสมทองเหลือง**	
	๑.๑ รมมันปูสร้าง ๑,๐๐๐ องค์ๆ ละ	๓,๕๐๐
	๑.๒ ปิดทอง จีวรดอกพิกุล สร้าง ๕๐๐ องค์ๆ ละ	๕,๐๐๐
๒.	**พระพุทธสุโขทัยรัตนมงคล ๕ นิ้ว รุ่นแรก เนื้อโลหะผสมทองเหลือง**	
	๒.๑ รมมันปู สร้าง ๑,๕๐๐ องค์ๆ ละ	๑,๕๐๐
	๒.๒ ปิดทอง จีวรดอกพิกุล สร้าง ๑,๐๐๐ องค์ๆ ละ	๒,๕๐๐
	๒.๓ เนื้อกระเบื้องผสมอิฐเก่าฐานชุกชี สร้าง ๕๐๐ องค์ๆ ละ	๕๐๐
๓.	**พระสังกัจจายน์มหาลาภ ๕ นิ้ว เนื้อโลหะผสมทองเหลือง**	
	๓.๑ รมมันปู สร้าง ๑,๐๐๐ องค์ๆ ละ	๑,๐๐๐
	๓.๒ ปิดทอง จีวรดอกพิกุล สร้าง ๕๐๐ องค์ๆ ละ	๑,๔๐๐
๔.	**พระปิดตามหาลาภ ๕ นิ้ว เนื้อโลหะผสมทองเหลือง**	

ลำดับ	รายการ
๙.	**พระผงเกศร-ว่าน ๑๐๘ พระแก้วมรกต, พระพุทธโสธร, พระพุทธชิน** **สมเด็จพระพุฒาจารย์ (โต), หลวงปู่ทวด, หลวงพ่อเงิน บางคลาน** สร้างพิมพ์ละ ๓๐,๐๐๐ องค์ จัดเป็นชุดรวม ๖ องค์ ชุดละ
๑๐.	**พระผงเกศร ๑๐๘ พระพุทธสุโขทัยรัตนมงคล วัดนก** พิมพ์เบญจภา นางพญา, พระรอด, ผงสุพรรณ สร้างพิมพ์ละ ๓๐,๐๐๐ องค์ จัดเป็น
๑๑.	**พระปิดตาจัมโบ้ ๑๐๘ ปี วัดนก**
	๑๑.๑ เนื้อผงมวลสารฐานชุกชีพระประธาน สร้าง ๓๐,๐๐๐
	๑๑.๒ เนื้อกระเบื้องโบสถ์ผสมอิฐเก่าฐานชุกชี สร้าง ๓๐,๐๐๐
	๑๑.๓ เนื้อผงใบลาน สร้าง ๑๐,๐๐๐ องค์ๆ ละ
	๑๑.๔ เนื้อผงตะไบ สร้าง ๑๐,๐๐๐ องค์ๆ ละ
	๑๑.๕ เนื้อผงแร่เงิน สร้าง ๑๐,๐๐๐ องค์ๆ ละ
	๑๑.๖ เนื้อผงแร่เหล็กน้ำพี้ สร้าง ๑๐,๐๐๐ องค์ๆ ละ

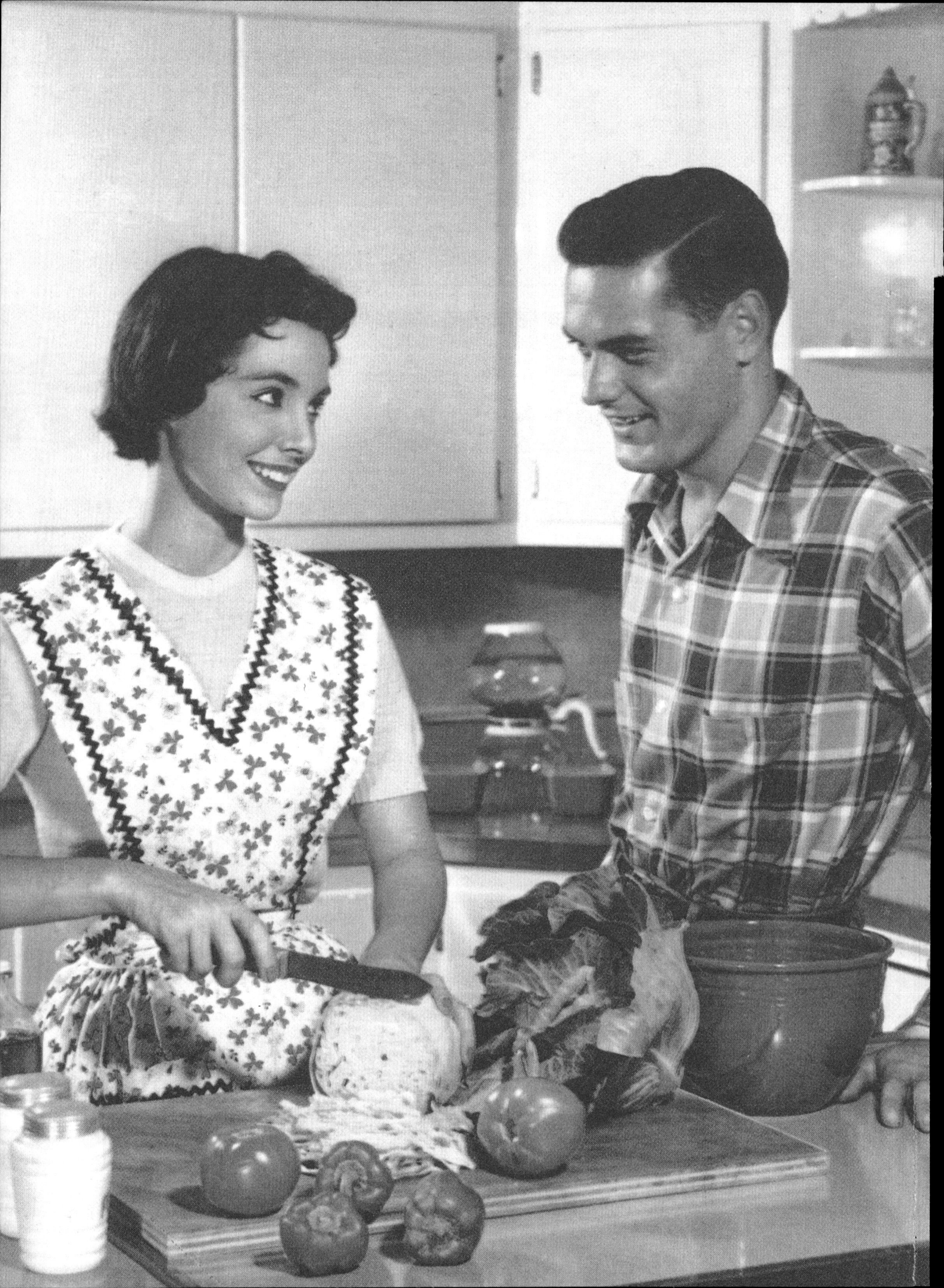

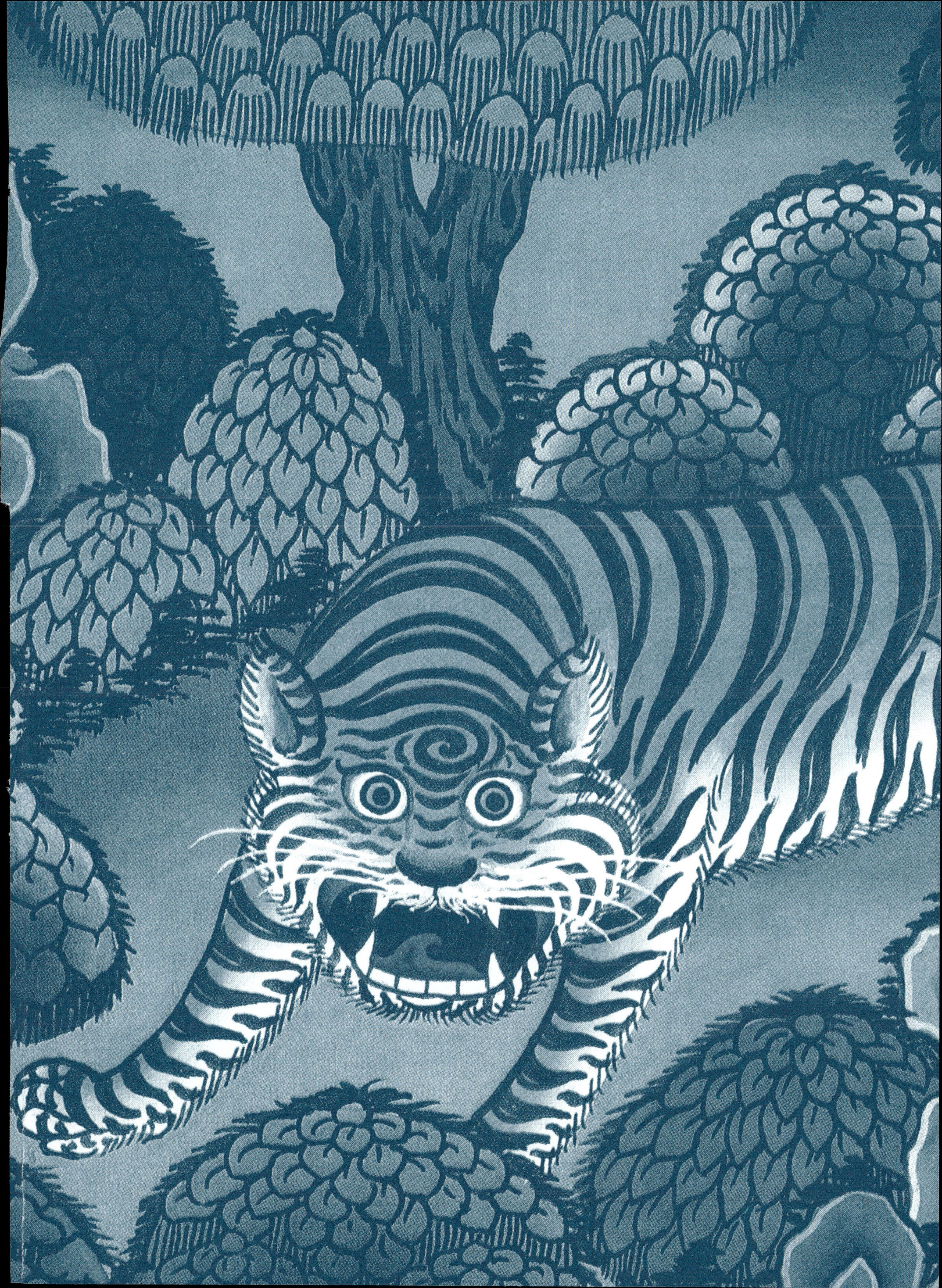

Published by the Shelagh Cluett Trust on the occasion of the exhibition 'Le Cabinet de Curiosités de Mademoiselle Clouette' at The Old Library, Chelsea College of Art & Design (9 Nov – 11 Dec 2010).

The Exhibition will travel to various venues along the Asian routes explored by Cluett.

Written & Curated by
Virginia Whiles

Co-Curated by
Johanna Garrad

Art Direction & Design by OK-RM (Oliver Knight & Rory McGrath)

Photography by
Nicole Bachmann
& Sarah Ainslie

Printed in Belgium by
Cassochrome

Archive & Website
Johanna Garrad
& Jack Rugg

www.shelaghcluett.com

ISBN 978-0-9567307-0-1